PRACTICAL ETHICS

GENERAL EDITOR: COLIN MCGINN

The purpose of this series is to provide clear analyses of topical and important moral issues written by experts in an accessible style suitable for both the student and the general public.

ANIMALS LIKE US

MARK ROWLANDS

VERSO

London • New York

First Published by Verso 2002
© Mark Rowlands
All rights reserved
The moral rights of the author have been asserted

1 3 5 7 9 10 8 6 4 2

Verso
UK: 6 Meard Street, London W1F 0EG
USA: 20 Jay St, Suite 1010, Brooklyn, NY 11201
www.versobooks.com

Verso is the imprint of New Left Books

ISBN 978-1-85984-386-4

British Library Cataloguing in Publication Data
A catalogue record for this book is available from the British Library

Library of Congress Cataloging-in-Publication Data
A catalog record for this book is available from the Library of Congress

Typeset in Garamond

To Emma

– an animal like me

CONTENTS

EDITOR'S INTRODUCTION

Colin McGinn

There are two ways in which things can have value: intrinsically or instrumentally. Life, liberty and the pursuit of happiness are intrinsically valuable – valuable in themselves, for what they *are*. Thus we promote these values, and enact laws and rules that respect and protect them. Money, automobiles and shampoo are instrumentally valuable – valuable as means for obtaining other things, ultimately things that have intrinsic value. Thus money can buy goods and services that increase happiness and sustain life. We tend to divide the world up into the instrumentally valuable things and the intrinsically valuable things, with the former serving the latter. And there is nothing wrong with this way of thinking – unless it makes the mistake of confusing what is intrinsically valuable with what is merely instrumentally valuable. Thus, as Kant observed, it is morally wrong to treat human beings as means and not as ends in themselves; it is immoral to accord them merely instrumental value.

The institution of slavery seems to do just that: the value of the slave is not measured in terms of his or her own happiness, liberty and life, but in terms of what the slave can do for the *intrinsically* valuable people. The slave is reduced to the level of the automobile – an instrument for the benefit of others. Slavery commits the cardinal error of treating an intrinsically valuable thing as if it had merely instrumental value; hence the denial of ordinary human rights to the slave. Moral enlightenment consists in seeing that this is the situation, and removing the perception that the slave is a mere instrument. Once this is done a whole new range of attitudes fall into place – attitudes of respect, concern, protection. Talk of dignity and freedom attaches itself to what was previously a mere tool. Intrinsic value replaces instrumental value.

The instrumental view of animals is deeply engrained in the human psyche. Animals are historically seen as valuable only in proportion to their contribution to the well-being of humans. The question is always what they can do for us – feed us, clothe us, entertain us, fight for us, comfort us. And, like slaves, they certainly have their uses – they make fine instruments in many ways. In the case of animals our perception of their nature is deeply colored by this instrumental view; we find it hard to think of them in any other way. Such is the force of tradition and habit, backed by self-interest. This conception even finds expression in the thought that animals were *made* to be our instruments – either by God or a helpful Nature. The *purpose* of animals – what they were designed for – is to serve human desires: they have no other reason to live. Thus whatever value they have is entirely dependent on what they can do for us. Even when we observe them in the wild, away from human domesticity, we think of them as spectacle, or perhaps objects of scientific interest.

This view of animals as human tools needs some moral and philo-sophical backing. If we are to treat them as tools, they have to be worthy of such treatment – they have to be the kind of thing that *can* be so treated. Obviously, they cannot be accorded rights, or else we would be violating their rights in using them as tools – much as slaves were not accorded rights. And they cannot have the kind of *nature* that precludes instrumental treatment; specifically, they cannot have minds or souls or personalities or feelings. For if they did, their status as mere means would come into question. Thus it has been very widely held that animals do not have minds or souls or feelings – either not at all or not "in the human sense." So even the death of an animal is not the end of anything that has any intrinsic value; though it may be instrumentally inconvenient for the "owner" of the animal (or convenient if killing the animal has some instrumental value). There is a package of tightly connected ideas here: the animal as instrument; the animal as morally off the map; the animal as mindless automaton.

Now, this entire conception has not been without its critics, from ancient times to the present. But it has only been in about the last thirty years that it has come under sustained and forceful attack. And the essential point has been that animals do *not* have merely instrumental value for humans, but rather count as ends in themselves; *their* life, liberty and happiness have intrinsic value. This change of perspective requires us to rethink our habitual conception of what an animal is – not a tool but something that has value in itself. Accordingly, we are gradually coming to see that animals are by no means mindless automata but rich sentient beings. We are coming round to the idea that this confers upon them certain rights and protections – that they *count* morally. We are shedding the idea – the prejudice – that an animal is just a tool that can be freely used and discarded, without consideration of its own interests. Those interests should be accorded the same consideration as anyone else's: it is not somehow less bad for an animal to suffer pain than a human – assuming the same degree of pain. The anatomical differences don't somehow make the pain less morally weighty, more negligible.

Imagine you were in the odd position of not knowing what species you belonged to – you have some weird sort of species amnesia. You also have an excruciating pain in your foot. Do you say to yourself: "Well, if I'm human this is a bad state of affairs and someone has the duty to help me; but if I'm an ape then it's really no big deal and no one has any responsibilities towards me"? That would be absurd, and the same absurdity attaches to similar thoughts about being eaten or vivisected or hunted. The species you happen to be can't make that kind of difference. Compare being in the dark about what race you belong to and considering the ethics of slavery: do you say "Well, if I'm white slavery would be a great evil, but if I'm black I have nothing to complain about"? Of course not: the inherent evils of slavery will be just as real no matter what race you belong to as a slave.

This is really just a way to put an old moral rule: *ask what you would feel like in the other guy's shoes.* If you wouldn't want it done to you, then how can you justify doing it to someone else? This is a maxim that promotes the recognition of *equality* – in the sense of not discriminating according to morally irrelevant characteristics. The only fair or just way to treat intrinsically valuable beings is equally: that is, according to their morally relevant characteristics, not irrelevant ones such as race or sex or species. This doesn't of course mean that such characteristics can *never* be used to make a selection: if I am auditioning for an actor to play the part of a black middle-aged man there is no moral objection to my choosing only individuals who are black and male. But when it comes to choosing someone to be a lawyer or a professor or baseball player, then such discrimination is wrong. In the case of animals, the question is whether species can be invoked to justify the radically different treatment we accord to humans and animals. For example, can it be used to defend the factory farming of animals, while admitting that this would be grossly immoral treatment of humans?

Such questions have been amply aired in recent years. Some philosophers have argued that on utilitarian grounds we cannot justify our treatment of animals: the pleasure we derive from using them as tools does not outweigh the suffering we thereby cause them. Others have argued that animals have natural rights that we routinely violate – such as the right not to be incarcerated without due cause. In the present book, Mark Rowlands extends these arguments by approaching the question as a question of social justice. Taking his cue from John Rawls' important work, he asks how we would want the world to be organized if we were behind the "veil of ignorance", not knowing which species we will belong to (essentially the same idea as I exploited above). Rawls was concerned with ignorance pertaining to the distribution of goods and opportunities in a human society; Rowlands asks the more radical question of what we would choose if we didn't know what species we were destined to belong to. And his point is that it would be irrational to favor the current set-up, since that might well make you one of the exploited animals – and hence a mere human instrument. This may seem like a fanciful way to make the point, but actually it is just an especially vivid way to bring out the old truth that you should always ask what you would feel if you were in a less lucky and privileged position. Justice requires that we not favor the group we *happen* to belong to.

Rowlands develops his case with great patience and skill, always attending to possible objections, taking the reader systematically through the

moral issues. First, he clarifies the general considerations in moral philosophy that are germane to the question of animal rights, and then he applies
these to various forms of animal use (or abuse). Both phases of the argument are essential and given equal weight: we need to get our principles
clear, and we also need to see how they work out in the real world. The
result is a marvelously lucid presentation of the issue, in which the reader
is never asked to take anything on trust; at every step Rowlands is careful
to make his case thoroughly and convincingly. Perhaps the gravest disad-
vantage animals labor under is that they cannot speak for themselves; they
cannot protest against their treatment – articulately anyway. But here they
have Mark Rowlands to plead their case, and they could not wish for a
more eloquent defender.

INTRODUCTION

Our treatment of many animals is not good. Anywhere. But in some places it is worse than others. In the following pages, what we do to animals is described, sometimes graphically. In order to avoid getting bogged down in issues of *who does what to animals where*, I have bracketed questions of variations in welfare law, and so variations in treatment, from country to country. The fact that battery cages for chickens are to be phased out in the EU from 2008, for example, does not alter the fact that they are not being phased out elsewhere. The fact that a brutal series of psychological experiments on dogs was carried out in the US is not in any way mitigated by the fact that they weren't carried out in the UK. This is a book about human treatment of animals, and about the large discrepancy between how it is and how it should be. It is a book about human treatment of animals in general, and not in any particular part of the world. If a certain precision is lost because of this, this is an unfortunate but necessary feature of the subject matter.

Colin McGinn encouraged me to write this; my thanks to him. And thanks to George Galfalvi at Verso for detailed comments, especially on chapters 2 and 3. Peter Rowlands was kind enough to read and comment on an entire draft. Anne Kennedy directed me towards some useful information on recent activities at Huntingdon Life Sciences.

My interest in animal rights began with a rather unfortunate journey I made about seven Christmases ago. I was making the ferry crossing from Rosslare to Pembroke to visit my parents for Christmas. About ten minutes before we docked at Pembroke, I looked up from my book to find my wolf-dog Brenin trotting merrily along the upper passenger lounge in the general direction of the restaurant – with various employees of Irish

1

ferries trailing in his wake. He had forced down the window of the car, climbed out, exited the car deck (which was supposedly locked), and navigated his way up five decks to the upper passenger deck. So, on the way back, attempting to avoid this scenario a second time, I left the window up a little further than usual. And he tore the car apart. Literally. Apparently old age was bringing with it certain separation issues. By the time I was called down to the car deck to be appraised of the situation, there was nothing left that was recognizably the inside of a car. Seats were gone, seat belts were gone, etc., etc. And the ceiling was hanging down in shreds. In order to be able to actually see out of the car as I attempted to drive it off the ferry and home, I had to remove the hanging tatters of the ceiling, and, noticing that the car deck attendant had a knife, I asked him for this. He seemed strangely reluctant to part with it, and eventually it emerged that he thought I was going use it to kill Brenin. I explained that while I may be somewhat irritated with the situation, I couldn't really hold Brenin responsible for what he had done. And on the rather uncomfortable drive home, as I sat in what was left of my seats, and attempted to see out of the window, I had ample opportunity to reflect on the idea of responsibility and its place in moral thinking. The first result was a book on animal rights, entitled (ingeniously) *Animal Rights*, published a few years ago. But, more generally, the role played by the idea that we cannot be held responsible for features that are beyond our control – which I here call the *principle of desert* – has its origin in that afternoon. Brenin is gone now, but lives on in this principle. My thanks to him.

1

DO ANIMALS HAVE MINDS?

If you were an animal in the seventeenth or eighteenth centuries, then one of the things you should have made a point of avoiding would be Cartesian scientists. If not, then, you could expect to find yourself nailed to a vivisection board, being slowly cut open. You would be conscious throughout. The Cartesian scientists did not believe in taking any steps to prevent your suffering or pain for one very simple reason: they did not believe you were capable of suffering or of feeling pain. In fact, they laughed at anyone who did think this. Philosophy is a dangerous thing; it can get you to believe all sorts of ridiculous things. And the average Cartesian scientist provides a classic example of someone, as we might say, in the *grip* of a philosophical theory.

The theory – and this is why Cartesian scientists were called "Cartesian" – stemmed from the seventeenth-century philosopher Ren Descartes.[1] According to him, human beings are very special things, in that they, and, in this world, they alone, possess minds. Now, for Descartes, the mind is the part of us that does the thinking. So, anything that does not have a mind, by definition, cannot think. Nor, according to followers of Descartes (although perhaps not Descartes himself – the textual evidence is disputed), can it feel. And from here it's a short step to Cartesian scientists nailing animals to boards.

The idea that animals cannot think or feel, of course, flies in the face of common sense. To begin with, if you start nailing animals to things they complain, and certainly do a pretty good job of imitating or *simulating* being in pain. Why would they squeal and struggle, etc., unless they were in pain? The answer Descartes and his followers gave was this: it's all *mechanical!* Imagine you were a toy maker, around Descartes' time. You specialized in toy animals. Internally, each of your animals was cunningly crafted, a complex arrangement of cogs, levers, pulleys, wheels, and so on. In particular, you arranged the innards of the animals you made so that when it was struck or received some kind of damage to its outer shell, inside this would cause various levers to engage various cogs and so on, which would cause, eventually, two wheels to rub together causing a loud screeching which sounded, for all the world, like a cry of pain. Of course, the toy is not really in pain; it's just a toy. But because the wheels rub together only when the toy is struck, and because the resulting screeching sounds so much like a cry of pain, it seems as if the toy is in pain.

If you can imagine this, then you are not far off understanding Descartes' view of animals. In fact, Descartes himself explicitly drew this sort of analogy. The French Royal Gardens were a sort of seventeenth-century EuroDisney. In particular, they contained a small society of hydraulically controlled robots, constructed so that when activated by an invisible water flow (initiated by visitors stepping on tiles), they moved, made sounds, and even played musical instruments. Moreover, their movements were designed to seemingly express states of mind. The arrival of strangers would cause a bathing Diana to hide in the rosebushes (thus simulating modesty), and cause Neptune to advance on them brandishing his trident (thus simulating anger). In this way, the robots seemed to have states of mind without really having them.

Animals, according to Descartes, were pretty much like the robots of the French Royal Gardens. The flow of water which drives the robots is replaced by what he called "animal spirits", and the tubes through which the water flows are replaced by nerve fibres. But the idea is the same. You kick a dog and this external stimulus causes stimulation of nerve fibres, which causes threads in the nerve marrow to be pulled. The threads pull open an orifice in the brain. This results in the release of vaporous animal spirits, which flow into nerves, which lead to muscles and tendons. This eventually causes, by inflation, the muscles and tendons to move. The dog's mouth opens, and it yelps. But there's no mental activity. The dog no more feels pain than the robot Diana feels embarrassment. In the case of animals, just as in the case of the robots, the lights are on but there's nobody home.

The activities of the Cartesian scientists are a classic example of the harm that philosophy can do. The problem is, however, that *we are all philosophers*. You are a philosopher, whether you know it or not, even if you have never picked up a book of philosophy in your life. We are, all of us, in the grip of various philosophical assumptions, presuppositions, hypotheses, even theories, about the way the world is, and about what matters in life. All of us, without exception.

So, before we start feeling too superior to our simple forebears, it's perhaps worth remembering that our present-day treatment of many animals is no better than that of the Cartesian scientists (if in doubt, read on). In fact, in some respects we are much worse than they. At least, they thought that animals were incapable of suffering. We are perfectly willing to accept that animals can suffer. It's just that many of us think this does not matter.

1 CAN ANIMALS FEEL PAIN?

But how do we know Descartes wasn't right? What reasons are there for thinking that animals can feel pain? After all, we can't get into the head of an animal, so how do we know what's going on in there? The answer is: in the same sort of way that we know another human being feels pain. How do you know that I feel pain? There are some human beings who, due to an abnormality in their nervous system, actually cannot feel pain. For them, life is hazardous in the extreme, since they can damage themselves, perhaps quite seriously, without being aware of it. How do you know that I am not one of those people? Well, I could, of course, tell you that I can feel pain. But this, in itself, is not decisive: I could be lying. In fact, there are no decisive tests that could establish, conclusively, that I can feel pain. However, there are a series of cumulative considerations, ones which, taken together, strongly suggest that I can feel pain. It is these considerations that strongly suggest that animals can feel pain also.

First, what is pain? Roughly, pain is an unpleasant sensory experience, typically (but not always) associated with bodily damage, and which typically (but not always) causes the individual who has it to try to avoid having more of it. This definition is a little sloppy, but it's probably good enough for our purposes. So, what reasons are there for thinking that animals (and other humans) can feel pain in this sense? There are basically three types of reason: behavioural, physiological, and evolutionary.

One reason for thinking that I am in pain is observation of my behaviour. First, I will systematically avoid, or try to escape from, things that typically cause pain. You won't find me putting my hand in the fire, leaning nonchalantly on the red-hot ring of my cooker, or changing the wheel on an improperly jacked-up car. Second, if I am unsuccessful in my attempts to avoid things that typically cause pain, then I am likely to either cry out for assistance, or more generally, engage in behaviour that we typically regard as expressive of feelings of intense discomfort. I am likely to cry out, scream and, more generally, swear profusely. Third, following my unfortunate run-in with things that typically cause pain, I am likely to avoid using the damaged body part, to expedite healing, possibly also reiterating behaviour of the second type (i.e. I limp around the house for the next few weeks, frequently muttering profanities).

Animals, of course, engage in essentially the same sorts of behaviour. First, they will systematically avoid (or try escape from) things that typically cause pain (the technical term is for these things is "noxious stimuli"). Second, if their avoidance or escape behaviour is unsuccessful, they will cry out, and engage in behaviour that we typically regard as expressive of feelings of intense discomfort. Third, following exposure to noxious stimuli, they will limit the use of an injured body part – for example, through immobilizing a damaged muscle by favouring another limb – to allow rest or healing.

So, there is a lot of behavioural evidence supporting the idea that Descartes was wrong, and that animals do feel pain. This evidence is, of course, not absolutely conclusive, but neither is it conclusive in the case of human beings. I might be an extremely good faker, for example, one skilled in avoiding noxious stimuli, and in pretending to feel pain when I do not. However, while the behavioural evidence is not decisive, it provides us with as much reason for thinking that non-human animals can feel pain as it provides for thinking that other human beings can feel pain. And that is very good reason indeed.

We have much more to go on than just behavioural evidence. Another important reason for thinking that animals can feel pain is provided by anatomical and physiological evidence. The neural mechanisms responsible for my behaviour after dropping the car on my foot are very similar to the mechanisms that are responsible for the cat's behaviour after I have stepped on its foot. That is, in humans, we know that pain behaviour following exposure to a noxious stimulus is controlled, or brought about by, certain types of neural mechanisms. We also know that there are similar neural mechanisms in all mammals and birds, and probably in all vertebrates. We know that the operation of these neural mechanisms in ourselves is accompanied by pain. And this provides us with good reason for supposing that their operation is accompanied by pain in other creatures too.

Most significantly, perhaps, the existence of *endogenous opiates* (or opiods) has been demonstrated in all mammals, birds, reptiles, amphibians, fish, and in some invertebrates such as earthworms and insects. Endogenous opiates, of which the endorphins are the most well known, are the body's natural opiates, and their function is to alleviate pain following major injury. It is thought that these opiates are involved in a survival mechanism that allows an injured animal – human or otherwise – to function normally until it has escaped immediate danger. So, the question is: why would an animal have a substance whose function was to alleviate pain unless it was capable of feeling pain? Now, one could always say: perhaps the endogenous opiates have another function in other animals? Perhaps, yes. But this seems uncomfortably like grasping at straws. By far the most natural explanation of the presence of endorphins and other opiates in non-human animals is that these animals can feel pain, and the endorphins are there to help them control it when necessary.

Moreover, all vertebrates and some invertebrates respond in similar ways to other, non-natural, pain controlling substances, like anaesthetics and analgesics. Why would substances that function to reduce or control pain have any effect on animals unless those animals are capable of feeling pain? Again, the most natural explanation of why analgesics and anaesthetics alter the behaviour of non-human animals is that these animals are capable of feeling pain.

The final reason for thinking that animals can feel pain is based on evolutionary considerations. At the time of Descartes, it was thought that human beings were very different from any other animal. Indeed, humans were not thought of as animals at all. The mind, the thinking part of us, was, according to Descartes, a non-physical thing, not really part of the physical world at all, but a soul or spirit that survived the death of our physical bodies. Only humans had this, animals were just physical machines. Now, however, we are in possession of so much evidence that emphasizes just how similar we are to other animals. In particular, we know that we have all had a common evolutionary history, beginning with chains of molecules floating around in the primeval soup. We share over 98 per cent of our DNA with chimpanzees. Indeed, genetically, there is a greater difference between chimpanzees and monkeys than between chimpanzees and us. We, and the other great apes, have a common evolutionary ancestor, and we split into separate species only – on the evolutionary timescale – very, very recently. Imagine you are standing on the east coast of Africa. You are holding hands with someone else, and they are holding hands with someone else, and so on. You form a chain of hands across the African continent, all the way to the west coast. The person standing at the water's edge in the west represents a molecular peptide chain, the first primitive proto-organism. You, standing at the water's edge in the east, represent the species *homo sapiens*. Then, we and the other great apes split from our common ancestor about thirty yards away from where you are standing. That's how close we all are on the evolutionary time scale.

Now, given that we all know this, doesn't it seem just a little implausible to suppose that pain is something that only humans and no other species has? Pain, certainly seems to have an evolutionary explanation. Animals have it so they will avoid noxious stimuli, and attempt to escape from such stimuli should they come across them. And, clearly, any animal that does not avoid/escape from noxious stimuli is not going to last very long. Things, perhaps, don't have to be this way. Perhaps we could have been hard wired to avoid such stimuli, so that we just avoided such things automatically, in the manner of an unconscious reflex response. But, the method evolution seems to have adopted in the case of human beings is to get us to avoid noxious stimuli by building into us a capacity to feel pain. And given the immense evolutionary continuity between us and other animals, it would be very surprising if evolution employed an entirely different method in other animals.

When we put the three different types of evidence together, when we add up behavioural, physiological, and evolutionary arguments, we end up with a compelling case for thinking that many non-human animals can feel pain. We have as much reason for thinking that, say, a dog feels pain when we kick it as for thinking that a human feels pain when we kick him or her. The only difference, of course, is that the dog cannot *tell* us that it feels pain, at least not in any way that we humans regard as conventional. Nor, with the likely exception of a few trained higher primates, can any other non-human animal. But the same is true of human infants and pre-linguistic children. We're still pretty confident that they feel pain. My point, then, is that given the three types of argument described above, we have just as much reason for thinking that non-human animals feel pain as for thinking that pre- or non-linguistic humans feel pain. And that, I think, is good enough.

2 OTHER BAD MENTAL STATES

Pain is a classic example of a *bad* mental state. That is, pain is a state such that anyone who has it would, typically, rather be rid of it. Typically, but not always. Mild pain can, perhaps, be quite pleasant when you associate it with (as you see it) some noble endeavour or achievement; think of the mild muscle pain that accompanies completion of your first marathon. Generally, however, those who have pain would rather be rid of it. The same goes for a broad class of other mental states, the most prominent examples of which are *fear* and *anxiety*.

Fear is an emotional response to a situation that is taken to be dangerous. This response involves heightened awareness and attentiveness to the environment, and is usually unpleasant. It is typically prompted by a known object in one's immediate environment, and the function of the response is to facilitate evasive or otherwise protective action. Anxiety, on the other hand, is somewhat more diffuse. Like fear, anxiety is an unpleasant emotional response and, also like fear, involves heightened attentiveness to the environment. However, whereas fear is typically prompted by a known or recognized object or situation, anxiety is prompted by a novel, unfamiliar, situation. This way of distinguishing fear and anxiety may be a little artificial. It is, however, useful. On its first visit to the vet's office, a dog may tremble, and this will be because of anxiety in the face of unfamiliar, thus potentially dangerous, surroundings. On its second visit (remembering, perhaps, the ignominious incident with the thermometer) the dog may whine or try to escape through fear of a remembered event (well, it would scare me anyway).

Just as in the case of pain, there is ample behavioural, physiological, and evolutionary evidence to support the idea that many animals suffer fear and anxiety. Behavioural evidence includes motor tension, as seen in shakiness and jumpiness, hyper-attentiveness, as seen in vigilance and scanning, and inhibition of behavioural repertoire in novel situations (a classic symptom of anxiety). There are also clear changes in autonomic activity that are, again, taken to be classic symptoms of fear or anxiety. These include sweating, pounding heart, increased pulse rate and respiration, frequent urination and diarrhoea.

Much significant neurophysiological evidence centres on the presence of *benzodiazepine* receptors in the mammalian central nervous system. All anxiety-mediating agents that affect humans – alcohol, barbiturates, and the like – work by acting upon these receptors. Studies on animals have confirmed that such substances act on the benzodiazepine receptors in mammals in precisely the same way, that is, through barbiturate and ethanol binding sites, chloride ion channels, and neurotransmitter binding sites. In short, anti-anxiety drugs have substantially similar effects on both humans and non-humans, and, crucially, work by producing very similar neurophysiological and neurochemical changes. The most natural explanation of these findings is that many non-human animals can suffer from fear and anxiety.

Finally, just as in the case of pain, there is a straightforward evolutionary explanation for why this should be so. Anxiety and fear have the same evolutionary benefit as pain. They both serve to increase the animal's awareness of and attentiveness to its environment, preparing the animal physiologically for rapid flight (or fight), thus facilitating its ability to escape or overcome the danger.

So, I think it is reasonably safe to conclude that, in addition to pain, many animals can feel fear and anxiety. At the very least, we have as much evidence for believing that many non-human animals can feel pain, fear and anxiety as we have for supposing that pre- or non-linguistic humans can feel these things.

This means that many non-human animals are capable of *suffering*, for suffering is an umbrella concept that we use to describe what it is to feel pain, fear or anxiety. That is, we *suffer* pain, fear and anxiety. To have these states is, typically, to suffer them. This is not always true. As we have seen, relatively minor pain can even be enjoyable to those of a certain bent (sadomasochists, marathon runners, assuming there is a difference between the two). The same is true of certain relatively minor levels of fear and anxiety. The surge of fear I feel before surfing a large break on a wind-swept Atlantic storm beach can be enjoyable and liberating. Moreover, the duration of the pain, fear, or anxiety is also relevant. It is not clear that the short, sharp, stab of pain I feel in my back after certain ill-advised movements is tantamount to suffering. Also relevant is the extent to which the situation that prompts the adverse mental state is under your control. It is not clear whether the perhaps intense terror that accompanies your walk to the boxing ring constitutes suffering, since the choice to fight is, ultimately, yours. Nevertheless, once the intensity and duration of your pain, fear or anxiety reach a certain threshold, and once the circumstances that prompt these states are sufficiently outside your control, you can, quite properly, be said to suffer these things. If animals are capable of feeling pain, fear, and anxiety, they are also capable of suffering.

3 GOOD MENTAL STATES

A bad mental state is one that anyone who has it would, typically, rather be rid of, and anyone who has had it would rather not have again. Conversely, a good mental state is one that anyone who has it would, typically, rather have more of, or anyone who has had it would like to have again. Typical examples of good mental states are *pleasure*, *enjoyment* and *happiness*. Animals, we have overwhelming reason to suppose, can have bad mental states. Can they also have good ones?

Pleasure, very roughly, can be defined as a feeling, such that any individual that has it, typically, regards it as desirable and/or wants more of it. The laboratory provides a lot less data relevant to answering the question of whether animals can feel pleasure. Laboratory studies, as we shall see, tend to be in the business of producing bad mental states in animals rather than good ones. Nevertheless, on the face of it, it would be extremely surprising if animals were capable of having bad mental states but not good ones. If animals – most vertebrates and probably some invertebrates – can feel pain, they are, by definition, conscious. Pain is an aversive mental state, and therefore, a motivational one: it motivates animals to avoid or escape from a noxious stimulus. The same is true of fear and anxiety. But pleasure is also a motivational state, one with roughly the opposite function as pain. It would, I think, be extremely surprising if evolution had equipped animals with consciousness, hence the ability to make use of negative motivational states like pain, fear and anxiety, but not to make use of a positive motivational state like pleasure. Therefore, we should expect, on general evolutionary grounds, that if an animal is capable of feeling pain, it is also capable of feeling pleasure.

In addition to this, there is also the obvious behavioural evidence that the higher mammals at least feel pleasure, as any dog or cat owner will attest (I doubt that controlled laboratory studies would provide evidence any more useful than this). Finally, neural pleasure centres, similar to those found in humans, have been identified in the brains of mammals, birds and fish.

If animals can feel pleasure, and, for the higher mammals at least, the evidence for this is almost as convincing as for the claim that they can feel pain, then they are also, more or less by definition, capable of enjoyment: just as pain is the sort of thing that is suffered, pleasure is the sort of thing that is enjoyed. What about happiness? Can animals be happy? This is more difficult, since the idea of happiness is multiply ambiguous. On the one hand, we often use the word "happiness" to refer to some kind of feeling or emotional state. In this sense, happiness corresponds pretty closely to pleasure or enjoyment. For example, we might describe someone sitting down with an ice-cold beer after running a marathon on a scorching summer's day as "happy." If the idea of happiness in this sense coincides with pleasure or enjoyment, then animals, if they are capable of pleasure, are also capable of happiness. On the other hand, we often use the word to describe a general disposition that someone might have. In this sense, we might say that the happy person was unhappy in their new job. This is not contradictory; it simply means that their normally sunny personality or disposition was temporarily clouded by feelings or emotions produced by their new occupation. It seems that there is no great impediment to regarding animals as capable of happiness in this sense either. Most people who have owned several dogs, for example, are quite capable of distinguishing different dispositions or temperaments, even within dogs of the same breed. Nina, one of my German Shepherds, for example, is always, as we might put it, "game for a laugh." What this means is that, no matter what the circumstances, she is always ready to play. A twenty-mile run behind the bicycle, from which she has collapsed into an exhausted sleep? No problem. Wake her up and she's ready to go again. You try this with Mabon, however, and you're likely to lose a hand. There is no great obstacle to recognizing certain types of disposition in dogs; nor is there any great difficulty in distinguishing sunny dispositions from the not so sunny (the number of digits on your hand can depend on your facility in this regard). So, in this second sense of happiness, animals can probably be happy too.

There is, however, a third sense of happiness in which animals may not qualify. We often use the word "happiness" in connection with some sort of life plan, and the question "Are you happy?" then, roughly, means, "Are your present activities conducive to, or consonant with, your overall life goals?" Animals, clearly, cannot be happy in this sense unless they are capable of making judgements about their lives as wholes. And it is most unlikely that they can do this

4 Do animals feel "in the same way we do"?

Today, it is only those who are severely in the grip of some theory, whether philosophical, psychological, religious, or broadly ideological, that seriously doubt that animals are capable of experiencing both bad and good mental states. Many people, however, argue that this fact does not matter, morally, because animals don't suffer pain, fear or anxiety "in the same way we do." Their suffering is, consequently, less important than that of human beings. What does it mean to say that they do not suffer "in the same way we do"?

Well, one thing it might mean is that animals can't worry about the sort of things we do. Suppose you and your dog have both fallen down a ravine, resulting in the pair of you having broken legs. You are both suffering. However, your suffering, it could be argued, is augmented, because you not only have the raw pain of the broken leg but the additional worry of how you are going to get out, whether anyone will find you, how you are going to afford the medical expenses, and so on. Clearly, your dog is not capable of worrying about the financial implications, or agonizing over whether, all things considered, private health insurance might have been a good idea. So, even if the pain of the broken leg is the same for you and your dog, you seem to be suffering more. It is because of your greater cognitive and imaginative powers, your ability to think about the future, and so on, that you suffer more. Therefore, it could be argued that humans, because of their greater cognitive, imaginative and speculative powers, typically suffer more than animals do in the same situations.

This conclusion, however, would be premature. The reason you suffer more than your dog does, in the imagined example, has more to do with the example than anything else. We could easily imagine another example where your dog, precisely because of its lesser cognitive, imaginative and speculative powers, suffers more. For example, you and your dog are taken into a room where you are both given a very painful injection. However, the situation is explained to you (the injection is necessary to save your life, the pain will be relatively short lived, there will be no complications, and then you will be allowed to go ... – you can fill in whatever other details you think are necessary or helpful). Your dog, however, knows none of these things, and so in addition to the pain of the injection, it has the anxiety associated with unfamiliar surroundings, strange people restraining it, and so on. In this case, your dog seems to suffer more than you do.

Indeed, recent work strongly suggests something very disturbing: animals, precisely because of their lesser cognitive, imaginative and speculative powers, actually feel pain more intensely than we do. That is, not only does your dog have to contend with the additional anxiety of unfamiliar surroundings and people, the pain the injection causes it is actually greater than the pain the injection causes you. According to at least one major pain physiologist, R.L. Kitchell, response to pain is divided into a sensory discriminative component and a motivational-affective component.[2] The first component is concerned with locating and understanding the source of pain, and the danger with which it is correlated. The second component is concerned with escaping from the painful stimulus. Kitchell argues that since the first component is more limited in animals, because of their lesser cognitive, imaginative and speculative abilities, the second component should, as a compensatory mechanism, be correspondingly stronger. That is, since animals cannot deal intellectually with injury and danger as we do, their motivation to flee must be correspondingly stronger. And what would provide a stronger motivation to flee? Easy: they hurt more.

When people claim that animals don't suffer "in the same way we do", what they are saying is probably right. But, unfortunately, they then tend to slide from this to the claim that animals "suffer less than we do." And this is almost certainly wrong. Not only do we have no evidence for the claim that animals, because of their lesser cognitive, imaginative, and speculative abilities, suffer less, in general, than we do, what evidence we do have tends to go the other way: animals suffer more.

5 Desires and preferences

We have excellent reasons, then, for thinking that many non-human animals are conscious, that they are capable of suffering mental states such as pain, fear and anxiety, and enjoying states such as pleasure and (two out of three forms of) happiness. We also have no general reason for thinking that they suffer or enjoy these mental states in any less a sense than we do. On the face of it, this seems enough to show that animals are also capable of having *desires*. It is difficult to see how one could suffer a perhaps intensely unpleasant state like pain without actively disliking it, and without desiring that it stop. Again, this is almost a matter of definition. A bad mental state, such as pain, is defined as one that anyone who has would, typically, rather not have, and anyone who has had would rather not have again. And to talk of what someone would rather or rather not have is to talk of their desires: it is to talk about what they want.

A consequence of this, also, is that many animals have preferences, for a preference is simply a special form of desire. Roughly, a preference is a desire for one alternative situation over another. An animal that is in pain, and desires that its pain stop, has a preference for a situation in which it does not have pain over one in which it does.

Some people, mostly philosophers, are not going to accept this so quickly. The reason is that they have a much narrower concept of desire (consequently of preference also). According to some philosophers, the notion of desire is closely bound up with the idea of *reasoning*. Suppose a dog is chasing a rabbit. It seems natural to say that the dog desires to catch the rabbit, after all why else would it chase it? However, according to some philosophers, if the dog genuinely desires to catch the rabbit, it must be able to engage in what is known as *practical reasoning* about how best to catch the rabbit, where this is a sort of means-ends reasoning. For example, "If I do X, then I will get Y" is a (simple) form of practical reasoning. So, merely chasing the rabbit is not enough; the dog must also be able to reason in this sort of way: if I chase the rabbit, then I will (or might) catch it.

When you think about it, this is quite sensible. Merely "going after" a rabbit is not going to be enough for desire. A bullet will "go after" a rabbit, if shot accurately. But there is no way that the bullet desires to catch the rabbit. So, in order to be convinced that the dog desires to catch the rabbit, we need to first be convinced that it is capable of engaging in this sort of practical reasoning. Similarly, to be convinced that the laboratory dog desires that its electrical shock induced pain end, we need to first be convinced that it can engage in practical reasoning about how to end it (e.g. if I jump over this wall, this will make the pain stop). So, the question we must ask is: can animals engage in practical reasoning?

There is, in fact, ample evidence that most vertebrates can engage in such reasoning. In fact, most of the work carried out this century on animal learning presupposes, at least implicitly, that they can do so. Consider, for example, the studies done by Martin Bitterman in the 1960s.[3] Fish can be trained to press their heads against particular plastic objects. For a correct choice of lever, as selected by the experimenter, they are rewarded with a meal worm. The fish will then learn to push only items of, say, a particular shape, and to ignore the rest. One would think that this type of learning is evidence that fish can at least reason to the following degree: "If I push this (rather than this), I will get that." However, to the experimenter in the grip of a behaviourist ideology, this is evidence of no such thing. Rather, the behaviour of the fish can be explained in terms of *conditioning*: force of habit created by the way the fish has been rewarded in the past.

Suppose, now, that you change the "answer." Whereas, before, the fish is rewarded for pushing square objects, it now gets rewarded for pushing round ones. The fish will eventually learn the new "answer" and act accordingly. If you change the answer back to the original, the fish will, eventually, work that out too. And so on. Bitterman discovered that if the same sort of experiment is done on amphibians, reptiles, birds and mammals, an important phenomenon is observed: they all become progressively quicker at learning the correct answer. When you reverse the answer the second time, amphibians, reptiles, birds and mammals all learn the correct answer more quickly than they did the first time. And they do so yet more quickly the third time, and so on. Fish showed no such improvement.

This indicates that a completely different type of learning procedure emerges with reptiles and amphibians. Since a fish takes, each time, just as long to learn the new answer, the fish's behaviour can be explained in terms of its prior conditioning. It is largely habit, so it could be argued, which pushes the fish first one way, then the other. That is, the force of habit created by the previous reward shape has to be overcome by the force of habit created by the new shape. Or, at least, that is Bitterman's interpretation.

However, the behaviour of amphibians, reptiles, birds and mammals cannot be explained in this way. When, say, a mammal's behaviour alters rapidly in response to a new reward shape, this suggests that its behaviour has *overcome* the conditioning created by the previous reward pattern. So, clearly, its new behaviour cannot be explained in terms of conditioning. Rather, its behaviour strongly suggests some kind of practical reasoning is taking place, specifically some kind of hypothesis formation and testing. Thus, practical reasoning seems to emerge, at the very latest, at the level of herpetofauna (i.e. reptiles and amphibians). Therefore, so too does desire.

This is a conservative estimate. Nothing in Bitterman's experiments rules out the possibility of fish having desires. Rather, the experiments indicate that we have far more compelling evidence for the claim that amphibians, reptiles, birds and mammals can engage in practical reasoning than we do for the claim that fish engage in such reasoning. Therefore, we also have more evidence for the claim that amphibians, reptiles, birds and mammals have desires than we do for the claim that fish have desires. It's also worth noting that more recent studies seem to indicate that .at least some fish do exhibit progressive adjustment in multiple reversal trials of the sort described above. These fish, therefore, do seem capable of a form of practical reasoning. If these studies are correct, then what seems to be crucial in determining whether fish exhibit the progressive adjustment indicative of practical reasoning is the size of the shoal to which they belong (once the size of the shoal reaches a certain threshold level, its members exhibit progressive adjustment).

The further we move from fish, the more confident we can be that the animal in question is capable of practical reasoning. Mammals, for example, exhibit a type of learning that is not evident in reptiles and amphibians. A probability learning situation is one where each possible response is rewarded a fixed percentage of the time, but where the rewarded alternative is varied at random. So, for example, let's suppose that a rat has a choice of pushing a red lever or a blue one. The rat is going to be allowed, say, 100 pushes. The red lever, let us suppose, will be rewarded sixty times, and the blue one forty times. However, within these parameters, the choice of rewarded lever is random. This is what's known as a probability learning trial. In these sorts of trials, fish adopt a strategy known as *matching*: they respond randomly, but in percentages that match the frequencies with which each alternative is rewarded. Rats and monkeys, on the other hand, adopt a strategy known as *maximizing*: they respond 100 per cent of the time with the more frequently rewarded alternative (in this case, the red lever). Birds occupy a curious middle ground. Like fish, they match on visual problems (e.g. where the reward is tied to the shape or colour of the object), but, like mammals, they maximize on spatial trials (e.g. where the reward is tied to the location of the object).

The matching strategy adopted by fish can, arguably, be explained in terms of conditioning. A sixty to forty response ratio simply reflects the conflicting forces of habit produced by a sixty to forty reward ratio. In contrast, when a mammal or bird adopts the maximizing strategy, it exhibits an independence from the habituation induced by the reward ratio, and this independence strongly suggests that some kind of practical reasoning – hypothesis formation and testing – is at work.

In conclusion, it may be true that, in order to genuinely have desires, an animal must have the ability to engage in practical reasoning. This is no obstacle to thinking that animals have desires, however, because we have excellent evidence for supposing that they are capable of engaging in practical, or means-end, reasoning (the examples described above merely scratch the surface). We can, at the very least, be confident that amphibians, reptiles, birds and mammals have this ability. Therefore, the claim that these sorts of animals have desires is unproblematic.

6 BELIEFS

The mental repertoire of animals has been gradually expanding as this chapter has progressed, and now includes pain, fear, anxiety, suffering, pleasure, (two out of three forms of) happiness, enjoyment, desires and preferences. Now, how about beliefs? Are animals capable of believing?

It may seem completely obvious that they are. Suppose a dog chases a squirrel up a tree, and then sits there barking. Does the dog not believe that the squirrel is in the tree? If it didn't, why would it be there barking at the foot of the tree? However, perhaps it merely sees the squirrel, and has no corresponding belief. To avoid this possibility, let's suppose the squirrel has disappeared; unbeknownst to the dog, it jumped to another tree, and vacated the area. (This is not implausible. Similar things happen to my dogs on a regular basis, although, usually with rabbits disappearing into scrub.) In this sort of case, does the dog not believe that the squirrel is in the tree?

Some philosophers have argued that it does not, and cannot, believe this.[4] The dog does not have the concept of a squirrel, and so cannot believe anything about squirrels. What is the concept of a squirrel? Basically, it's a set of sentences that specify crucial information about what a squirrel is. Plausible examples of these sentences would be ones like: "A squirrel is a mammal"; "A squirrel has fur"; "A squirrel has four legs"; "A squirrel has blood flowing through its veins"; "A squirrel has a skeleton", and so on. These, and other things, are, many have argued, the sorts of things you have to know in order to know what a squirrel is. These sorts of sentences, then, specify the concept of a squirrel.

For the dog to have the concept of a squirrel it must have a set of beliefs of the sort specified in these sentences. That is, it must believe that squirrels are mammals, that they have blood flowing through their veins, that they have fur, skeletons, and so on. If it does not have these beliefs, it does not have the concept of a squirrel, and so cannot believe anything about squirrels. In particular, it cannot believe that the squirrel is in the tree (the same points can also be made about its having the concept of a tree). But, it is argued, the dog is not going to have many of these beliefs. Does the dog, for example, have the concept of a skeleton? If not, how can it believe that squirrels have skeletons? Does it have the concept of a mammal? If not, how can it believe that squirrels are mammals? Therefore, it does not have the concept of a squirrel. Therefore, it cannot have any beliefs about squirrels.

It is quite easy to see that there is something wrong with this argument. Suppose you are an explorer, and have come across a hitherto undiscovered tribe in a remote region of the world, a tribe that has had no contact with any other society. Let's suppose the men and women of this tribe are terrified by your camera. After months of study, you think you have worked out why: you hypothesize that they believe the camera will steal their souls. The example is a familiar one. Now, who knows if this hypothesis is correct, but the important point is that it *might* be correct: it's the sort of hypothesis that might turn out to be right, or so it seems.

But, wait a minute! The tribesmen and women have no idea what a camera is. They have no idea of its internal workings, no idea of what it produces (pictures, if your hypothesis is right, are frozen souls for them). They no more have the concept of a camera than the dog has the concept of a squirrel. So, since they don't have the concept of the camera, they can't have any beliefs about the camera, including the belief that the camera will steal their souls. So, why are they terrified?

What has gone wrong? Basically this: we have assumed that *our* concept of the camera is the only concept. Consequently, we are confusing *what* the tribesmen and women believe with the *way* that they believe it. A tribesman clearly does not have our concept of a camera (if he did, he wouldn't be terrified), but he can still believe *of* the camera, of this object that we point at him, that it will steal his soul. We may not be sure of how he represents the camera to himself, we may not be sure, that is, of his concept of the camera, but we can be sure, nonetheless, that his belief is a belief about the camera.

We can make the same sort of point about the dog. The dog may not have *our* concept of a squirrel. We may not know how the dog thinks about the squirrel, how it represents squirrels to itself, whether it distinguishes squirrels from rabbits and other small animals or whether it lumps them all under a broad, partly self-referential, category like "eat-able thing!" or "chase-able thing!" We may not know, that is, anything about the dog's concept of a squirrel. Nevertheless, we still know that the dog thinks *of* this squirrel, *of* this thing that it has been chasing, that it is up there.

Dogs, and other animals, in all likelihood, see the world very differently from us. Their beliefs, correspondingly, are probably very different from ours. Often we may have difficulty working out the *way* they believe things, the concepts in terms of which they represent the things they think about. But we can still be reasonably certain not only *that* they have beliefs but also *what* those beliefs are about.

7 AUTONOMY

To summarize the argument so far. Most vertebrates have the ability to suffer pain. Many of them can also suffer fear and anxiety and enjoy pleasure and (two out of three forms of) happiness. In addition to this, most of them, certainly amphibians, reptiles, birds and mammals have desires, preferences (a type of desire) and beliefs, and the ability to engage in at least rudimentary forms of practical reasoning. They also have, and this is implicit in the discussion so far, the ability to direct their behaviour on the basis of what they desire, prefer and believe, and to use their practical reasoning abilities to guide their actions in accordance with these desires, preferences and beliefs. This, after all, is what desires, beliefs and practical reasoning abilities are for: to make a difference to behaviour. And what this means, in at least one sense of this difficult philosophical term, is that animals, at least many of them, are *autonomous*.

Like most philosophical terms, "autonomy" is ambiguous. At least two different senses need to be distinguished. In the first sense there is what I shall call *weak* autonomy. An individual acts autonomously in the weak sense if he or she acts intentionally, with understanding, and without controlling influences that determine the action. First, to act autonomously, you must act intentionally: you must mean or intend to act in the way you do. Your action is what you meant to do, and not an accident or reflex response. Second, to act autonomously, you must understand what it is you are doing. If you willingly sign the consent form for electro-convulsive therapy, but have no idea what this therapy entails, you are not acting autonomously. Third, in order to act autonomously, you must act in the way you do because of what you want and believe, and not because someone is forcing you by, say, putting a gun to your head.

In this sense of autonomy, the weak sense, many animals can act autonomously. A wolf stalking its prey acts intentionally, with understanding, and without outside coercion or compulsion. Any creature that has beliefs and desires, and can act on the basis of these beliefs and desires, where this action is perhaps mediated by way of appropriate practical reasoning, is capable of autonomy in this weak sense. All the evidence suggests, then, that this type of autonomy can be exercised by mammals and birds, and even by reptiles and amphibians.

Sometimes, however, when philosophers talk of autonomy, they have something stronger in mind. Autonomy, in what we can call the *strong* sense, requires something more than just the ability to act intentionally, with understanding, and without outside coercion or compulsion. It requires, in addition, the ability to critically reflect, or think about, your reasons for acting, and, in particular, to think about whether these are good or legitimate reasons. For example, one way of developing the notion of strong autonomy is in terms of the idea that you must act not only on the basis of what you want, but also that, after critical reflection on what you want, you want to have those wants you have; that is, you want to want what you, in fact, want. It is reasonably clear that the vast majority of animals, with the *possible* exception of some higher primates such as chimpanzees or gorillas (and even here the evidence is suggestive rather than conclusive), are not capable of autonomy in the strong sense.

8 SUMMARY

All the evidence we have suggests that the vast majority of vertebrates possess a complex mental repertoire. It seems overwhelmingly likely that all of them can feel pain, and that many of them can, in addition, suffer "bad" mental states like fear and anxiety, and enjoy "good" mental states like pleasure. Some of them might even be describable as happy (at least in two out of three senses of that term). All the evidence we have also suggests that mammals and birds, and even reptiles and amphibians, have desires and preferences and, concomitantly, at least rudimentary practical reasoning abilities. Furthermore, since desires and practical reasoning abilities are useless without beliefs (it is no good desiring food if you are incapable of having a belief about how to go about getting it), we have every reason to suppose that these sorts of animals also have beliefs. Finally, as possessors of desires, beliefs, and practical reasoning abilities, mammals and birds, and even reptiles and amphibians, must, it seems, be regarded as capable of a form of autonomy, autonomy in the weak sense.

Many of you are going to regard these claims as stunningly obvious, and wonder why I've bothered to spend the past 10,000 words on them. Basically, I agree with you. The reason I have spent so much time arguing for the obvious is that so many people have not, and many still do not, accept the obvious. For so many decades, the scientific orthodoxy was that animals could not think or feel, that their behaviour could always be explained in terms of reflex, of conditioning, and other essentially non-mental processes. For so many decades the philosophical orthodoxy was that animals could not think or feel, that to do this requires language, and animals have none. Today, both these orthodoxies are increasingly being recognized for the nonsense they are; but it does take time to get nonsense out of our system.

Establishing the mental life of non-human animals is, from a moral point of view, a result of great importance. What it shows is that animals are *mental subjects*. The life of an animal has an *inside*; an animal can experience its life as going a certain way, as going well or badly. And this is what is crucial. There is *something that it is like* to be an animal. An animal is the sort of thing that can fare better or worse, things can go well or badly for it. Of course, we can talk about things going well or badly for inanimate objects; things go badly for my car if I crash it into a wall, for example. But this is different: the car has no perspective on this. The car does not experience things going well or badly for it; animals do.

I am going to argue that the capacity for life to go well or badly, better or worse, in this sort of experiential sense that animals have but cars lack, is enough – or, as philosophers say, *sufficient* – for something to count morally. If you are the sort of thing for which things can, in an experiential sense, go well or badly, better or worse, then you count morally. Other people are, then, morally obligated to take you into account, to consider you and the impact their actions will have on you, when they deliberate and act. So, that animals have a mental life, that things can, in an experiential sense, go better or worse for them, is a crucial first step in the case for animal rights.

2

THE MORAL CLUB

1 THE INS AND OUTS OF THE MORAL CLUB

Tennis balls are small, round and furry. So too are baby rabbits. Yet those of us of a non-psychopathic persuasion would be horrified at the thought of playing tennis with (i.e. "utilizing" rather than "against") a baby rabbit. And this is not simply because rabbits don't bounce properly! Most of us are perfectly willing to allow that our treatment of animals raises at least some moral issues. We are quite willing to allow that we have to consider the impact of our actions on animals. Having knocked all the balls over the fence, we can't just pick up the nearest baby rabbit and start serving with that. That would be morally outrageous. We all know this. This, essentially, is why we have laws prohibiting cruelty to animals.

One way of putting this is to say that we view many animals as things that are *morally considerable*. And to say that we regard something as morally considerable is to say that we regard it as the sort of thing that counts morally – the sort of thing that should, morally speaking, be considered when we decide what to do. To get clear about this, think of morality as a *club*. Some things are in the club, and some things are not. If you're in the club, then you count morally. You are morally entitled to be treated with consideration, and whatever follows from this. If you're in the club, that is, others have a moral obligation to treat you with consideration; to consider the impact their actions will have on you. If you're outside the club, on the other hand, then you don't count morally, and no one is under any obligation to consider you and the impact their actions will have on you.

Humans provide the clearest examples of things that are in the club. All humans, we are inclined to suppose, are entitled to be treated with consideration, and consequently each of us has the moral obligation to treat others with consideration. Tennis balls provide equally clear examples of things that are outside the moral club. Tennis balls cannot be treated with consideration. Treating something in this way is a matter, at the very least, of respecting its interests, and tennis balls don't have interests. Consequently, when deciding what is the best thing to do, morally speaking, you don't have to consider the impact of your actions on tennis balls, how your actions will affect their welfare, and the like. You have to consider what you do *with* tennis balls, since this may affect the welfare of things that are in the moral club; but you do not have to consider what you do *to* tennis balls.

The crucial difference between rabbits and tennis balls, of course, is that the former are, whereas the latter are not, *conscious*. Rabbits have, in the sense explained in chapter 1, an experiential welfare: life can, experientially speaking, go better or worse for a rabbit, but not for a tennis ball. Consciousness seems to play a central role in determining what we let in, and what we exclude from, the moral club.

On the other hand, while they may be in the moral club, animals seem to have a peculiarly second-class status. Staying with rabbits, if reincarnation is true (and personally I don't believe it for a second), then if you come back as a rabbit, you must have messed up badly in your previous existence. Here is just one of the things that might happen to you. Someone drips an irritating substance in your eye at regular periods for up to three weeks. If you are lucky, you will spend these three weeks in only extreme discomfort before you are killed. If you are not so lucky, then you can look forward to weeks of agony, during which you are prevented from scratching or in any way touching your eye. Then you are killed. Dark karma indeed! Personally, I think I would opt for tennis.

Animals are in the moral club, because we accept that they deserve some form of consideration. But they are very definitely second-class club members. We give them some consideration, but not much. Certainly not as much as we give human beings. I am going to try and show that this is a morally unacceptable position. It is morally unacceptable because it is *inconsistent*. Inconsistent with what? Basically, with the rules of the moral club. If we checked club rules, we would see that a radical *egalitarianism* holds within the club. *All members are equal members.* And so it is unacceptable, morally unacceptable, to accord one member less consideration that another. Consciousness may be what gets you in the club, but once you're in, your status is equal to every other member of that club.

2 MORAL ARGUMENT: THE ZEN APPROACH

Talk of the moral club, and who is in and who is out, is potentially ambiguous. Just as with any club, we can talk of who *is* allowed in the club and who *should* be allowed in the club. Non-whites actually were (and in some cases unofficially still are) excluded from certain social and sporting clubs, but not many of us today (hopefully) would say they *should* be thus excluded. Similarly, when we talk of the moral club, it seems we can talk not only of who *is* in the club but, also, who *should* be in it. For example, I said that consciousness was a necessary credential for admission to the club. This, it seems, is the way things *are*, but is it the way things *should* be? After all, it excludes many things that at least seem to have value – 1000-year-old redwoods, complex and detailed ecosystems, and so on. Now, nothing I say actually entails that such things do not count morally.[1] However, I do think that if a case is to be made for new membership – a case, that is, for the claim that something that isn't in the moral club *should* be in it – then this case will have to derive from moral beliefs and principles that we actually do hold. The same is true for arguments concerning the status of members within the club. All moral claims, I think, ultimately arise from principles we already believe. And nowhere is this truer than in the case for the moral claims of animals. The key to moral argument – arguing morally for anything – is working out what we already believe. And this, in fact, is not as easy as you might suppose.

The idea of moral argument has had a bad time recently. "Argument", in this context, doesn't mean disagreement, spat or squabble, nor even, necessarily, a dispute. Argument, in the philosophical sense, is a process of supporting what you believe by giving reasons or citing evidence. And this, many people suppose, can't be done in the case of moral beliefs. We often hear that morality is *subjective*, in that what is right or wrong depends on the feelings or opinions of people, and so can vary from one person to another. We are also often told that morality is culturally *relative*, in that moral codes and standards vary from one society to another. Either way, it does not seem to leave much room for the idea of moral argument. What need is there to rationally support your moral beliefs, if they are simply expressions of your feelings? That would be like justifying the feeling of pleasure you get when you eat ice cream. Feelings, ultimately, are just things you have or don't have. Beyond a certain point, at least, they are not the sorts of things that can or need to be justified. Similarly, if moral standards are simply the rules that happen to be in force in any given society, then justifying any moral claim is simply a matter of saying, "Look! This is what we do here!"

Now, I don't happen to believe that moral standards are really subjective or relative in these senses. But it doesn't really matter anyway. I am going to show you how to argue morally, even if your opponent believes moral standards are relative or subjective. To do so, you have to bend like a reed in the wind.

Here is one way to argue morally. First, take a general moral rule or principle like, say, "Thou shalt not kill." This is a general rule since it does not apply to any particular person. It doesn't say thou shalt not kill Bob, for example. Nor is it restricted by time, place, method, etc. ("Thou shalt not kill Bob in the study with a dagger", etc.). Then you try to get people to believe it. Then, when you have got them to believe it, you show them that a particular action, involving a particular person, time, place, method, and so on, is wrong. You did kill Bob in the study with a dagger? Then what you did was wrong. Why? Because: "Thou shalt not kill", i.e. killing is wrong.

Now, for me, this method of moral argument has always seemed to lack a certain finesse. But, my aesthetic sensibilities aside, it isn't going to be a very effective method against someone who claims that morality is relative or subjective. Then, it's highly likely that you are going to find yourself subjected to a litany of stories about cultures where killing is just hunky-dory, and they get on fine thank you very much. The point is that any attempt at moral argument that relies on general rules or principles that nobody could reasonably contest has a problem: such principles are often contested, and sometimes quite reasonably. If the history of moral philosophy has taught us anything, it has taught us that.

To avoid being given a lecture on cultural anthropology, it's wise to adopt another strategy, one with more refinement and effectiveness. *You work with what they give you.* You don't try to foist any general moral principle on your interlocutor; instead, you find out what general moral principles they already believe, and you work with those. Most people will give you plenty of material to work with.

So, this is how it goes. You want your opponent to believe some claim, call it proposition X. Let's suppose that you believe proposition X for various reasons, and you want to convince your interlocutor of the truth of X also. So, first, you find out what they believe. Suppose you find out they believe proposition Y. It doesn't matter so much whether you believe Y, you can use it anyway. So, if all goes well, you then show that if they believe Y, they must also believe X. Proposition Y logically entails proposition X, at least loosely. So, if they believe Y, they must also, logically, believe X. If they do not, they are being inconsistent. Chances are, it won't go this smoothly. Perhaps you can't get straight from Y to X. Perhaps, however, you can show that proposition Y entails proposition Z, and proposition Z entails proposition X. So, if they believe Y then, again, they must also, to be consistent, believe X. The result is the same even if the route is more tortuous.

Once you have reached this stage, your interlocutor faces a choice. Either they must believe X (which you want them to do), or they must abandon Y. If they try to hold on to Y but still not believe X, then they are being inconsistent. So, your strategy will work best if Y is a claim they will really want to hold onto. The more you can get at their most cherished beliefs, and use those, the greater your chance of success in convincing them. How can this strategy work? It works because we don't always realize or appreciate the implications of what we believe. Our beliefs are often complex, and we don't fully understand their meaning; consequently we don't always appreciate their consequences.

It is not just individuals, but also communities, that can have beliefs. This may sound odd, but all it means is that a large percentage of the individuals in a community adhere to a belief, and that, consequently, the belief plays a role in shaping the customs or practices of that community. Just as with individual people, the beliefs of a community can be more or less deeply ingrained. Some of a community's beliefs are relatively superficial ones that the community can jettison without too much difficulty. Other beliefs run to the very core of the community; they are beliefs that the community could not abandon without, in effect, becoming a very different type of community. Moreover, just as an individual can fail to understand all the consequences of their beliefs, including their most fundamental ones, so too a community can exhibit the same sort of failure.

The argument for animal rights, to be developed in this and the next chapter, does not involving foisting any unwanted moral rules or principles on anyone. Rather, I am going to work with principles we already have. These general moral principles are etched deeply into our moral community, consequently into the moral consciousness of each one of us. We have failed to properly understand the consequences, the logical implications, of these principles. For they entail, I shall argue, that our duties, our *moral* duties, to animals are far more substantial than we commonly think. That is, the fundamental moral principles that shape our own moral community are incompatible with our present attitudes towards and treatment of animals. And consistency, then, requires that we change our behaviour and attitudes.

What are these fundamental moral principles? The first is what we can call the *principle of equality*: all people are created equal.[2] The second we can call the *principle of desert*: people should not be blamed (or praised) for things that are beyond their control. I am going to try and show that once we properly understand these principles, what they mean and where they come from, we will also realize that they require some very radical changes in the way we treat non-human animals. Animals are in the moral club as fully paid up, hence equal, members.

3 ARE WE ALL CREATED EQUAL?

All people, we are told, are created equal. What does this mean? Does it mean everyone is born into the same social or economic group? Obviously not. Some are born with the proverbial silver spoon in their mouth; most of us are not. Does it mean that everyone is born with the same talents and abilities? The same innate level of intelligence? Again, clearly not. We all differ in our abilities. Some of us will be sporting superstars, most of us won't. Some will be Einsteins or Beethovens, some of us will be completely talentless in these arenas. Whether we like it or not, it is a simple fact about the world that people come in different shapes and sizes, with different physical abilities, different intellectual abilities, different creative abilities, and so on. Some people are born stunningly handsome, athletically gifted and with IQs of 153. Others are not so lucky. We are all different; and a lot of this has to do innate features, features with which we were born. So where does this leave the idea that we are all created equal?

In fact, it leaves the idea perfectly intact. The claim that all people are created equal does not refer to any supposed physical, intellectual or artistic equality. If it did, the claim would be clearly false. Instead, the claim refers to what some people call *moral equality*. This does not mean that all people are equally morally good or morally bad. It is fairly obvious that some of us behave much better than others. And most of us occupy a portion of the moral spectrum between, say, Mother Teresa and St Francis of Assisi, on the one hand, and, say, Hitler and Pol Pot on the other. So, to talk of moral equality is not to say that everyone is a moral equal in this sense. It does not mean that everyone is equally good or bad. In fact, to talk of moral equality is not to *describe* the world at all. To talk of moral equality is not to say how the world *is*, it is to say how the world *should be*. The function of such talk, that is, is not to describe but to *prescribe*.

When we talk of moral equality, what we are talking about, in an admittedly vague and poorly understood way, is the idea that all people deserve *equal consideration*. This, to reiterate, is not a description of the way the world is; it's a sad truth that many people are not treated this way. Rather, it is a claim about what people are morally entitled to: every person is entitled to be treated with consideration equal to that accorded anyone else. This, properly understood, is what the principle of equality means.

Of course, this is all very rough. What does it mean to treat everyone with equal consideration? This is not an easy question, and I don't even pretend to have a complete answer. Neither, as far as I can tell, does anyone else. But, at the very least, we can say that treating everyone with equal consideration requires giving every person's *interests* due weight. Everyone's interests should be taken into account. We all have interests – interests in staying alive, remaining or becoming healthy, finding a partner, and so on. In fact, each one of us, at any given time, has many thousands, perhaps millions, of interests, whether we are aware of them or not. Now, not all of these can be satisfied. I may have an interest in getting a job, and you might have your eye on that same job. Clearly, at least one of us is going to be disappointed. So, to say that all interests should be given due weight and consideration does not require that we should attempt to satisfy the interests of everyone: that would be impossible.

Nor, in fact, does it require that we treat everyone the same. This is simply because different people have different interests. You might have an interest in opera, and I might have one in mud wrestling. So, the principle of equality does not require that my interest in opera be taken into account, or given due weight and consideration, for the simple reason that I have no such interest. Similarly, you might have an interest in being screened for the gene that causes sickle cell anaemia. I have no such interest because I know that I cannot possess this gene (although I may have an interest in *you* being screened for the gene). Interests vary from one person to another, and for various reasons. Therefore, the precise treatment to which someone is morally entitled under the principle of equality can vary from one person to another also. The principle of equality simply requires that we take each person's interests into account. It does not entail that they have the same interests. Therefore, it does not entail that they should be treated the same.

Identifying exactly what is involved in giving due weight and consideration to the interests of everyone is, in fact, where the hard work really starts. Philosophers have been arguing about this for a long time, and different moral theories give very different accounts of what is involved here.

Happily for us, we don't need to get into all that. For our purposes, it is enough to point out what the principle of equality rules out rather than what it rules in. And what it rules out is a general discounting of any person's interests. That is, we cannot fail to take a person's interests into account simply because of who and how they are. If I don't like you, for example, or if I disapprove of your lifestyle, then that is no excuse for me to completely ignore or disregard your interests. To do this would be to contravene the principle of equality.

Of course, it may be that a person can abrogate their right to have their interests fully taken into account. If someone commits a heinous crime, for example, do we not, in consequence, often regard his or her interests as less important? This, actually, is a difficult issue. For example, is the prisoner's interest in remaining free not given due weight, simply because we incarcerate them? Or is it that, after giving their interest due weight and consideration, we decide that it is outweighed by the public's interest in remaining safe? Tricky issues, and happily we don't need to solve them. All that we need to do, for the purposes of the argument for animal rights, is to point out that *if* there are ever cases where a person's interests should not be accorded equal weight, this is always because of something they have *done*, and something for which they are *responsible* (the issue of responsibility will be explored further towards the end of the chapter).

4 WHY SHOULD WE BELIEVE THE PRINCIPLE OF EQUALITY?

The principle of equality, then, is the claim that the interests of everyone should be accorded equal weight and consideration. While we are not too sure what this principle requires, we are sure what it rules out: a general discounting of someone's interests, at least where this is unconnected to anything they have done or for which they are responsible. But why should we believe the principle of equality?

It is a curious fact that although moral philosophers tend to agree about little, there is fairly unanimous agreement that the principle of equality is a valid moral principle. Why should this be? The reason stems from the connection between this principle and an even more basic one. And this more basic principle is, as philosophers sometimes say, *constitutive* of our moral thinking. By this, they mean that it is essential to our moral thinking; that it is so central to the way we think about morality that it would be difficult, or impossible, to imagine what morality would be like without this principle. The principle can be stated like this: *no moral difference without some relevant other difference.*

This may sound cryptic, but it's really quite simple. An example might help. Hitler is an archetypal example of someone who is morally bad; very bad in fact. What made him bad? Well, different ethical traditions give different answers. What are known as *consequentialist* moral theories emphasize the consequences of actions. The rightness of wrongness of an action, according to consequentialism, depends solely on its consequences. So, if you are a consequentialist, you will probably believe that Hitler was a bad person because his actions had such horrendous consequences. On the other hand, what are known as *deontological* moral theories emphasize the intentions of the person performing the action: the rightness or wrongness of an action depends, at least in part, on the intentions of the person performing the action. So, if you are a deontologist, you will probably think that Hitler was a bad person because, at least in part, of the intentions or motives that he had for his actions.

We don't need to adjudicate between these two alternatives. Suppose there is a person who does the same things as Hitler, with the same intentions as Hitler, and with the same consequences. He starts a world war, sends six million people to the gas chambers, and so on. And he does so for precisely the same reasons as Hitler, that is, with exactly the same motives. In this case, it would *make no sense* to say that Hitler was a bad person but that this other person is not. If Hitler is bad, and if this other person does exactly the same things as Hitler for the same reasons, then this other person *must* be bad also. You would, broadly speaking, be contradicting yourself if you were to say that Hitler was bad but that this other person was not.

The point is that a difference in moral evaluation – judging something to be morally good, bad, or neutral – only makes sense if it is based on a difference in other qualities. In fact, not only must there be a difference in other qualities, this difference must also be a *relevant* one. So, if this other person lacked the familiar silly moustache, this would not be a relevant difference. Nor would it be relevant difference if this other person carried out his atrocities in, say, east Asia instead of Europe. Nor would it be a relevant difference if this other person were a woman rather than a man.

We morally evaluate not just people, of course, but a whole range of things: actions, rules, attitudes, institutions, customs and so on. But the same point applies no matter what it is we are evaluating: no moral difference without some relevant other difference. Take actions, for example. If two people do exactly the same thing, in exactly the same circumstances, for exactly the same reasons, with exactly the same results, it would make little sense to say that one action is good but the other bad. If the one action is good, then the other one must be good also. And vice versa. The principle *no moral difference without some relevant other difference* applies to anything – persons, actions, rules, institutions, motives, practices, habits or whatever – that can be morally evaluated.

A consequence of this is that if we are to justify a difference in the way we treat two people and, in particular, in the consideration and respect we accord them, then we have to be able to point to a morally relevant difference between them. Throughout history, of course, there have been very different ideas about what constitutes a morally relevant difference. Philosophers such as Aristotle and Nietzsche, for example, were what are known as *perfectionists*: they believed that level of excellence was a morally relevant factor. So, an Einstein, a Mozart, or, to use Nietzsche's favourite example, a Goethe, might deserve extra consideration – basically, have more moral rights – than the average person in the street simply because they were "better" (in, of course, senses defined by Aristotle and Nietzsche). And, not so long ago, it was commonplace to hear that a difference in race or gender was a morally relevant difference.

Today, however, with our opinions shaped as they are by the democratic ideal, we no longer hold these views (or, hopefully, most of us don't). As we shall see, there are good reasons for this, ones that will be explored later in the chapter. For now, we can simply note that the moral equality of all people, the idea that everyone is deserving of equal consideration, stems from our belief that there are no morally relevant differences between people together with the claim that there can be no moral difference without some other relevant difference.

This means that the principle of equality is on a very secure foundation. Moral philosophers, as I said, don't tend to agree about all that much. However, no one, but no one, is going to mess with the principle of no moral difference without some relevant other difference. The principle is so central to our moral thinking that we simply cannot imagine what morality would be like without it.

5 THE PRINCIPLES AT WORK

The idea that there can be no moral difference without some relevant other difference provides a really good example of how some moral principles work. Most of us have probably never even explicitly thought about or formulated this principle. Its effect on the way we think about morality is profound, but subterranean; it tacitly, rather than explicitly, shapes our moral thinking. Moral principles (or *meta-moral* principles – principles about moral principles) are often like this. This is one of the reasons we often don't comprehend the consequences of what we believe: sometimes we are not even explicitly aware of what it is we believe.

How does all this apply to animals? To develop the argument for animal rights, we start off with the principle of equality. That is:

Premise 1: human beings are entitled to be treated with equal consideration.

We then add what I have argued is the basis of this principle, the idea that there can be no moral difference without some relevant other difference, which, in this case, has this specific form:

Premise 2: there can be no difference in the entitlements of members of two groups unless there is a relevant difference between members of those two groups.

That is, if members of one group are entitled to be treated with consideration, and if there are no morally relevant differences between them and members of another group, then members of that other group are entitled to be treated with the same consideration. Then, we add the controversial premise:

Premise 3: there are no morally relevant differences between humans and (many) non-human animals.

No one can really contest the first premise; the principle of equality is a deeply rooted component of our communal moral thinking. And no one can contest the second premise, for that is simply an expression of the idea that there is no moral difference without some relevant other difference, and this is what explains, and provides the logical basis of the principle of equality. So, if we also accept the third premise, we get the conclusion:

Conclusion: (many) non-human animals are entitled to be treated with consideration equal to that accorded humans.

The problem is, of course, premise 3. Many people think that this claim has simply got to be wrong. After all, human beings are very different from all non-human animals, and can do things no non-human animal can do. So, in the eyes of many, premise 3 is wrong, and, therefore, the argument doesn't work. I am going to try and show, however, that premise 3 is true: while there are many differences between humans and other animals, these differences are not relevant ones, not ones that are relevant to the level of consideration and respect animals deserve.

So, we have to ask ourselves two questions. First, what are the principal differences between humans and other animals? Second, are these differences morally relevant ones?

6 IS BEING HUMAN MORALLY RELEVANT?

The most obvious difference between us and other animals is precisely that they are not human. This is a difference, of course. But is it a relevant one?

It's difficult to see how it could be. Species membership is, ultimately, a genetic category. That is, the particular species to which you belong depends on what genes you have. To be a human being, and not a member of some other species, is a matter of your possessing a certain set of genes, a certain genetic profile. And it is difficult to see how genes, in themselves, could be morally relevant factors. Whether you are white or black, for example, depends on which genes you possess. And differences of genetic profile here are not, we now accept, morally relevant differences. So, why should possession, or lack of possession, of certain genes be any more morally relevant in the case of species? It is difficult to see why.

Suppose, for example, there is intelligent life on other planets. We have all watched enough of (the various versions of) *Star Trek* to get our heads around the idea that there might be various species of extraterrestrials, perhaps more advanced than us, who have developed cultures and societies that we would admire should we become aware of them. Now, I'm not, of course, claiming that there exist such species. We simply don't yet know. But, my present point concerns not fact but *principle*. If there were such species, would we want to say that their members possess no moral rights simply because they are not members of the human race? It is difficult to see what the rationale for this could be. Would you want to say that Data possesses no moral entitlements, simply because he is an android? Or that Worf possesses no rights, simply because he is Klingon? Sticking with science fiction, how about ET? My point is not that these fictional characters exist (I may be a philosopher, but I'm not that mad). Rather, my point is that the idea that species membership is the crucial factor, determining who has rights and who doesn't, automatically rules out creatures such as these having any moral rights. And this seems implausible and unwarranted. It is not that such creatures exist, but that *if* they existed they *would* be plausible contenders for individuals who deserved to be treated with consideration and respect. We couldn't legitimately rule out their moral status simply because they were not human. And this means that being human is not what is crucial, morally speaking.

We can make the same point in a slightly different way. Suppose you found out that you were a genetic anomaly. While you look and act human, scientists have discovered that you possess a radically different genetic profile, so different, in fact, that you are not human at all. Imagine, for example, a sort of *Island of Dr Moreau* scenario. You began your existence as a fertilized non-human ovum. Then, through a combination of genetic manipulation, vivisection, surgery or whatever, you were transformed into something that looked, acted, and felt human. Indeed, not being aware of your origins, you spend your life thinking that you are human. Scientific testing eventually reveals your mistake. Would you then accept that you don't, in fact, have any moral status? That the consideration you thought you were due, as a human being, was inappropriately applied and should now be withdrawn? Presumably, you would not accept this, and rightly so. Even after your true genetic status has been revealed, there is still a clear sense in which you are the same person you always were. What has changed is your understanding of the biological category to which you belong; but this revision has not changed your identity as the particular person you are. You still feel the same, you have the same memories, the same history, the same emotions, thoughts, feelings, and the like. Whoever you were before your genetic status was revealed, there is a clear sense in which you are still that person. Then, surely, whatever consideration and respect you thought you were due before the discovery of your true genetic character, you are still due after the discovery. And, if this is right, species membership cannot be what is crucial, morally speaking.

These examples are, of course, somewhat far fetched; but this is not a significant drawback. What we are examining by way of these imagined examples is our *concept* of morality. That is, we are examining how we *think* about the notion of moral entitlement; of what makes an individual entitled to a certain sort of treatment. One way of facilitating this process of concept examination is by considering various imagined examples or situations, and often the more outlandish the example the more helpful it is in this regard. We could also use the same process for more mundane and well understood concepts. We might, for example, examine the concept of, say, a bachelor by imagining various features that bachelors might have. Then, when we find that we cannot, without contradicting ourselves, imagine a married bachelor, this tells us something about the concept of a bachelor: the concept of a bachelor logically excludes the concept of being married. The reason we do not do this with mundane and well-understood concepts is precisely because they are mundane and well understood. There is no point in clarifying these sorts of concepts; we already understand them perfectly well. However, part of what we are doing in the case of moral inquiry is clarifying the nature of the moral concepts we use. And, in this case, the concept we are trying to clarify is, as some philosophers call it, that of *moral considerability*; of what it means to be morally entitled to consideration or respect.

In this light, what the above thought experiments tell us is that the concept of moral considerability is *not* closely tied to the concept of species membership. In certain circumstances at least, we would be quite happy to extend the umbrella of moral consideration beyond the boundary of our species. We would, it seems, be happy to extend moral consideration to beings like Data, Worf, and ET, if they existed; and, likewise, to at least some of the things that emerge from the island of Dr Moreau. Being a member of the human species, then, cannot be what is crucial in deciding who has moral rights, or who deserves to be treated with consideration and respect. So, we cannot rule out the moral status of other animals simply because they are not human.

7 Is LOOKING HUMAN MORALLY RELEVANT?

The thing about Data and Worf is that they look human. More or less. So, too, does our imagined refugee from the island of Dr Moreau. ET doesn't; but Spielberg did infuse him with various humanlike mannerisms, gestures and so on. And, besides, he looks vaguely humanoid. So, perhaps, the morally crucial feature is looking human, at least vaguely. Other animals don't deserve to be treated with equal consideration and respect simply because they don't look human. Can this be right?

A moment's thought should, I think, convince us that it cannot. In particular, the suggestion falls victim to what we can call the *elephant man scenario*. John Hurt played the eponymous, and hideously deformed, man in the 1981 film (and since my knowledge of the actual historical figure is restricted to what I can remember from the film, I shall focus on the celluloid version of events). Now, Hurt's famous line from film, one upon which various impressionists and stand-up comedians dined out for years, was "I am not an animal!" If the arguments to be developed in this book are correct, then Hurt is expressing his point in a misleading way. But the fundamental idea underlying it is sound. The idea is that it does not matter what he looks like, it is the mind within that counts. The treatment to which he is entitled is not diminished one iota by his rather unfortunate appearance. He can run the full human gamut of thoughts, feelings and emotions. And the consideration and respect he is due derives from these things, rather than the way he looks.

It is true that the elephant man still looks more or less human. But surely the same point would be true no matter how much make-up had been applied to John Hurt. No matter how hideously deformed the elephant man was, even if his deformity had reached a point where he was no longer recognizable as a human being, at least not from outer appearance, this would in no way detract from, diminish or undermine the consideration and respect he was, morally, due. It is what is happening on the inside that counts morally, and not the outer appearance. Beauty, we all know, is only skin deep; moral considerability is not.

8 IS INTELLIGENCE MORALLY RELEVANT?

So, it seems that what is happening "on the inside" is what is crucial in determining whether something morally deserves equal consideration. That is, what is crucial is the sort of mind, rather than the sort of body, an individual has. However, as we saw in the previous chapter, many non-human animals have quite complex minds. In common with human beings, they can suffer pain, fear and anxiety and enjoy pleasure and (two out of three forms of) happiness. Amphibians, reptiles, birds and mammals can also believe, desire, and engage in at least rudimentary forms of practical reasoning (as can, probably, some forms of fish). And the more we ascend the evolutionary ladder, the more complex their mental capacities become. Therefore, if we are to justify the claim that there is some vast moral gulf between humans and non-human animals, such that humans do, but animals do not, deserve to be treated with consideration, then we are first going to have to identify some relevant mental difference between humans and animals.

The most obvious mental difference between humans and other animals is level of intelligence. Humans are, in a nutshell, much smarter than other animals. This is a difference, but is it a morally relevant one? Does the gap in intelligence between them and us justify our present attitudes towards and treatment of non-human animals?

Again, it is very difficult to see how this suggestion is going to work. In particular, the suggestion falls victim to what is known as the *argument from marginal cases*. While it is true that *most* humans are more intelligent than *most* other animals, there are some humans for which this is not true. Some humans, for example, are born with moderate to severe brain damage, resulting in significant diminution of their mental powers. Some humans are not born this way, but become this way either through accident or through the sort of degenerative brain disease associated with old age (or eating improperly rendered beef, for that matter). For these desperately unlucky human beings, it is often not true that they are more intelligent than, say, the average dog or horse, and in many cases may be significantly less intelligent. Indeed, even normal human infants and very young children do not obviously possess any more intelligence than the average higher mammal, and significantly less intelligence than many of the higher primates. Therefore, if you want to claim that animals, because of their inferior intelligence, lack various moral entitlements, then you are also going to have to claim that these human beings lack those entitlements also.

If this is so, why not treat them in the same way we now treat animals? Why not hunt them, wear them, experiment on them, even use them for food? If intelligence is what is crucial, morally speaking, and if it is legitimate to do all these things to animals because they lack intelligence, then it should be morally legitimate to do the same things to those human beings who, for whatever reasons, are no more intelligent than the animals which we do these things to. This is simply a matter of consistency; *if*, that is, intelligence is what matters morally. Now, a few total psychos aside, it seems fairly safe to assume that the vast majority of us (myself included, I hasten to add) are not in favour of hunting the mentally deficient. Nor are we in favour of vivisecting babies or turning the brain damaged into handbags. Unless you are very ill, you will regard these suggestions as morally outrageous. Why? Because despite the gulf in intelligence between them and us, these unlucky human beings still have moral rights; they are entitled, morally entitled, to avoid this sort of treatment. We would be badly disregarding their moral rights if we were to hunt, wear, eat or vivisect them. This, I hope and believe, is what most of us think. And if this is what we do think, we cannot be relying on intelligence as the morally decisive factor determining who has, and who does not have, moral rights.

9 THE ARGUMENT FROM MARGINAL CASES

What counts against the idea that level of intelligence is a morally relevant difference is one version of what is known as the *argument from marginal cases*. It is worth having a look at this argument further, since it is a logically very powerful argument that applies to other things besides intelligence. The argument, in a generalized form looks like this. First, we take some proposal for what counts as a relevant difference between humans and animals. So:

Premise 1: X is proposed as a morally relevant difference between humans and non-human animals.

The next step is to point out that not all humans have X, whatever that is:

Premise 2: There are certain human beings who do not possess X.

This gives us the conclusion:

Conclusion: Therefore, either (a) those humans possess no more moral rights than animals, or (b) the claim that X is a morally relevant difference must be abandoned.

The argument is so powerful because it applies no matter what X is, as long as it is true that some human beings do not have X (so, it wouldn't work for a property like "being human", which by definition all humans have; but it does work for most other properties). In the above case, X designates a certain level of intelligence. But it could refer to almost any proposed difference between humans and non-human animals. Some people, for example, have proposed use of language as the morally relevant difference: humans count morally because they can use language, animals do not because they can not. Now, it is difficult to see how language use, in itself, has any relevance to morality; but let's overlook this. For if language use is proposed as the morally relevant difference between us and them, then we can easily run the argument from marginal cases in exactly the same way as we did in the case of intelligence. That is, we can point out that certain human beings are unable to use language (for whatever reasons – brain damage, infancy, disease, raised by wolves, etc.). And would you want to deny moral rights to these humans? If, along with most reasonable people, you think these humans do possess moral rights, then you have no basis for denying that animals possess the same rights. Unless you are willing to allow that humans who can't use language have no moral rights, you can't (consistently) claim that animals lack rights because they don't use language.

The argument from marginal cases provides us with a powerful argument that applies to almost any suggested morally relevant difference between humans and animals. Whatever feature is proposed, ask yourself: "Do all humans have it?" If they don't, then ask yourself: "What about those humans who don't have it?" This argument, almost single handedly, rules out most of the suggested relevant differences between humans and animals. Differences there may be, but, as the argument from marginal cases shows, these differences are almost certainly not morally relevant ones.

Is there any way of getting around this argument? It seems the only option available to someone who wants to insist that there is some morally relevant difference between humans and animals is to bite the bullet, move to Psychoville, and claim that certain human beings – the brain damaged, infants, the senile, etc. – who do not live up to the required level of intelligence (language use, or whatever is your favourite example of a supposedly relevant difference), do not, in fact, possess moral rights, and do not deserve to be treated with equal consideration.

This position, however, seems implausible for at least two reasons. First, remember the consequences. If certain sorts of human beings lack moral rights, and, so, if we don't need to consider or respect their wishes, then why not, say, conduct painful experiments on them? Why not test cosmetics on them? Why not saddle up the horses, release the hounds, and chase them over the countryside? They wouldn't want us to do any of this, of course. Who cares? According to the present suggestion, these humans lack moral rights, including the right to be treated with consideration, because they fall below the threshold level of intelligence. If these suggestions are unacceptable to you, as I assume they will to most people of a non-sociopathic persuasion, then you should reject the claim that humans deficient in one or another respect – intelligence or whatever – thereby lack moral rights.

Second, there is a profound logical problem with the claim that a difference in, say, intelligence, is a morally relevant difference. The problem is that it seems impossible to non-arbitrarily settle on any relevant level of intelligence. Suppose, for example, there were a species of extraterrestrials, vastly more intelligent than us. And whereas the average human intelligence on the IQ scale is around 100, the aliens' level of intelligence, on the same scale, averages over 500. Accordingly, they suggest 300 as the cut off point for the possession of moral rights: any individual with an IQ of 300 or above should be treated with equal consideration and respect, anyone who falls below that threshold should not. Presumably, we would all be very unhappy with their choice of threshold level, since we all fall below it. We would probably claim that 300 is a morally arbitrary figure. But what makes 300 any more arbitrary than, say, a level of fifty? Or ten? Once we set our own likely scores aside, all seem equally arbitrary. And this strongly suggests that intelligence is a not a morally relevant feature, but a morally arbitrary one.

Space does not permit me to deal with all the possible suggestions for morally relevant differences between humans and animals. Intelligence is simply the most common one. But, hopefully, I have said enough to give you some idea of just how difficult it is to identify any such difference. It's not just difficult. No one has ever succeeded in identifying such a difference. Indeed, no one has even come close to a remotely plausible suggestion on this score. The reason for our difficulty here, I think, is clear: *there is no such difference*. And, if this is correct, there is no justification for the differential treatment we accord humans and animals. And, therefore, much of our current treatment of animals is, in all likelihood, very wrong indeed.

10 WHAT ABOUT POTENTIAL?

Potential is something you often see dragged into the debate about animal rights. In particular, some people claim that the comparison of the intelligence of babies and animals is illegitimate. Although it may be true that babies and young children are no more intelligent than, say, dogs and horses, and significantly less intelligent than the higher primates, nevertheless, babies and young children have the potential to be more intelligent than these animals, and in the normal course of things will fulfil this potential.

The appeal to potential, however, is not going to save us from the problem of marginal cases. There are still large numbers of human beings who, for one reason and another, do not have the required sort of potential (e.g. the potential to develop their intelligence above the level of other mammals). Those children with severe brain damage, or those adults at an advanced stage of Alzheimers, for example, do not have this sort of potential. So, we could still run the argument from marginal cases using these groups of human beings. And, would we really want to say that these humans do not count morally? I hope not.

But, this aside, there are serious problems with thinking that potential is a morally relevant feature anyway. You have the potential let's suppose, to be Prime Minister of Britain. Does this mean that you now have the rights or entitlements of the Prime Minister? Clearly not. At most, it means you *potentially* have the rights and entitlements of the Prime Minister. So, potential never gives you actual rights or entitlements, it gives you only potential ones. So, it is difficult to defend the claim that the potential of babies and young children gives them rights or entitlements that animals don't have. At most it can give them potential rights, but not actual ones. And a potential right is, for all intents and purposes, no right at all. Young children no more have additional rights because of their potential for intelligence than you have additional rights because of your potential to be Prime Minister.

11 THE PRINCIPLE OF DESERT

In addition to the principle of equality, there is another principle that plays an enormous role in shaping our moral thinking. I'll refer to this as the *principle of desert*. In moral philosophy, the word "desert" has nothing to do with arid or otherwise desolate regions of the earth. Instead, it has to do with the idea of people, as we sometimes say, *getting their just deserts*. "Desert", that is, is the abstract singular term that comes from the word "deserve." Your desert, in the moral sense, is what you *deserve*.

The best way of understanding the role of desert in our moral thinking, is to see it not as functioning independently of the principle of equality but, rather, in tandem with it. The principle of equality is based on the idea that there can be no moral difference without some relevant other difference. The principle of desert tells us that some differences are not relevant ones. Which differences? Those that we have not in any way earned or merited; those that are, so to speak, *beyond our control*.

Too see how this might work, remember the perfectionists, Aristotle and Nietzsche, mentioned earlier. They thought that level of "excellence" (as defined by them) was a morally relevant difference between people, so that "excellent" people actually merited more moral consideration than average people. Typically, perfectionists think that the usual standards of morality do not apply to excellent people; these standards are for, as Nietzsche put it, the *herd*. Perfectionists, however, still accept the idea that there is no moral difference without some relevant other difference; they simply think that level of excellence is a morally relevant difference.

How would you argue against a perfectionist? Both you and he (or she) believe in the idea that there is no moral difference without some relevant other difference. You just have very different ideas of what constitutes a morally relevant difference. One way of arguing would be to bring in the idea of desert. People, you might argue, should get what they deserve. And, in particular, people do not deserve to be blamed or penalized for things that are beyond their control. The level of excellence of a person, for example, their intelligence or their artistic creativity, is not something that a person generally has much control over. Within certain limits at least, the intelligence or creativity of a person is a matter of the way they are born, or of early childhood influences; and neither of these are things over which the person has much control. So, a person who, for whatever reason, is lacking in intelligence or creativity does not deserve to be penalized for this. In short, level of excellence is a not a morally relevant feature because people do not deserve or merit their level of excellence.

The principle of desert is probably best understood as a combination of two claims, one about the notion of *praise*, the other about the notion of *blame*. And these two claims are, almost but not quite, two sides of the same coin. First, a person does not deserve to be praised for things for which he or she is not responsible. Second, a person does not deserve to be blamed for things for which he or she is not responsible. You would neither praise nor blame a person for being born with blue eyes. This is something beyond their control; it is, metaphorically speaking, nature's choice not theirs. Neither would you praise or blame a person for being born male instead of female, black instead of white. Nor, almost as obviously, would you praise someone for being born a genius, or blame them for being born mentally disadvantaged. All these things are beyond our power. We are not responsible for them, therefore they merit neither praise nor blame.

If we are careful, we can translate this into a point about moral entitlement. Your entitlements are simply the things to which you are entitled, and so your moral entitlements are the things to which you are morally entitled. Not all entitlements are necessarily moral ones. There are, for example, legal entitlements, and unless you think all laws are necessarily moral (i.e. morally correct), not all legal entitlements will be moral ones. So, first, let's be clear that I am talking only about moral entitlements, not entitlements of any other sort.

So, with this qualification in mind, we can formulate the principle of desert in terms of the idea of moral entitlement. As formulated, it looks like this. The moral entitlements you have cannot be diminished by things over which you have no control. That is, your moral entitlements cannot be reduced by things or circumstances for which you are not responsible. Being born with blue eyes does not reduce your moral entitlements because it is something over which you have no control. Neither, by the same reasoning, are your entitlements diminished by your being born black (or white), male (or female). Nor are your entitlements diminished by your being born mentally or physically disadvantaged. All these things are beyond your control. Therefore, they have no bearing on the things to which you are morally entitled. Why? Because taking away a person's moral entitlements is, in effect, a form of punishment, and no one should be punished for things that are beyond their control.

Careful readers will have noticed that when I formulated the principle of desert in terms of the idea of moral entitlement, I used only the negative, or blame-based, version of the principle. That is, I used only the idea that you should not be blamed for things that are beyond your control. I did not use the idea that your moral rewards are unaffected by things beyond your control. This is because I seriously doubt that the positive, reward-based, account can be translated into the language of moral entitlement. We sometimes say, for example, that a person who becomes seriously ill *deserves* our sympathy. But becoming seriously ill is not, presumably, something over which they have any control. So, if they are indeed entitled to our sympathy, this seems to show that their moral entitlements can be *increased* by circumstances over which they have no control. This certainly adds a wrinkle or two to our thinking about the connection between responsibility and desert. However, for the purposes of this book, this does not really matter. For my purposes, and for the case I want to develop for animal rights, the important idea is that your moral entitlements cannot be *diminished* by circumstances for which you are not responsible, or over which you have no control. Whether they can be increased by such circumstances does not really matter.

The fundamental moral entitlement, as I said earlier, is the entitlement to be treated with equal consideration. Any other entitlements that we have almost certainly derive from this one. So, the right not to be tortured, not to be killed unnecessarily, to live your life, within certain limits, as you choose, to have access to education, and so on: all these stem, in the end, from the entitlement to be treated according to the principle of equality. So, the principle of desert, basically, amounts to this: *your entitlement to be treated with equal consideration cannot be diminished by things or circumstances over which you have no control.*

12 WHAT ANIMALS DESERVE

If you are in the moral club, then you have moral entitlements, and others are under the obligation to treat you accordingly. That is what the club is: an entitlements club. But getting in the club in the first place is not something for which you are responsible, or over which you have any control. For example, on most accounts, you get into the moral club if you are the sort of thing that is conscious or sentient or (what may or may not be the same thing) the sort of thing that has interests. But being the sort of thing that is sentient is not something over which you have any control; you are simply born that way. Similarly, being the sort of thing that has interests is nature's choice, not yours.

The principle of desert, accordingly, applies only to things that are *already* in the moral club. That is, it applies only to things that already have interests. The principle of desert that is, is not a principle about how to get in the club, but a principle about the status you have once you are in that club. What it says, basically, is that *within* the moral club, any difference in status between two individuals cannot be the result of circumstances that are beyond the control of those individuals. That is, for any two individuals that are entitled to be treated with consideration, any difference in the amount of consideration they are due, morally speaking, cannot be the result of circumstances over which those individuals have no control. There can be no difference in status within the moral club as the result of eye colour, for example, since that is something for which you are not responsible. Neither, for the same reason, can there be any difference in status within the club because of race, gender, or innate intellectual or physical abilities. All these are beyond anyone's control, and differences between them cannot, therefore, provide a justification for differences in the amount of consideration and respect different individuals are owed.

The principle of desert, then, is a principle concerning what we might call *differential* moral entitlement: differences in the amount or degree of consideration people are due. What it says, in a nutshell, is that if there is any difference in the amount of consideration different individuals are owed (assuming they are owed anything – assuming, that is, they are in the moral club) these differences cannot be the result of *unearned* or *unmerited* factors; they cannot be the result of factors beyond those individuals' control.

In many cases, it is difficult, perhaps practically impossible, to separate those things that are beyond our control from those that are not. Take genius, for example. Genius, we are sometimes told, is ten per cent inspiration and ninety per cent perspiration. I don't know if this is true, but if it is then genius depends not just on what you are born with, for which you are not responsible, but also on the work you put in, for which you are. But, there again, how responsible are you for having the ability to work hard? Jim Courier, a tennis player always slated for lack of inspiration but praised for abundance of perspiration, claimed that the capacity to apply himself and put in the necessary hard work was a talent, therefore a form of inspiration. And perhaps he has a point. Perhaps the ability to work hard is something shaped by innate endowments, or inculcated in you by certain features of your early childhood. And you have no control over these things.

As a matter of fact, neither I nor anyone else really has any idea of the extent to which we are responsible for our skills, aptitudes, and other behavioural characteristics. Perhaps we are responsible for all of them, perhaps for some, perhaps for none of them. For the purposes of this book, however, none of this matters. The relevant feature, for our purposes, is one over which we can be absolutely 100 per cent certain we have no control whatsoever: our *species*.

The principle of equality tells us that all members of the moral club should be treated with equal consideration unless there are morally relevant differences between them. The principle of desert tells us that any feature that we have for which we are not responsible, hence have not in any way earned or merited, is not a morally relevant feature. If we put these together, we get the claim that animals deserve less moral consideration than us only if there is some difference between us and them which we have earned or merited. But, there is no such difference.

Race and gender differences between two people are morally irrelevant precisely because these have not been unearned or merited; you are simply born belonging to a particular race and gender, and there is nothing you can do about it. Similarly, differences in innate intellectual or physical abilities between two people are not morally relevant, again because these differences have not been earned or merited. Your innate intellectual and physical abilities are nature's choice, not yours. If you are born grotesquely unprepossessing, athletically clueless, and with an IQ of seventy-three, you don't thereby have any less moral entitlements than someone born more fortunate. Why not? Because this, in effect, is to penalize you for circumstances over which you have no control. And this, if the principle of desert is right, is morally wrong.

Clearly, however, the species to which you belong is not something over which you have any control: it is not, that is, something for which you are in any way responsible. So, therefore, species is morally irrelevant. A dog, for example, is in the moral club because we recognize that our treatment of it does raise moral issues. That's why we have laws prohibiting cruelty and the like. We have such laws because dogs, and many other animals, have a welfare; things can, experientially, go better or worse for them. But if the dog is in the moral club then, by definition, it deserves moral consideration. But the principle of desert tells us that consideration it is owed cannot be diminished by any features or circumstances over which it has no control. But which species it belongs to is clearly something over which it has no control. Therefore, the consideration it is owed cannot be reduced by the fact that it is a dog rather than a human. And, clearly, the same goes for any other animal that is in the moral club.

The same point also applies to the innate intellectual endowments that go with being a member of one species rather than another. We are tempted to suppose that a dog is worthy of less consideration on the grounds that it is significantly less intelligent than us (or most of us at any rate). But, again, this difference is something over which neither we nor the dog have any control. This is the way we are born, and not something we earn. Therefore, innate intellectual abilities must also be irrelevant to the consideration one is owed.

Animals, therefore, as acknowledged members of the moral club, deserve to be treated with consideration equal to that accorded human beings. There are, I think, contrary to popular wisdom, no second-class members of the moral club. Anything that is in the club is in it equally. At the very least, we cannot discriminate within the club on the basis of species, or anything that goes with species, because an individual's species is not something over which they have any control.

13 WHAT DOES ALL THIS MEAN?

The reaction of many to these arguments is that they just can't be right. OK, one might think. We can treat animals with *some* consideration. But *equal?* That's just ridiculous! I admit, it does sound strange. But why? Probably because it conjures up images of animals being treated in the same way humans are now treated. Pigs being taken to school. Subsidized visits to the opera for dogs. Killing a cat being punishable by the same penalties as killing a human. And so on. And this is, of course, all ridiculous. However, none of this is required by the idea that we treat animals with consideration and respect equal to that we accord humans.

The principle of equality, the requirement that we treat animals with equal consideration and respect, demands only that we give their *interests* the same weight that we would give to the corresponding interests of human beings. Now, of course, there is nothing here which says that they have the *same* interests as human beings. Animals have some of the interests of humans, but by no means all of them. And often their interests diverge wildly from human ones. This, by itself, is enough to make us realize that the principle of equality does not require that we treat animals the same way we treat humans. It does not require us to educate pigs, for they have no interest in being educated, just as dogs have no interest in opera, subsidized or otherwise. The principle of equality tells us only that when a human and an animal have the same interest, we should, when deciding what to do, give equal weight to each interest. So, in no way, then, does it tell us we have to treat humans and animals the same.

But this still can't be right, surely? What about cases where humans and animals have the same interest? Both a human and, say, a dog can plausibly be regarded as having an interest in staying alive. Suppose, a human and a dog were both trapped in a burning house. You only have time to get one of them out. Does the principle of equality not mean that there is nothing to choose between saving the human or saving the dog? That you might as well toss a coin to choose? And, surely, this is wrong. Would it not be wrong to let the human die so you can save the dog?

However, again, none of this follows from the principle of equality. The issue of dying, and what's wrong with it, will be discussed at much greater length in chapter 4. Here, however, we can make some preliminary points. Suppose you have grown a tree from a sapling. You did this because you wanted this particular species of tree in your garden. Year in and year out, rain or shine, you were out in the garden fertilizing it, watering it, talking to it, and generally nurturing it. Your neighbour, on the other hand, wants the same sort of tree in his garden. He, however, calls up the garden centre, and has them deliver and plant a full-grown version of the tree in his garden. You both, it seems, have an interest in having this species of tree in your respective gardens. In one sense, we could even say that you and your neighbour have the *same* interest: the interest in having tree of species X in your garden. Suppose, however, that an unexpectedly early frost kills both of the trees. Would there not be a clear sense in which you have lost *more* than your neighbour? You had, in some intuitively clear sense, far more invested in your interest than your neighbour did in his.

Consequently, when your tree dies, you lose more than does your neighbour when his tree dies. The moral of this fable is that just because two interests *seem* to be the same, it does not mean that they *really are* the same. Consequently, one person can lose more than another by having what seems to be the same interest thwarted.

We can make the same point about the human and the dog. It may be that the human loses more in dying than does the dog. If this is true, then the human has a greater interest in staying alive than the dog does. And if this is true, the principle of equality requires that we save the human instead of the dog. And, more generally, in cases where humans seem to have the same interests as animals, it does not necessarily mean that they actually have the same interests. It may be that, in having the relevant interest thwarted, the human loses more than does the animal. Or it may not be: whether or not this is true will probably vary on a case-by-case basis.

However, I shall argue in chapter 4 that a typical human probably loses more in dying than does a typical non-human. If this is correct, then we can justifiably choose to save the human before the dog. This, as we shall see, proves to be a very minor concession. Most of the issues that affect animals in no way involve this sort of "who would you save?" scenario; these are very much abnormal circumstances. On the contrary, in normal circumstances, most of the good we can do for animals comes at only minor inconvenience to ourselves.

14 SUMMARY

Our moral thinking is governed by what I called the *principle of equality*: all people should be treated with equal consideration. This means, very roughly, that, in our moral decision-making, we should weigh the interests of all people equally. The justification for the principle of equality is the idea that there can be *no moral difference without some relevant other difference*. However, this means that the principle of equality applies not just to humans but, also, to all those things that are not relevantly different from humans. While there are many differences between humans and other animals, none of these differences are morally relevant ones, since all such differences are either morally arbitrary (e.g. species membership) or fall victim to the *argument from marginal cases* (e.g. intelligence). Therefore, the principle of equality encompasses not just humans but also at least some non-human animals, and we should treat these animals with consideration equal to that we accord human beings. This claim is further supported by another principle central to our moral thinking: the *principle of desert*. If we are in the moral club, and thus have moral entitlements, then these entitlements cannot be diminished by factors or circumstances over which we have no control. But species, like gender, race or eye colour, is not something over which we have any control. Therefore, our moral entitlements cannot be diminished in virtue of our belonging to one species rather than another. There is no moral difference without some relevant other difference, and, according to the principle of desert, any feature that we have over which we have no control is not a feature that can go into making a relevant difference. Finally, the claim that the principle of equality applies to animals as well as humans does not have the ridiculous consequences one might think. It does not require that we treat animals the same as humans. And it does not entail that, in the case of major life and death decisions, there is nothing to choose between humans and animals.

3

JUSTICE FOR ALL

The argument so far. The way we think about morality is organized around two crucial principles. The principle of equality claims that, in the absence of any morally relevant differences, you are entitled to as much consideration as anyone else; and this is true irrespective of whether you are human or animal. The principle of desert claims that, if you are owed consideration in the first place, then the amount of consideration you are due cannot be diminished by factors or circumstances over which you have no control. These two principles operate in tandem. The first tells us that, whether or not you are human, you are morally entitled to as much consideration as anyone else, as long as there are no morally relevant differences between you and others. The second tells us, in effect, that if you have no control over the differences between you and other individuals – human or not – then those differences are not morally relevant ones. Each principle on its own provides a powerful argument for animal rights. If we put the two together, the strength of the case is increased even more.

Any adequate moral theory must be appropriately sensitive both to the idea of equality and to that of desert. And this means that when we start looking at specific moral issues involving animals – using them for food, experimenting on them, and so on – then we will have to find a way of interweaving both ideas. How can this be done? The approach I favour derives, loosely, from the work of the Harvard philosopher John Rawls, although the way I develop his idea differs in many ways from Rawls' account.[1] In fact, Rawls probably wouldn't at all like what I've done with his idea. Too bad.

1 THE ORIGINAL POSITION

Imagine, or try and imagine, that you know nothing about yourself. You don't know your gender. You don't know your race. You have no idea about your place in society, whether you are rich or poor, white collar or blue collar. Nor do you know how lucky you have been in the distribution of natural talents. When God handed out intelligence, beauty, athleticism, charm and all the other useful things to have, you have no idea whether you were at the front of the queue or outside having a quick smoke. You do not even know which things you value, which things you regard as good or bad, and have no idea of what you desire and what you aspire to. In short, you know nothing about yourself. You have no specific information about the sort of person you are.

This is a description of what Rawls calls the *original position*. In this position you are behind a *veil of ignorance*; you are ignorant of any facts about yourself and the sort of person you are. It is from this sort of ignorance that, Rawls thinks, we should try to work out what an ideal human society should look like.

You may have already worked out the rationale for this idea of the original position. It's all to do with dividing things up fairly. Suppose you and your friends are watching a game on TV and, as usual, have ordered a pizza. Being a greedy and bellicose lot, the division of pizza has, in the past, been a source of acrimony between you. Disputes have been common over which slice is the biggest, who has the lion's share of the toppings, etc. What is the best way of ending these disputes? Easy. Make sure that the person cutting the pizza does not know which slice he or she is going to get. Make them choose last, or, at the very least, don't tell them what the order of choosing is going to be (so there is a possibility that they will choose last). A fair distribution of pizza is ensured by the fact that the person slicing it does not know which slice he or she is going to get. Because of this, any basis for partiality or bias in the way they cut the pizza has been removed. The rational thing for the pizza cutter to do, then, is to cut the pizza evenly. And, if this is the *rational* course of action in the original position, then, so Rawls' idea goes, it is the *fair* or *just* course of action in the real world.

This is essentially what is going on in the original position. If you are deprived of all specific information about yourself – your sex, gender, talents and abilities, values, goals and so on – and then asked, "What sort of society would you like to live in?" the answer you give is likely to be a fair or just one. Any basis for partiality or bias in your answer has been removed along with this knowledge. If you had this information, information about the sort of person you are, then you might be tempted, perhaps unconsciously, to choose a world that suited your abilities and requirements. But removing this information also removes the possibility of such bias. Since you don't know who you are, in choosing how you would like society to be, you are choosing a society that is best for everyone.

This, then, is Rawls' original position. My spin on this differs slightly, in ways that will soon become apparent, from Rawls'. To register this difference I'll talk about the *impartial*, rather than original, position.

2 BRINGING IN EQUALITY AND DESERT: THE IMPARTIAL POSITION

As Rawls himself points out, there are lots of different ways of setting up the original position. The impartial position, I shall call it, is the version of the original position shaped by the principles of equality and desert. Any version of the original position is, of course, going to be shaped by the principle of equality. If you don't know who you are, then you have no way of being biased towards yourself; any grounds for bias have been removed by the veil of ignorance. So, the idea of the original position clearly allows us to incorporate the idea of equality into our moral thinking.

What is not quite so obvious, but nonetheless equally true, is that the original position also allows us to incorporate the idea of desert. The principle of desert provides, in effect, a justification for excluding knowledge of certain information about oneself. In what I call the impartial position, the features of yourself that you know nothing about are precisely those features over which you have no control. Properties like gender, race, innate intellectual and physical endowments, are all excluded behind a veil of ignorance precisely because they are properties over which we have no control. They are, that is, features that we have in no way earned or merited. In the impartial position, knowledge of which of these features we have is excluded because they are morally irrelevant features. And they are morally irrelevant because we have no control over whether or not we have them.

The impartial position, then, is the version of the original position where the properties excluded behind the veil of ignorance are precisely those properties that we are not responsible for having. They are the properties for which the choice of whether or not we have them is not ours but nature's. In this way, we can mesh together the ideas of impartiality and desert in our moral reasoning.

3 The exclusion of species (and everything that goes with it)

Consider, now, the species to which you belong. Is this something over which you have any control? Is it something you have in any way earned or merited? Clearly not. Being human is something over which neither you nor I have any choice. It is an undeserved property in the sense that we are simply born that way. Therefore, by the principle of desert, the property of belonging to a particular species is as morally arbitrary as race, gender, or eye colour. So, in the impartial position, knowledge of your species is also something that should be excluded behind the veil of ignorance. That is, one of the things you have to imagine you do not know is to which species you belong. But since we must exclude knowledge of our species behind the veil of ignorance, so too will we have to exclude everything that goes with being a member of a particular species. This means that innate intellectual endowments that go with being human must also be excluded. Certain capacities for complex rational inference, an IQ within a certain range, and so on – all these must be excluded behind the veil of ignorance for we have no control over whether or not we have them. The choice is nature's, not ours.

It is true that we sometimes talk of improving or developing our intelligence. In other situations we talk of trying to be reasonable (i.e. rational). And these ways of talking suggest that intelligence and rationality are things that might be worked upon, developed, even improved. And, if this is correct, it's simply not true that rationality and intelligence are things for which we are not responsible: we can earn or merit them just as we can earn or merit many other features. Therefore, there is no reason to exclude them behind the veil of ignorance.

This line of argument is not going to work. Take intelligence. Recent studies suggest that intelligence – at least if that's the thing you think IQ tests test – can be improved with practice. That is, if you practice IQ tests, you will get better at them. However, this is neither surprising nor relevant. First of all, any improvement you show through practice is strictly limited. Work as hard as you like, you're not going to improve more than about twenty per cent. Now, no one, presumably, is going to claim that a twenty per cent difference in IQ is a morally relevant difference. It is not as if anyone with an IQ of twenty points or so above average thereby has more moral entitlements or rights than someone of average intelligence. This strongly suggests that whatever increase in intelligence can be gained through hard work and determination is not morally relevant anyway.

Second, if you increase your intelligence by twenty points through hard work and practice, this is only because you have a foundation of intelligence to build on. You're not going to get an IQ of 120, for example, unless you already have one of 100 to work with. But this foundation of intelligence is not something you've earned or merited. It basically goes with being born a biologically normal member of the human species and not having too dreadful a childhood; and neither of these things have you earned. But, then, the increment to your IQ is not something you have fully earned either.

In short, in the impartial position, we should exclude, behind a veil of ignorance, knowledge of which species we belong to, and therefore, also, knowledge of all those features that go with being a biologically normal and environmentally not too unfortunate member of that species. Then, when we imagine ourselves not knowing who we are, or even what we are, we ask ourselves this question: *How would I like the world to be?* Since you do not know who or what you are, in choosing for yourself, you thereby choose for everyone and everything. Any basis for partiality or bias has been removed by the circumstances of the impartial position. Then, whatever is *irrational* for you to choose in the impartial position is *immoral* for you to choose in the real world. That, in a nutshell, is what justice is all about.

4 MORAL AGENTS AND MORAL PATIENTS

One advantage of the impartial over the original position is that it allows us to be properly sensitive to the important distinction between moral *agents* and moral *patients*. A moral patient, roughly, is anyone (or anything) that is deserving of moral consideration. That is, a moral patient is anything whose welfare you are morally obliged to consider when you act. If you have to, morally speaking, consider the impact of your actions on some thing, that thing is, by definition, a moral patient. A moral agent, on the other hand, is something that is capable of moral *thinking* or *reasoning*. That is, when faced with a particular choice, a moral agent is able to ask itself, "What is the right thing to do here?" Then it is able to at least attempt to work out the right answer to this question by bringing to bear on the situation impartial moral rules and principles. Note that to be a moral agent, you don't *actually* have to do bring impartial moral principles to bear on a situation – some moral agents can be selfish and blinkered people indeed. Rather, to be a moral agent you have to be *capable* of bringing such principles to bear, and working out on this basis what is the right thing to do.

All moral agents are moral patients, but not all moral patients are moral agents. All human beings are moral patients. Most are moral agents also. But not all. Humans who are only moral patients include: the severely brain damaged, the moderately brain damaged (for certain types of brain damage), the permanently insane, the temporarily insane, the senile, infants, and young children. All these sorts of human beings are (or can be) incapable of bringing impartial moral principles to bear on a situation and, by doing so, working out what is the morally correct course of action. Nevertheless, most would accept, these people are clearly moral patients. We ought, morally speaking, to consider the impact of our actions on them. We ought not, for example, to torture them for fun simply because they are not moral agents. Human moral patients are the interesting class of human beings who have rights but not responsibilities.

Knowledge of whether or not you are a moral agent is also something that should be excluded in the original position. Being a moral agent is an unearned, hence undeserved, property. Whether or not one has the capacity to assess a situation morally, and bring impartial moral principles to bear in working out the correct course of action, is something that is beyond your control. You are either born with the relevant intellectual abilities in place, and then undergo a relatively normal process of social development or you are not and/or you do not.

Of course, whether or not you are a moral patient is also something beyond your control, so that knowledge is also something that should be excluded in the original position. But that is OK, because if you are not even a moral patient, this will have absolutely no effect on the choices you should rationally make in the impartial position. To work out why, let's suppose you are in the impartial position, and knowledge of all your unearned properties, including the species to which you belong, whether you are a moral agent or even a moral patient, has been excluded. You then ask yourself: *how would I like the world to be?* An irrational choice in the impartial position is an immoral choice in the real world. Will you choose a world where only humans have rights or entitlements? That would be irrational, for you don't know which species you will belong to. Will you choose a world where only moral agents have rights? That, again, would be irrational; you may turn out to be only a moral patient.

How about moral patients? Will you choose a world where moral patients are favoured over things that are not even moral patients? Yes, you can choose this, and you can do so rationally. The reason is that if you are not even a moral patient, there is no point in worrying about how the world is: it won't make the slightest bit of difference to you. If you are a rock, or a tree, or a tennis ball, then, however the world is, it won't matter to you. Indeed, nothing will matter. On the other hand, if you are conscious, or have interests, then you have a welfare. Things can, then, go better or worse for you; better or worse in an experiential sense. Then you will be, at the very least, a moral patient. So, although being a moral patient is an undeserved property, and so should be excluded from the impartial position, this will in no way affect the choices you should rationally make in this position. Put the knowledge that you are a moral patient behind the veil of ignorance. You should, rationally, make exactly the same choices as you would if you were in possession of this knowledge.

At the beginning of this section, I said that one of the advantages of the impartial position, over Rawls' original position, is that the impartial position allows us to be properly sensitive to the distinction between moral agents and moral patients. According to Rawls, his account of justice applies only to individuals who have what he calls a *sense of justice*. And you have a sense of justice, in Rawls' sense, only if you are capable of thinking and reasoning morally. In other words, the original position is restricted to moral and rational agents. One of the things you know, in Rawls' original position, is that you are a moral agent. And this means that moral patients fall outside the scope of justice, as defined by Rawls.

We have already seen how many humans are moral patients without being moral agents. If we use Rawls' conception of the original position to guide our moral thinking, then all these people will fall outside the scope of morality. These people, then, cannot be treated unjustly. They have no moral rights or entitlements, and so we cannot violate their rights or entitlements in the way we treat them. In our treatment of them, in effect, *anything goes*.

This, at least on the face of it, seems intolerable. If you torture a young child, then you certainly seem to be doing something wrong. And what you are doing is wrong, it seems, because of the harm it does to the child. The torture is something he or she is morally entitled not to have to endure. What we need to account for this very strong intuition that all (or most) of us have is a more inclusive version of the original position. And this is precisely what the impartial position gives us. Motivated by the principles of equality and desert, in the impartial position you are denied knowledge of any property you haven't earned, including knowledge of your species, the innate abilities that go with being a member of that species, and of whether you are a moral agent or moral patient. The limits of morality, on this approach, are the limits of the things you could worry about being. You could not, rationally, worry about being a rock, for if that is how the world turned out, nothing would matter to you anyway. But you could rationally worry about being a pig or a cow or a dog. From the perspective of the impartial position, the limits of morality, that is, are the limits of all those things that have a welfare, in an experiential sense. And, in deciding how these things are to be treated, we follow the *golden rule*: if a choice is an irrational one in the impartial position, then it is an immoral one in the real world.

5 IS THE IMPARTIAL POSITION POSSIBLE?

Talk of the impartial position is, of course, metaphorical. It is what philosophers sometimes call a *heuristic device*: an aid to thinking. That's all it is. When we talk of the impartial position, we are not talking about a situation you might literally find yourself in. It is not as if you can be "in" the impartial position in the same way you can be in a house or car or country. In fact, the impartial position is not even a *possible* or *imaginable* situation, let alone an actual one. No one can really lack all knowledge of his or her unearned properties. Indeed, no one can even imagine himself lacking all this knowledge.

In what sense, then, can you ever be *in* the impartial position? We get closer to the relevant sense of "in" when we look at an expression sometimes applied to athletes when they are performing particularly well. We sometimes say that they are "in the zone." I use this only to show that we sometimes use the word "in" to refer not to a place one can be, but to a way of doing something. That is the relevant sense of "in." To be in the impartial position is to be doing something in a certain way. But doing what? Basically, *reasoning in a certain way, or in accordance with certain restrictions*. You are in the impartial position when you reason in the following sort of way. "As a matter of fact, I have property P (e.g. maleness). But what if I didn't have this property? How would I like the world to be then? More precisely, what principles of morality would I like to see people adopt if I didn't have P?" You are "in" the impartial position, in the only meaningful sense in which you can ever be in it, when you engage in a process of reasoning of this type.

In the impartial position, property P could be any unearned property:

gender, race, species, intelligence, moral agency, and so on. To be in the impartial position, then, you have to repeat this process for all unearned properties; all of them have to be put behind the veil of ignorance. However, there is no need for you to put all your unearned properties simultaneously behind the veil. You do not need to ask yourself, "What moral principles would I like to see adopted if I had no knowledge of *any* of the (unearned) properties I now know myself to have?" This question is not required. All that you need to do, to be in the impartial position, is to ask yourself about each of your unearned properties in turn. So, you ask yourself the following sort of question. "I, in fact, have the property of being male (or female). But what if I did not have this property? How would I like the world to be then?" Then, you repeat for your other unearned properties, in a one-by-one, piecemeal, way.

Also, which property you bracket will depend on which question you are trying to answer. If you are trying to work out how to construct a society free of racial discrimination, then ask yourself: "I have the property of being white (or black, or whatever). But suppose I didn't have his property. How would I like the world to be then?" For the question of how we should treat animals, however, the central question is: "I have the property of being human. But suppose I didn't have this property. How would I like the world to be then?" Indeed, we can be a lot more specific than this. Suppose, for example, we were trying to work out the moral status of veal farming. Then, the impartial position simply requires that we pretend we don't know if we are a human or a veal calf. Then, we ask ourselves, "How would I like the world to be?" That is, would we prefer it if the world contained the practice of veal farming or would we prefer it if it didn't? The important point is that, in order to be in the impartial position, you don't have to imagine that you lack all the properties you know yourself to have. One at a time will do, depending on what question you are trying to answer.

Remember also that the idea of imagining is an ambiguous one. Suppose you are to imagine yourself not being male. What does that mean? Well, it could mean two different things. On the one hand there is *imagining that* you are female. On the other, there is *imagining what it is like* to be female. If you are a male, then in order to be in the impartial position with respect to questions about gender equality, you have to ask yourself this question: "Suppose I did not have the property of being male. How would I like the world to be then?" If you are male, then in doing this you have thereby imagined *that* you are not male. But this does not mean that you have imagined *what it is like* to not be male. Nothing about being in the impartial position requires that you succeed in this second feat of imagination. Being in the impartial position only requires imagining *that*, not imagining *what it is like*. This is good, because imagining what it is like is notoriously difficult. I'm not at all sure I have the ability to imagine *what it is like* to be female. But, and this is the real problem, even if I succeeded in imagining this, I would have no idea if I had succeeded in imagining it.

Some people object to giving moral status to animals on the grounds that we cannot imagine what it is like to be them. This may be true, but is completely irrelevant. We don't need to imagine what it is like to be animals to give them moral rights any more than men need to imagine what it is like to be women, in order to give them moral rights.

6 THE ROLE OF RATIONALITY: THE IMPARTIAL POSITION AS AN IDEAL

Once we have set up the impartial position, and asked the moral question that interests us, we follow what we call the *golden rule*: if a choice is irrational in the impartial position then it is immoral in the real world. This rule, of course, raises the question of the extent to which we can ever be truly rational. If we are blinkered, short-sighted, biased and self-preferential in the real world, what reason is there to think that we can banish these shortcomings just because we are allowing our reasoning to be governed by certain restrictions? The answer is, unfortunately, that we cannot be sure of this. In fact, it is most unlikely that we will ever succeed in being truly rational and impartial in our moral reasoning and deliberation. No matter. *We can still do our best.* Philosophy is often, as the philosopher Wittgenstein put it, a battle of the will as much as of the intellect: a battle to follow our rational faculties wherever they may lead, and in as exacting a manner as we can manage, in spite of a temptation not to do so. The impartial position is an ideal, something to which we aspire, and no worse for that. Even if we can never be completely "in" it, we can do our best to immerse ourselves in it, in its rules and restrictions, as far as we can and to the best of our ability.

7 SUMMARY

The idea of the *impartial position* gives us a powerful *heuristic device* or method, for addressing moral problems and issues. The impartial position is motivated by the requirement that our moral thinking conform to both the principle of *equality* and the principle of *desert*. The impartial position incorporates the principle of equality by way of the requirement that you do not know who or what you are. It incorporates the principle of desert by way of the requirement that all unearned properties be similarly excluded behind the *veil of ignorance*. The impartial position is not literally a place or situation. It is a way of doing, not a place of being. You enter the impartial position, in the only meaningful sense in which you can ever enter it, when you allow your reasoning about moral issues to be governed by certain restrictions, namely that you imagine – in a one-by-one, piecemeal manner – *that* you do not know whether you have any of the unearned properties you do in fact, have. You then ask yourself: "If I did not have property P, how would I like the world to be?" In answering this question, you follow the *golden rule*: if a choice is irrational in the impartial position, then it is immoral in the real world. We may not be ideally rational, but in answering this question, we can do our best.

4

KILLING ANIMALS

The idea of the impartial position gives us a powerful imaginative device for thinking about the moral questions and issues surrounding our treatment of animals. In chapters to come we shall take an in-depth look at issues such as raising animals for food, experimenting on animals, whether for scientific or cosmetic purposes, keeping animals in zoos, and keeping them for pets. First, however, we need to look at an even more basic question. It concerns something we do to animals all the time, often without thinking about it. We kill them.

1 LIFEBOAT SCENARIOS

People sometimes claim that the whole idea of animal rights is absurd because, if you take it seriously, it means that it is as wrong to kill, say, a cow, pig or dog, as it is to kill a human being. Sometimes this point will be made graphic by way of what we can call a *lifeboat scenario*. If you were on a lifeboat, and had to choose between saving a human being and saving a dog, which would you save? Lifeboat scenarios don't necessarily involve lifeboats. Here is another one. If you run into a burning house and are forced to choose between saving a puppy and a baby, which do you save?

The idea underlying all lifeboat scenarios (whether involving lifeboats or not) is something like this. You find yourself in a situation where you are forced to choose between saving a human being and saving a member of some other species. The exigencies of the situation allow you to save only one. Which do you save? Actually, this way of putting it is not quite right. The question is not what you *would* do in any particular situation, but what you *should* do; because what you would do is not always what you should do. I once owned a wolf, to which I was very attached, and who knows? Perhaps I would have hauled him up into the lifeboat (rescued him from the burning house, etc.) and left you to drown (burn). But what I *would* do, in any particular situation is not necessarily what I *should* do. The relevant question, in a lifeboat situation, is not what you would, but what you should do.

The idea behind this question is that anyone who believes in animal rights will have to say that it is equally legitimate to save the dog as to save the human being. You might as well flip a coin. And this means that the idea of animal rights is absurd, or fundamentally misguided; because we all know that the right thing to do is save the human. In this chapter, I want to show that this common belief about animal rights simply isn't true. Any sane animal rights account will be able to allow that, in most situations, it is, morally speaking, better to save the human being. In most situations, but not in all.

However, we should be careful not to go too far in this direction. Tom Regan, one of the ablest philosophical defenders of animal rights, actually endorses the claim that, in any given lifeboat situation, it is morally correct to save the life of one human being over *any number* of animals. If a situation arose where you had a choice of saving one human being or, say, one million animals, you should choose to save the human. Indeed, this is true no matter how many animals are involved – ten million, 100 million, or whatever – you should always save the human. I think this goes too far. Much too far. And, in this chapter I shall try to explain why.

Lifeboat scenarios work by getting us to think about the *relative value* of human and non-human life. The guiding intuition behind them is that the life of a human is, in some sense, worth more, has more value than, the life of an animal. This, to most of us, will seem obvious. But why? For it to be obvious, do we first not have to know in what the value of human life consists? If we don't know this, how can we know that human lives have more value than non-human ones? So, in what does the value of human life consist? The life of a human has value; that is undoubtedly true. But what gives it this value?

This, to say the least, is not an easy question. The hardest part is not so much working out the answer, but working out how to even approach the question. How do you even *begin* to answer a question like this? Well, one way of doing it is to ask another question: *what's so bad about dying?* Death is what takes life away. So, if we can work out what's so bad about dying, this should tell us something about what is valuable about life.

2 THE EPICUREAN ARGUMENT

Death, whatever else it is, is not something that occurs *in* a life. Death, as Wittgenstein put it, is the limit of a life, and a limit of a life is not something that can occur within that life, any more than the limit of a visual field is something that can occur within that field. If we accept this, then we are immediately presented with a well-known argument, associated with Epicurus, an argument that death cannot be something that harms us. It goes like this. Death cannot harm us because while we are alive death has not yet happened (and so can't have harmed us yet), and after we are dead there is nothing left to harm. Death can't harm us until it actually happens, but when it happens we are no longer around for it to harm. So death does not harm us. What, if anything, is wrong with this argument?

3 NAGEL ON DEATH

The classic response to the Epicurean argument is provided by Thomas Nagel.[1] According to Nagel, the argument fails because it overlooks the irreducibly relational character of a certain type of harm: harms of *deprivation*. Consider an analogy. A person who suffers severe brain trauma and is reduced to a mental age of, say, three months, can be perfectly happy both before and after the trauma. The harm consists in the relation their former state bears to their latter. The analogy is, of course, imperfect, most obviously because, in this case, there is a subject of whom the harm can be predicated both before and after the injury (although it is not clear that it is the *same* subject). Nevertheless, Nagel argues that the harm of death should be understood in similarly relational terms.

> There are goods and evils which are irreducibly relational; they are features of the relations between a person, with spatial and temporal boundaries of the usual sort, and circumstances which may not coincide with him either in space or time. A man's life includes much that does not take place within the boundaries of his body and his mind, and what happens to him can include much that does not take place within the boundaries of his life.[2]

This raises the question of the connection between a person and those things that happen outside the boundaries of that person's life. These occurrences must, of course, happen to, or be undergone by, the person, and not somebody else. And so we must be able to answer the question of how a person can be the subject of an occurrence that may not actually occur until that person is no more. Nagel's answer centres on an appeal to *hopes* and *possibilities*.

> A man is the subject of good and evil as much because he has hopes which may or may not be fulfilled, or possibilities which may or may not be realized, as because of his capacity to suffer and enjoy.[3]

The satisfaction, or otherwise, of hopes, and the realization, or otherwise, of possibilities, can depend on circumstances that exist or occur outside the temporal boundaries of a person's life. Therefore, if we understand death in terms of the deleterious consequences it has for the satisfaction of hopes and the realization of possibilities, we can understand how death can be a harm for us, even though it occurs outside the temporal boundaries of our lives.

Will this suggestion work? Not, I think, as it stands. The appeal to hopes and the appeal to possibilities are far from equivalent. And the appeal to possibilities, in particular, is especially problematic.

In ethics, appeals to possibilities generally turn out to be problematic, in one way or another. Consider, for example, a well-known argument against attempts to explain the moral entitlements of someone or something by appeal to their possibilities or potentialities. I'm potentially a

Formula 1 racing driver, indeed, potentially I'm a very good Formula 1 racing driver. The best, even. Michael Schumacher would be losing serious amounts of sleep if he knew how good I am – potentially that is. However, this does not mean that I *actually* have the rights or entitlements of a Formula 1 racing driver. The Ferrari team would, presumably, be singularly unimpressed if I were to show up at practice and ask them where my car is. And, unaccountably, supermodels are not exactly beating a pathway to my door. To say that I'm potentially a Formula 1 racing driver gives me no actual rights or entitlements. At most, it gives me only *potential* rights or entitlements. In general, the potentiality of having a certain property P does not actually give you the entitlements that go with P, it only potentially gives you those entitlements.

The idea that death is a harm because of the possibilities of which it deprives us is in danger of running into an analogous problem. If death is a harm, then, it is natural to suppose, this is because it deprives us something that is, broadly speaking, of *benefit*. But if it deprives us of things that we have only possibly, then there is a danger that we'll be committed to the view that death deprives us only of possible benefits. And then the danger is that we'll be committed to the claim that death is only a possible harm. To avoid this conclusion, we would have to endorse not only the claim that possibilities are things we *actually* have – which, I think, is not incoherent – but also the claim that the entitlements that possibilities bring with them are things we *actually* have. And this is extremely implausible.

These sorts of problems inherent in the appeal to possibilities are well known. Unfortunately, I'm less persuaded by them than I used to be. I now think that an appeal to possibilities or potentialities can play a legitimate role in moral reasoning about harm and entitlement, it's just that we have to be very careful in understanding precisely what role this is. In particular, it's not necessarily the role we think it is. I'll return to this later.

In any event, this type of problem does not, I think, get us to the heart of what's wrong with Nagel's appeal to possibilities. The real problem is that possibilities are, as we might say, *promiscuous*. This means two things. First, there are far too many of them. Second, it is not clear what makes a possibility mine (or yours). These features make them unsuitable for understanding the sense in which death harms us. If I were to drop dead now, then this would, in my view at least, be rather unfortunate (at least for me). But this is not because the possibilities that I become (i) Emperor of the Known Universe, (ii) a Formula 1 racing driver, (iii) an estate agent, or (iv) a (sentient) teapot, thereby go unrealized. All these are, in some sense, possibilities, but they are, I think, irrelevant to understanding why my death is a harm for me. They are irrelevant for somewhat different reasons, of course. I have no desire to be an estate agent (or a teapot, for that matter). Death does not harm me by depriving me of possibilities in which I am in no way interested. The possibilities of being a Formula 1 racing driver or, indeed, Emperor of the Known Universe, do, in some sense of interest, interest me. If God, for example, were to come along and offer these to me, I would be much more inclined to accept than if He offered me a job at the local realtors. However – except for a few speeding tickets – I've never actually acted in such a way as to make the actualization of these possibilities more probable. It is not clear that the harm of death can be understood in terms of possibilities in which I would be interested, but not sufficiently interested to take steps to increase the probability of their actualization.

Nagel seems to recognize that his appeal to possibilities is problematic. This is why he states that "we still have to set limits on how possible a possibility can be for its nonrealization to be a misfortune."[4] This is true, but does not get us to the heart of the problem. The possibility of my being an estate agent is significantly higher than of my being a Formula 1 racing driver, and this, in turn, is significantly more likely than me becoming the Emperor of the Known Universe. But it is not clear that the non-actualization of the possibility of my being an estate agent harms me any more than the non-actualization of the possibility of being a Formula 1 racing driver or, indeed, Emperor of the Known Universe.

It is the promiscuity of possibilities that lies at the heart of the problem. The original problem – the one that the appeal to possibilities was meant to solve – was the problem of how a person could be connected to occurrences that lie outside of the temporal limits of that person's life, such that the person could be said to undergo those occurrences. That is, the problem was of finding a way of *binding* that person to those occurrences. Appeal to possibilities merely replaces this problem with one of explaining what binds a person to his or her possibilities. And this, ultimately, is because possibilities are promiscuous; there are far too many of them, and, hence, there is nothing in a possibility that makes it intrinsically mine (or yours).

4 LOSING A FUTURE

The problems with Nagel's *possibilist* account of death strongly suggest that we need an *actualist* alternative: the harm of death is to be explained in terms of features that an individual actually – and not merely possibly – possesses, and so actually loses when she dies. It's pretty clear that Nagel is right about one thing. Death is a harm. And if death is a harm, then it seems it can only be what's known as a *harm of deprivation*. Death harms its victims because it deprives them of something. But what? Well, life obviously. But we are trying to explain the value of life in terms of what death takes away. So, to say that death harms us because it takes away life is not getting us very far. We need a more substantial answer.

One thing that death takes away from us is a *future*. Think about what goes into your life at any given moment. What this can be will vary from species to species and, within certain limits, from one human to another. For humans, what goes into one's life at any given time may be a constellation of experiences, beliefs, desires, goals, projects, activities, and various other things. If you attend to the experiences, beliefs, desires, goals, projects, and activities that you have, undergo or perform at any given time – say now – then suppose that there is a time later than the present and, you are, or might be, having, undergoing and performing the same sorts of things at this later time, then you understand the gist of what I mean by the future. That is, I use the term "future" simply as shorthand for these sorts of things. When we die, we lose a future in this sense. This is why death harms us. Simple.

The sheen of simplicity, however, is only apparent. The idea of losing a future is, when you think about it, a very strange one. And its strangeness comes from the strangeness of the idea of the future. The future does not yet exist. So how can you lose it? Indeed, you can lose a future only if you in some sense now have one. But how can you have something that does not yet exist? What this seems to show is that the ideas of *having* and *losing* in this context have a somewhat different meaning from when they occur in other, more usual, contexts. It is possible to have a future, but not in the same sense in which one might have broad shoulders or a Rolex watch. And when a murderer deprives you of your future, the sense of deprivation is quite different from when age deprives you of your shoulders, or a mugger deprives you of your watch.

We can, in fact, distinguish three quite different senses in which something can be said to *have* a future. To begin with, there is the *minimal* sense in which everything that exists has a future (as long as it is not instantaneously destroyed). This book that you have in front of you – the physical object that you hold in your hands – has a future at least in one sense. This means, simply, that there are times later than the present, and the paper will exist at those times. Of course, if you decide to consign the book to the flames, then the book will no longer have a future. Throwing it in the fire will cause it to lose a future: as the flames consume the last portion of it, there will be no time later than the present at which this individual book will exist. Clearly, everything has, and just about everything can lose, a future in this sense. There is a way of using the word "harm" according to which it makes sense to say that the book is harmed when you throw it in the fire. But clearly, the harm is very different in this case from the harm suffered when someone's life is taken away. This is, I shall argue, because the sense of deprivation is also very different in the two cases.

It is also worth noting that having a future in this minimal sense can have no bearing on morality. It is not as if the book has moral entitlements simply because it has a future in this sense. And, it is not as if we should commiserate with the book on its losing a future when thrown into the fire. Therefore, it would be difficult, to say the least, to generate any moral claims based on the idea that it is wrong to deprive an individual of a future in this minimal sense.

If we want to understand what's so bad about dying, we need to look at other, more substantial, ways in which something can have a future. The only way to do this, consistent with the actualist approach, is by focusing on certain types of mental state that are, as we might say, *future-directed*. The idea is that you can have a future because you actually have now, at the present time, certain states that, in some sense, direct you towards times later than the present. The paradigmatic examples of such states would be *desires*, *goals*, and *projects*.

In what sense is a desire future-directed? Well, here's one. Desires can be *satisfied* or *thwarted*. My desire for a beer will be satisfied if I walk to the refrigerator and get one. It will be thwarted if, for example, I open the refrigerator door and find the shelves bare. Satisfying a desire typically takes time. It takes time to walk to the refrigerator and open myself a bottle. And this is *one* sense in which desires are future-directed: satisfying them takes time. The same is even more obviously true for goals and projects, both of which are, in all essentials, longer-term desires. My project of training six days a week takes time, as does my goal of becoming an Olympic triathlete. (Or, at least, these things would take time if I actually did or had them.) Desires can be satisfied or thwarted, and goals and projects can be fulfilled or unfulfilled. And satisfying and fulfilling take time.

Therefore, I now, at the present time, have states that, in a reasonably clear sense, *direct me towards the future*. We all do. This is not to say that all desires are necessarily future-directed. One might, for example, desire that the past be other than it was (or is, depending on your view of the past). Nevertheless, many desires, almost certainly the vast majority, are future-directed in that their satisfaction takes time. Since the future does not yet exist, the only way a person can have a future, in any non-minimal, non-possibilistic, sense is if they now, in the present, have states that direct them towards a future. These presently existing states are future-directed: they relate a person to her future and thus allow her, in a metaphorical but perfectly meaningful sense, to *have* that future. Therefore, as a first approximation, we can say that a person has a future, in a non-minimal sense, if he or she possesses certain future-directed states.

However, this is only a first-approximation, and glosses over a crucial distinction, a distinction between two types of future-directed state. A state can be future-directed in two different ways. On the one hand, it may be a state that involves, as part of its content, a *concept* of the future. We can call such a state a *conceptually future-directed state*. On the other hand, a state can be directed towards the future in that although it contains, as part of its content, no concept of the future, the state does, nonetheless, require for its satisfaction that the possessor of the state persist beyond the present moment. I shall call this a *non-conceptually future-directed state*. The distinction is, I think, important to understanding our moral intuitions about the harm of death.

5 CONCEPTUAL AND NON-CONCEPTUAL REPRESENTATIONS OF THE FUTURE

There is a big difference between the following two situations, and in the kinds of mental state involved.

Situation 1 I desire some pizza. To satisfy this desire, I must get up and walk across the room to the refrigerator, grab the leftover slices and eat. My desire is future-directed in that in order for it to be satisfied, I must persist for at least a few moments into the future – as long as it takes for me to accomplish the necessary steps. The desire, in this sense, directs, or binds, me towards a future.

Situation 2 You are asked to list your plans for the future, what you hope to get out of life, where you hope to be in twenty years time, and so on. In order to satisfy or fulfil these plans and goals, you, of course, need to persist into the future. So, your plans and goals are future-directed in this sense. But there also seems to be something more in the way in which they direct you into the future. For, in this case, it is explicitly recognized by you that the plans and goals you have are things "for the future." You recognize, that is, that they are things that cannot be satisfied now, but to which your present behaviour and actions can help make a contribution. You want to be an Olympic triathlete; that is why you are now spending every day running, swimming and cycling. You recognize that your efforts now are directed at something that cannot happen now but might, if you are lucky and diligent, happen in the future.

The second situation, but not the first, involves a *concept* of the future. My desire for a slice of pizza is future-directed in the sense that its satisfaction requires that I persist into the future. But my having this desire does not require that I think, or even be able to think, to myself, "My eating the pizza, which will satisfy my desire, is an event that will take place in the future." In order to have and satisfy this desire, by itself, I need have no concept of the future. The desire is one that *involves* the future, and does so quite centrally, but it does not involve, and having it does not require, a *concept* of the future. However, in the second type of situation, it is explicitly recognized that your present desires and actions (e.g. the desire to get your 10K time below forty minutes, and the effort you put into satisfying this desire) are desires and actions that are directed towards further goals, ones that cannot be satisfied now but only in the future. So, in the second situation, you must have the ability to explicitly think about, or represent, the future. Desires that you have in the second situation presuppose, and only make sense in terms of, a concept of the future.

The upshot of all this is that there are two different ways in which a mental state, such as a desire, goal or project, can direct you towards the future. There is, as in the case of my desire for pizza, what we can call a *non-conceptual* way, one that does not involve an explicit concept of the future. Second, there is, as in the case of your goal of becoming an Olympic triathlete, a *conceptual* way, one which does involve an explicit concept of the future. So, to mark this distinction, I am going to talk about mental states that are *conceptually future-directed*, or conceptually directed towards the future, and mental states that are *non-conceptually future-directed*, or non-conceptually directed towards the future.

Given that there are these two different ways – conceptual and non-conceptual – in which a state can be directed towards a future, there are also two different ways in which an individual can have a future. An individual can have a future in a *non-conceptual sense* if he, she, or it has mental states that are non-conceptually future-directed. An individual will have a future in a conceptual sense if he, she, or it has mental states that are conceptually future-directed.

6 LOSING A FUTURE AND THE HARM OF DYING

I have supposed that death is a bad thing because it deprives us of a future, understood in a non-minimal sense. Now, however, we see that it is possible to have, non-minimally, a future in two different ways, a conceptual and a non-conceptual one. The question we now need to look at is whether this makes a difference to the harm or badness of dying. Is dying worse for someone who has a future in a conceptual sense than for someone who has a future only in a non-conceptual sense? I shall argue that it is.

We can understand the sense in which someone possesses a future in terms of the idea that she, at the present time, possesses states that direct or bind her to a future that does not yet exist. There is, I think, an intuitive sense in which someone who has a future in a conceptual sense is more closely, or intimately, bound to their future than someone who has a future in only a non-conceptual sense. Is this anything more than an intuition, or can we back it up with argument? If we are to do so, the same general actualist strategy must be followed: we must explain not only the connection to the (as yet non-existent) future, but also the *strength* of that connection, in terms of states that the subject (actually) possesses in the present. Can this be done?

I think, to a considerable extent, that it can. A person who has a future in a conceptual sense is far more able to orient and organize his or her present behaviour, and discipline and direct his or her present desires, to achieve a desired future state than someone who does not. The person spending all his free time running, cycling and swimming so he can become an Olympic tri-athlete in later life is investing much of his present time and energy in this future goal, and such investment is possible only because he has an explicit concept of the future. The greater strength of this person's connection to the future is, thus, explained in terms of the greater disciplining, orienting, and regimenting of the person's present behaviour, desires and other mental states. And this greater disciplining, orienting, and regimenting is made possible by the fact that he possesses a concept of the future, and, on the basis of this, a desire that the future be a certain way.

Most of us, at least to some extent, have a tendency to "live for tomorrow." Much of what we do in the present we do not for the sake of the present but for the future. After all, this is what becoming educated, building a career, remaining faithful to one's partner despite temptation, watching one's weight, taking out life insurance, and so on, are all about. But even simple, mundane decisions, often so trivial as to be barely noticeable, are often infected by the future. No, I won't have one more drink, or I'll suffer tomorrow. No, I won't have that Twinkie, it'll ruin my appetite. For some of us, our orientation towards the future borders on the neurotic. But even for allegedly normal people, much of what we do in the present, perhaps the vast majority of what we do, only makes sense on the basis not only of the future but, more importantly, of our *concept* of the future.

An individual who has a concept of the future, and on the basis of this is conceptually directed towards her future, has more invested in that future than someone whose connection with her future is only non-conceptual. Such a person has more invested in her future since she is explicitly orienting and organizing her present behaviour, and disciplining and directing her present desires, on the basis of a conception of how she would like her future to be. Without a concept of the future, this cannot be done. Therefore, for this reason, I'll use the following terminology. An individual who has a future in a non-conceptual sense I shall say has a future in a *weak* sense. But an individual who has a future in a conceptual sense has, I shall say, a future in a *strong* sense. The difference between strong and weak possession of a future, therefore, ultimately reflects a difference in the amount a person has *invested* in that future.

Someone who has a future in a strong sense, orienting much of their present behaviour, and disciplining many of their present desires, towards a conception of how they would like their future to be, is more closely tied, or bound, to their future than an individual who has a future in only a weak sense. Therefore, a person who has a future in a strong sense has more to lose, in losing a future, than a person who possesses a future in only a weak sense.

If this is not already clear, consider the following analogy. Two people get to the Olympics, to compete in the triathlon. One has trained for years, oriented her life, organized her behaviour and disciplined her desires, to achieve this goal. The other is a lazy, shiftless athlete who has reached the Olympics through, let us suppose, mistaken identity. Neither wins a medal. We sometimes talk of a person "losing out" on the medals. If this is indeed a loss, then it seems that the greater loss is suffered by the first athlete, since she has organized her life around achieving this goal. Much of her life was lived for the sake of a future goal, which she did not achieve. She had, in a clear sense, more invested in getting a medal than did the other athlete. Therefore, her loss is greater.

I am basically making a similar point about the harm involved in losing a future. The more you have invested in the future, judged in terms of the organization, orientation, disciplining, and regimentation of your present behaviour and desires, then the more you lose when you lose that future. If you have a future in a conceptual, or strong sense, then, when you die, you lose more than if you had a future in only a weak, non-conceptual, sense. Death is a greater harm for those who have a future in a strong sense, for in dying they lose more than those who have a future in only a weak sense.

So, we arrive at a three-way classification of the senses in which you can have, and consequently lose, a future. Something that has a future in a strong sense is more closely tied to, and has more invested in, its future than something that has a future in only a weak sense. And something that has a future in a weak sense is more closely tied to, and has more invested in, its future than something that has a future in only a minimal sense. Therefore, something that has a future in a strong sense has more to lose in losing its future than something that has a future in only a weak sense. And something that has a future in a weak sense has more to lose in losing its future than something that has a future in only a minimal sense. Therefore, all things being equal: death is worse for something that has a future in a strong sense than for something that has a future in a weak sense, and death is worse for something that has a future in a weak sense than for something that has a future in only a minimal sense.

7 The length and quality of a future

Death harms us, I have argued, because it takes away a future. This presupposes that having a future is a good thing. However, one obvious feature of futures is that while everybody has one, not everybody has as much of one. So, if having a future is a good thing, then, it seems, all things being equal, that having more of a future should be better than having less of a future. All things being equal, more of a good thing is better than less of it. There are, of course, dissenting voices. Achilles reputedly opted for a short and glorious life over a long and mundane one. And Roger Daltrey once told us that he hoped he'd die before he got old. Nevertheless, Achilles later came to rue his decision, and there are no indications that Roger Daltrey has any suicidal inclinations now that he is, manifestly, old. And, anyway, Achilles, presumably, would have opted for a long and glorious life, given the choice. Why? Well, typically if our life is going well enough for us to value it, then we would rather more of it than less of it. All joy, as Nietzsche put it, wants eternity. And if joy cannot be realistically expected for most of us, if reasonable contentment is the best we can hope for, then it is still true that we will generally want more of it than less of it.

Now, I'm afraid, I'm going to have to side with Achilles and the young Roger Daltrey on this. Not the short and glorious life stuff. Rather, the idea is that the value of the life of an individual *at time t* in no way depends on the length of the future awaiting that individual. Thus, when death strikes an individual at time t, the value that death takes away *at that time* is in no way dependent on the length of the future that individual would otherwise have had. This is for the simple reason that while a future is something that one can – now, at the present time – legitimately be supposed to have, having a future of a certain length – a long one as opposed to a short one, for example – is not. Having a future, in the only meaningful sense in which we can be said to have one, is a matter of being the subject of certain future-directed mental states. But having a future of a certain length cannot be accounted for in these terms. I can explain how I can possess a future – even though the future does not yet exist – in terms of my possessing now, at the present time, states that direct me towards a future. But my having a future *of a certain length* cannot be similarly explained – not in terms of states that I now possess at the present time. I could be hit by a bus, for example. Having a future of a certain length is, partially but crucially, something beyond my control, and cannot be secured by states I have at the present time. And this means that having a future of a certain length is something I have not actually but *potentially*. Therefore, being robbed of a future of a certain length – as opposed to a future *per se* – is not something that harms me, but only something that potentially harms me. Death does not harm me by taking away a future of a certain length – it only potentially harms me by doing so. Conversely, my life has no more value because I (potentially) have a future of a certain length. At most, my life has potentially more value because I (potentially) have a future of a certain length. Having a future of great length is not a value-adding property of a life.

Nonetheless, this is quite compatible with our taking the anticipated length of a life into account when we deliberate in contexts of life and death. If we find ourselves aboard the lifeboat, for example, we can, *legitimately* take into consideration the likely or anticipated lengths of the future lives of those we must choose to save or abandon. We must clearly distinguish two different things. First, there is the question of the value of life at the time of death. If death occurs at time t, what value is it that death takes away at that time? Second, there is the question of the value that a life would have at a future time t+1 if that life were to continue to this future time. In contexts of life and death decision-making, our reasoning can be legitimately guided by factors in addition to the value of a person's life at the time of death. It can be guided by considerations of the value that life would have at a future time if it were to continue to that time.

Suppose we have a person, Bob, who at time t has a future in the sense that, at t, he possesses various future-directed mental states. Bob, thus, at t, actually possesses a future. At t, however, he only potentially possesses a future of a certain length. Therefore, having a future is a value-adding characteristic of Bob's life, but having a future of a certain length is only a potentially value-adding characteristic of his life. This notwithstanding, it is still true that if at time t+2, Bob turns out to be still alive, and thus to have had a long life, then this fact will be something that has added value to his life at t+2 (and progressively during the interval from t to t+2). All things being equal of course, and if we buy into the more of a good thing is better than less idea. Suppose, now, that Bob dies at t+1. Then, again assuming all things are equal and more of a good thing is better than less, the value added will, accordingly, be less. Therefore, one of the things we know in contexts of reasoning about the relative values of lives is that if Bob lives until t+2, then his life will *at that time* have extra value, value that it would not have had if he lives only until t+1.

When we reason about the relative value of lives, as in lifeboat situations for example, our reasoning is often guided not simply by questions of the value of the life of an individual at time t, but also by considerations of the future value of the life of that individual, the value it would have a times later than t. In such deliberations, we seem to be guided by the desire to produce the most value, and less concerned with *when* that value is produced. And it is not clear that this concern is illegitimate. Life and death decision-making, at least of the abstract philosophical variety, is usually conducted under conditions of profound ignorance. In a lifeboat situation, for example, when we are faced with two individuals that both have a future in a strong sense, and we have to decide who will live and who will die, we often have nothing to go on other than the prospective length of their futures. Nonetheless, we are willing to push the idea of future-produced value to greater lengths than this. Much greater lengths. A common intuition, for example (unless, of course, you're Peter Singer or Michael Tooley), is that the death of an infant is as great a harm, or an even greater harm, than the death of a normal adult human being. To the extent that this intuition can be rationally defended (and I'm not claiming that it can), and to the extent that it is based on genuinely moral rather than prudential concerns (and I'm not claiming that it is), it must be in terms of the idea that, in contexts of life and death, we are primarily concerned to produce, or safeguard, value and only secondarily concerned with when this value is instantiated.

The length of a future, then, contributes nothing to the value that death takes away when it takes away a future, at most it contributes only potentially to this value. This is compatible with our taking the anticipated length of a person's future into account, in contexts of life and death decision-making, if we assume that we can, in such contexts, be primarily

– and legitimately – concerned with producing, or safeguarding, value and only secondarily concerned with when this value is instantiated.

We can, I think, take essentially the same line with regard not just to the length of a future but also to other features that a future might have. The idea of *quality of life* often crops up in contexts of life and death decision-making. But the *quality of a future* subsequent to time t is not a value-adding characteristic of a person's life at t – for the same reason that length is not a value-adding characteristic of that life at t. The quality of a future cannot be explained in terms of features actually possessed by the subject of the life at t. It is, therefore, not an actual, but a potential, value-adding characteristic of the life of that subject. Nevertheless, if we suppose that in our reasoning about life and death we are primarily concerned to produce or safeguard value, and are only secondarily concerned with when that value occurs, and if we assume that a higher quality of life – however that is measured – adds more value to a life than a lesser one, then we can legitimately include such considerations in our ethical decision-making.

This separation of the idea of *possession of a future* from the idea of *possession of a future of a certain length*, or *possession of a future of a certain quality* is important. It allows us to avoid what is commonly taken to be the principal objection to *deprivationist* accounts of death – accounts that understand the harm of death in terms of the idea that it deprives us of something. The objection is that whenever continued life would be of overall negative value to an individual – because of it's extremely low quality – then that individual would not be harmed by painless murder. By clearly distinguishing the possession of a future by an individual from the possession of a given quality of future, we can avoid this objection. One is harmed by the fact that one's future is taken away. The harm of death consists in losing a future, and not losing a certain quality of future. So to end a person's life – one's own or that of another – on the grounds of its quality in no way obviates the harm that is death, for this is not a function of that quality. Don't misunderstand me. This is not an argument against euthanasia (or suicide for that matter). To say that death is a harm because of the loss of a future does not entail that it cannot be outweighed or overridden by other harms. My claim is one concerning in what the harm of death consists. It is not a claim about the status of that harm relative to other harms. There are, I think, worse things than death.

8 Back to the lifeboat

With all this in mind, let's head back to the lifeboat. And let's start by taking the simplest scenario: a straightforward choice between saving a human and saving a dog. What do you do? Or, more accurately, what *should you do*? To answer this, you put yourself in the impartial position, as you must when trying to reason morally. In the impartial position, you don't know if you are going to be the human or the dog. So, does this mean that it's a toss up between saving the human or the dog? Are the two morally equivalent? Not at all. Because, while you do not know if you are human or not, you do know that humans, typically, possess a future in a strong sense. What about dogs? Well, it seems likely that they possess a future in only a weak sense. This may be incorrect, but it is difficult to see that dogs orient much of their present behaviour, and discipline many of their present desires, on the basis of their conception of how they would like their future to be. And, if this is right, then the typical dog has far less invested in its future than the typical human, who does orient her behaviour and discipline her desires on the basis of such a conception. Whether dogs have a conception of the future that allows them to orient their present behaviour and discipline their present desires in this sort of way is what is known as an *empirical* question. That is, it is not the sort of question that can be answered by the pronouncements of some philosopher sitting in an armchair, but only detailed study of dog behaviour. But, at the very least, in the impartial position, one of the things you will know is that it is *far more likely* that humans have futures in the strong sense than do dogs. We know that most humans, above a certain age and with no serious impairment of cognitive abilities, possess a future in a strong sense. We don't know this about dogs, and much of the evidence we have seems to point the other way.

So, if this is right, then one of the things you will know in the impartial position is that *if* you turn out to be human then, in dying, it is *probable* that you will lose more than a dog does when it dies. Note that this is not the same as knowing you are human. In the impartial position you do not know this. But you can still know what humans and dogs have to lose, relative to each other, when they die. That is, in the impartial position, you can, without knowing whether you are the human or the dog, know that *if* you are the human then you will – probably – lose more in dying than *if* you are the dog.

Therefore, it would, from the perspective of the impartial position, be irrational to save the life of the dog. You don't know whether you are the human or the dog, but you do know, or at least strongly suspect, that *if* you are the human you will lose more in dying than if you are the dog. So, rationally, it would be wise to opt for the human, rather than the dog, to be saved. But, remember that an irrational choice in the impartial position is an immoral choice in the real world. Therefore, in the real world, the morally correct choice is to save the human rather than the dog.

So, we have avoided the objection with which we opened this chapter. The animal rights position does *not* entail that human and non-human lives are of equal worth. It does not entail, therefore, that lifeboat situations are the moral equivalent of flipping a coin; that it is equally morally legitimate to let a human die as to let a dog die. The supporter of animal rights can consistently claim that, all things being equal, the morally correct choice in a lifeboat situation is to save the human. It is morally right to save the human because, typically, the human has more to lose in dying than does the non-human. Easy, right? Well, actually, no. In morality, nothing ever is.

9 COMPLICATIONS: THE LENGTH OF THE LIFE LOST

Dying is a bad thing, I have argued, because it takes away a future. This presupposes that having a future is a good thing. This is not always true, of course, but it is generally true: this is one of the reasons why not many of us commit suicide. So, one of the things you will know, in the impartial position, is that most futures are good things to have. Now, as I argued earlier, the length of a future is not something that adds value to a person's life – it is something that only potentially adds value to that life. But, as I also argued, this is compatible with our taking the anticipated length of a future into account in our moral reasoning and decision-making. With this in mind, consider a few more lifeboat scenarios.

Lifeboat 1 The choice is between two humans: pulling a baby out of the sea or pulling out an adult. Babies, we have overwhelming reason to suppose, have a future in only a weak sense, not a strong one. Babies cannot conceptually represent the future to themselves, nor orient their present behaviour and discipline their present desires to bring about their desired conception of the future. So, which should we save? We put ourselves in the impartial position, so we don't know if we are going to be the adult or the baby. It seems like no contest: the adult has a future in the strong sense, the baby only in the weak sense. So we should save the adult, right? Maybe not. One of the things we will know in the impartial position is that babies, while less connected to their future, still, typically, have more of a future than adults. So, while babies have a future in only a weak sense, and adults have it in a strong sense, perhaps the greater magnitude of the baby's future outweighs the stronger connections of the adult?

Which way do your intuitions go? Should you save the adult or the baby? It's not easy; issues of life and death rarely are. The very fact that we are likely to disagree over this, that different people will have different intuitions about what is the right thing to do, shows that, in terms of moral importance, the strength of a person's connection to their future does not, necessarily, outweigh the length of that future. We can perhaps make some headway by breaking down the lifeboat situation into several different scenarios. In each scenario, the choices might be between saving a baby and (i) saving a young child, (ii) saving a teenager, (iii) saving a twenty-something, and so on. Indeed, we could, if necessary, break each of these categories down into smaller ones. In each case, you put yourself in the impartial position. In the first case, you don't know whether you are a baby or a young child. In the second, you don't know if you are a baby or a teenager. And so on. In each case, you have to ask yourself: "If I didn't know which I was going to be, which one should I opt to have saved?" Whatever you decide is rational for you to choose in the impartial position is also morally right to choose in the real world.

Horrible decisions many of these would be. Most of them would also be very difficult decisions. Indeed, in many situations, there simply may not be one correct answer. It is true that what is rational to choose in the impartial position is morally right to choose in the real world; but the idea of rationality is itself a very difficult one. There is no guarantee that even a perfectly rational analysis of a situation will yield one correct solution. Perhaps there are many, equally rational, therefore equally correct, solutions. In any case, since we are not perfectly rational, in real life we just have to do the best we can. Guided by the knowledge constraints of the impartial position, we must work out what we think is the most rational choice in any given case, and then use that to decide what we think is the morally correct decision or course of action.

Even with our imperfect rationality, we can easily accept that some decisions are more rational than others. Suppose, to make this graphic, the choice is between pulling someone aged twenty into the lifeboat and hauling in someone aged eighty. In the impartial position, you do not know which of these you will be. How should you choose? Well, one thing you will know in the impartial position is that both people – probably – will have futures in the strong sense. Only probably, of course: the twenty year old may have severe brain damage, and the octogenarian may be at an advanced stage of Alzheimer's. But there is a reasonable possibility that both will have futures in the strong sense, and this is something you will know in the impartial position. However, you will also know that it is highly likely that the twenty-year-old will have much more of a future than the octogenarian. This may not turn out to be right: the twenty-year-old may be hit by a bus after getting off the boat. But the overwhelming probability is that the twenty-year-old will have much more of a future than the eighty-year-old. This is not something that adds value to the twenty-year-old's life – but only something that potentially adds value to his life. Nevertheless, you know that, in the absence of countervailing evidence, at a later time t (say forty years down the road) it is far more likely that the twenty-year-old is alive than the eighty-year-old. And the value that exists in the world at this time t will, therefore, be a function of the continued existence of the twenty-year-old and not the eighty-year-old. And this is something that can legitimately be included in your moral deliberations.

Therefore, given that you do not know which one of these you will be, the rational choice would be to opt for having the twenty-year-old saved. It's not that the twenty-year-old has more to lose in dying than the eighty-year-old – they both lose the same. Rather, it's that the twenty-year-old, in virtue of going on to live a longer life, will at a later time t, bring value into the world that the eighty-year-old, having died, cannot bring. Therefore, it would, I think, be rational in the impartial position to opt for saving the twenty-year-old over the eighty-year-old. And if this is the rational choice in the impartial position, then it is the moral choice in the real world.

Sorry if I am labouring the obvious. I think most people will accept that it is right to save the twenty-year-old before the eighty-year-old, all other things being equal. I labour it partly because it provides an illustration of the impartial position at work: the idea of the impartial position explains and justifies an intuition that most of us share about this lifeboat situation. Also, I use it because I want to set up another claim, one that many will regard as far more controversial.

Lifeboat 2 The choice is between pulling out of the sea a normal adult human being and a (normal, adult, but young) dog. However, you know the human being has only a very short time to live; say fifteen minutes. How do you know this? Well, suppose you witnessed the placement in his neck of a small explosive device, with a charge large enough to blow a hole in his carotid artery (and apologies to John Carpenter for stealing the plot line to *Escape from New York*). The result of this explosion will be his certain death, and let's suppose that these explosive devices never fail and their removal is impossible. So, the person's imminent death, in fifteen minutes time, is as certain as anything can be. Who should you save: the man or the dog? In the impartial position, you don't know which you are going to be. So, from the perspective of this position, which would it be rational to save? I suggest that it would be irrational to opt for the saving of the man. If you turned out to be the man, then you would not have a future that progressively added value to the world. If you turned out to be the dog, you could have a whole life in front of you, a life that would progressively add value as it proceeds along its course. So, rationality dictates that we opt for saving the dog. And if this is the rational decision in the impartial position, it is the morally correct decision in the real world.

If this is correct, then it shows that a human life is not *always* more valuable than that of a non-human animal. The scenario is, of course, extremely far fetched. But this is not important, because what we are after are moral *principles*. One moral principle many people believe is that human life always has more intrinsic worth or value than the life of any non-human creature. I have argued that this is not, necessarily, so. The value of your life is a function, first, of how closely you are tied to your future, and, second, how much of a future you have to be tied to (although this latter value is something that exists only as the future unfolds). Typically, humans, having a future in a strong sense, are more closely tied to their future than animals, which have their future in only a weak sense. But the closeness of ties to the future can sometimes be overridden by great disparities in the amount or size of the future one is tied to. This is why it is morally correct to save a baby over, say, an octogenarian. This is also why it is morally right to save the young dog over the man who is certain to die in fifteen minutes time. In the impartial position, you don't know whether you will be the baby or the octogenarian, the dog or the man. The rational course of action, in these circumstances, is to choose that the baby and the dog, respectively, be saved. The huge disparity in the length of the futures involved overrides the stronger ties the other two have to their respective futures.

Most of the time humans have more to lose in dying than animals. This is because of their stronger ties to their future. Therefore, most of the time, the death of a human is worse than the death of a non-human animal. But, this is not necessarily so, and it is not always so.

10 A COMMON FALLACY

Before we go on, it's worth pausing to point out a common fallacy some people commit when thinking (or, more likely, not thinking) about the ethics of killing animals. I have accepted that the death of a human is, typically (but not always and not necessarily), worse than the death of an animal. Therefore, if you kill an animal, you do something wrong, but not as wrong as if you killed a human. Some people tend to slide from the claim that killing humans is worse than killing animals to the claim that killing animals is morally OK. But this isn't going to work. It's like arguing that since mugging someone is not as bad as killing them, then mugging is morally OK. And, let's face it, that's not going to stand up in court. More generally, you cannot excuse the infliction of harm on someone (or something) on the grounds that it is not as great as the harm you *might* have inflicted on him or her.

11 IMPARTIALITY ON THE LIFEBOAT

The idea that the harm of death consists in losing a future, together with the idea that there are three different ways in which you can have, and lose, a future, allows us to avoid the typical objection to the idea of animal rights: that it entails that the death of an animal is morally equivalent to the death of a human. It does not entail this. Humans, typically, but not necessarily and not always, lose more in dying than do animals because humans are more closely bound to their future than animals.

What we also have is an account of why killing an animal is wrong: it deprives that animal of a future. It is true (probably) that it has a future in only a weak sense, but, nevertheless, in dying it loses a future. Holding on to a future, even in this weak sense, is unarguably a vital interest of the animal, for if this interest is thwarted, then all its other interests are automatically thwarted too. The animal may have less invested in its future, but in losing a future it still loses out on all the opportunities for satisfaction that the future brings with it. So, that an animal has a future in a weak sense, that it loses this future in dying, and that this loss is, for it, a very bad thing; these are all things that you will know in the impartial position.

So, we have an account of why killing animals is wrong, but also of why it is not as bad as killing humans. We require one more thing from this account. We require that it does *not* entail that the life of a human being is worth an unlimited number of animal sacrifices. Some defenders of the idea of animal rights have actually endorsed this claim. Tom Regan, for example, in the process of developing a sophisticated defence of animal rights, finds himself endorsing what he calls the *worse-off principle*:

> Special considerations aside, when we must decide to override the rights of the many or the rights of the few that are innocent, and when the harm faced by the few would make them worse-off than any of the many would be if the other option were chosen, then we ought to override the rights of the many.[5]

Then, the idea is that since humans lose more in dying than do dogs, for example, it is legitimate, according to the worse-off principle, to sacrifice an unlimited number of dogs in order to save the life of a single human.[6] This, I think, is one instance where Regan has got it wrong. Suppose you are a doctor, at a battlefield or accident, and you have a choice. There is a group of, say, ten people, who will lose their legs if you do not treat them fairly quickly. There is also another person who will die if you do not treat him immediately. Unfortunately, the treatment this person requires will take many hours, during which time the ten people will lose their legs. Therefore, you have a choice: saving the life of one, or saving the legs of ten. According to Regan's principle, you should choose to treat the dying man and let the ten lose their legs. This is because, I think we can assume, dying is a greater harm than losing your legs, and according to the worse-off principle, you should act so as to avoid the greater harm, even when the lesser harm is suffered by more people. In fact, it does not matter how many more people suffer the lesser harm. If the number of people who were to lose their legs were a hundred, a thousand, a million etc., it still would not matter. You should, according to the worse-off principle, act to save the life of the one person, even if one million were to lose their legs as a result. Do you agree? I don't.

The idea of the impartial position allows us to avoid this conclusion. The guiding insight, the golden rule, is that if a choice is irrational in the impartial position then it is immoral in the real world. So, what would the rational choice be in the impartial position? Should you, rationally, opt for a world where the doctor saves the life of the one man or the legs of one million? Well, if the group of people liable to lose their legs were as large as this, then surely the rational choice would be to opt for a world where the doctor treats this group. (We don't need to get into technicalities like how one doctor is going to treat a group this large. These will simply detract us from the principles we are trying to identify.) You don't know, of course, whether you will be the one who would die without treatment, or one of those who would lose their legs without treatment. And if you turned out to be the person who dies without treatment, then you will lose more in dying than the others lose when they lose their legs. But the odds are a million to one against you being this person. You would lose more, that's true; but the chances of you doing so are so small that the rational choice would almost certainly be to opt for a world in which the doctor chooses to treat the larger group.

The other limiting case is where both groups number only one person; that is, one person will die if not treated immediately, the other person will lose her legs. In this case, the rational choice in the original position would again, surely, be to opt for a world where the doctor chooses to treat the dying person first. In the impartial position, you do not know which of these you might be, but you do know that if you turn out to be the dying person, then you stand to lose more than the person who will lose their legs.

So, in a fifty-fifty situation like this, the rational choice would be to opt for the person who would be harmed most, or who stands to lose most, to be helped first. But where there is a great disparity in the size of the groups, as in the million-to-one situation imagined above, then the opposite would seem to apply. Somewhere between even odds and a million to one we have a grey area, where we are not sure what is the rational decision to make. How does this apply to animals?

Regan allows, indeed insists, that the harm suffered by a human in dying is greater than the harm suffered by a non-human in dying (although not for the same reasons as I defended earlier). Therefore, his worse-off principle entails that whenever we have to choose between saving a human and saving an animal or animals we should save the human. This applies no matter how many animals are involved. If we find ourselves in a situation where we have to choose between saving the life of one human being and one million dogs then we should, according to Regan, choose to save the one human and let the million dogs die.

The position I advocate differs significantly from this. In the impartial position, as the size of the group of dogs increases, so too does the chance that you will turn out to be one of them. Therefore, what also increases is the irrationality, from the perspective of the impartial position, of opting for a world in which the one human is saved at the expense of the dogs. It is true that if you turned out to be the human you would lose more in dying than any of the dogs. But as the size of the group of dogs increases, the chances of you being that human correspondingly decrease. If you have a choice of saving one human versus a million dogs, then the chances of you being that human are a million to one. In the impartial position, then, the rational decision would be to opt for a world where the dogs were saved at the expense of the human. But if this is the rational decision in the impartial position, then it is the morally correct decision in the real world.

Moral reasoning, on my understanding, is a complex process of weighing, calculating, assessing and evaluating potential gains from potential losses but, crucially, where all this is done from a position of ignorance: the impartial position. In moral reasoning, we try to do the best we can for ourselves. We try to be as mean, selfish, and acquisitive as we can be. It's just that in contexts of moral reasoning, we should pretend we do not know who or what we are. Therefore, in trying to do the best for ourselves, we automatically do the best for everyone.

So, we should not think that the life of a human being is worth the lives of an unlimited number of animals. The life of a human may, typically, be worth more than the life of an animal; typically but not always or necessarily. A human life may, indeed, be worth the lives of several animals. But somewhere this stops. It stops wherever the complex calculation of potential benefits and losses, performed from the perspective of the impartial position, says that it should stop.

12 Summary

Death is harmful. The harm of death consists in the fact that it *deprives its victim of a future*. However, there are three different senses in which something can have a future: *minimal, weak*, and *strong*. Therefore, there are also three different senses in which that thing can lose a future. It is worse to lose a future had in a strong sense than to lose a future had in a weak sense; and it is worse to lose a future had in a weak sense than to lose a future had in a minimal sense. The magnitude of the loss a thing suffers in losing a future is neither a function of the anticipated length of their future, nor of its anticipated quality. However, we justifiably include considerations of length and quality of a future into our moral decision-making on the grounds that they are determinants of the value of a life as it progressively unfolds. Thus, in our moral deliberation, great disparities in the length of a future lost can sometimes outweigh stronger ties to that future.

Most humans have a future in a strong sense. Most, perhaps all, non-humans have a future in only a weak sense. Therefore, humans, typically, lose more in dying than animals do. Therefore, again typically, it is worse to kill a human than a non-human animal. This is not always true. Some humans, those with various forms of brain damage for example, are no more strongly tied to their future than are animals. Also, if the anticipated future of an animal is substantially greater than that of a human, this can offset – at least from the point of view of our moral decision-making – the stronger ties the human has to its future. Finally, the fact that a human life is typically more valuable than that of an animal does not mean it is right to allow any number of animals to die in order to save a single human life.

This chapter has been couched in very general terms; and to some this will seem unsatisfactory. If it is not right to allow an *unlimited* number of animals to die in order to save a single human life, then *precisely how many* animals is it right to let die to save that human? It is this sort of question that will be asked by those who like their morality black and white. The problem is that moral decision-making simply isn't like this. Or, it's hardly ever like this. But there is another reason I haven't pushed for precision here. As we shall see in the coming chapters, most of the time the decisions we have to reach about our treatment of animals are *not even close*. There is no need to agonize over the precise balancing of potential benefits versus potential losses. *It's not even close*. Unlike lifeboat scenarios, it's not as if there are vital human interests at stake which we have to weigh carefully against the similarly vital interests of animals. Most of the time, our mistreatment of animals stems from our letting relatively trivial human interests outweigh even the most vital interests of animals. Nowhere is this more so than in our raising and killing of animals for food. It is to this that we now turn.

5

USING ANIMALS FOR FOOD

Working out what is morally right and what is wrong amounts to choosing how you would like the world to be, but choosing this from the perspective of the impartial position. In doing this, you follow the golden rule: *if it is irrational to choose a situation, institution, or course of action in the impartial position, then it is immoral to choose this situation, institution, or course of action in the real world.* Even in the impartial position, however, our power to choose a world is limited. We can shape the moral, social, economic and political relations that exist in our ideal world, but we have no say over its natural order. We have to assume the laws of nature as presently given. We cannot choose a world, for example, where the second law of thermodynamics doesn't apply, so that there is no need for us or any other animal to eat in order to survive. Our brief concerns the moral order not the natural one.

Would it be rational, from the perspective of the impartial position, to choose a world where humans use animals for food? In the impartial position, not knowing if you are going to be human or an animal eaten by humans, would you opt for a world like the present one? If you did, then far from being rational, you would be a raving lunatic.

1 CHICKENS

Suppose you are chicken. First you are born. And that, I'm afraid, is about as good as it is going to get. You will be born either a "layer" or a "broiler."

100

That is, your destiny will be to lay eggs or to be eaten. If you are a layer, but are male, then your flesh will be deemed not good enough for eating and your life will, accordingly, be short. If you are lucky, you will be gassed. Chances are, however, that you will be thrown into a plastic sack and allowed to suffocate under the weight of other chicks. Alternatively, you might simply be ground up while still alive. In the United States alone, at least 160 million of you and your brethren will suffer this fate every year, and in the UK the number is close to twenty million.

If, on the other hand, you are a layer and female, your troubles are just beginning. First, probably when you are between one and ten days old, you will find yourself being *debeaked*. That is, a guillotine-like device with a red-hot blade will slice off your beak. Just be thankful you weren't born in the 1940s: then it would have been burnt off with a blowtorch! But this won't hurt will it? After all, aren't beaks simply horny outgrowths? Isn't it just like cutting nails, or something like that? Actually, no. Under the beak is a highly sensitive layer or soft tissue, infused with nerve endings. It's something like the layer of skin under the human nail. So, debeaking would be like trimming nails if your preferred method of doing so involved ripping through half your finger as well. And, as if debeaking isn't bad enough in itself, there is a significant chance that it's going to be more or less botched as well. Perhaps the blade is too hot, in which case your mouth will be badly blistered. Perhaps it is not hot enough, in which case an extremely painful growth is likely to appear at the end of your mouth. Perhaps the severance of your beak is incomplete, causing torn tissue in the roof of your mouth. And having too much of your beak sliced off, almost as far as the nostrils, is not an unlikely occurrence. Why is the procedure likely to be botched? Sheer numbers. Battery egg farms range in size from tens of thousands to several million chickens. That's a lot of beaks to get through. And this sort of repetitive job, where the financial rewards, meagre as they are, are tied to quantity rather than quality, is almost inevitably accompanied by mistakes; lots of them.

After your beak has been sliced off, you will be sent to a "grow out" house. At one time, this might have been a relatively idyllic time in your life. You might actually have been allowed to move around freely, perhaps even outdoors (in the belief that this would make you tougher, and better able to withstand the rigours of life in a cage). Now, in all likelihood, you will be put in a cage in a large shed. There you will remain until you are about twenty weeks old, and ready to start laying.

Following a second debeaking, you will be moved to a battery cage in a laying facility. If you are in the US, the cage will be approximately twelve by twenty inches; if you are the EU it will be approximately forty-six by fifty-one centimeters. You will share this rather palatial residence with anywhere between three and six other birds. (As the price of eggs goes up, so in all likelihood will the number of your roommates. The increased mortality rate overcrowding brings is more than compensated by the increase in egg production.) This, admittedly, is a little cramped. Being a bird of average size, at rest you need around 637 square centimeters to be able to sit down comfortably. If you wanted the luxury of turning around, then you would require 1,681 square centimeters. The standard twelve by twenty inch cage, shared with four others, gives you about 300 square centimeters. Total. Just to be clear on the sort of dimensions we're talking about here, 500 square centimeters is about the size of a sheet of A4 paper. If you're a very lucky bird, and share your cage with only three others, then you have 375 square centimeters. Either way, you can forget about stretching your thirty-inch (seventy-five-cm) wingspan.

Stretching and turning around are not the only things stymied by your close confinement. Any possibility of normal social interaction has pretty much gone also. Chickens have evolved as social creatures, and essential to the stability of any group of chickens is a form of social hierarchy known, colloquially, as the "pecking order." In more normal conditions, chickens lower down the order stay out of the way of their more dominant conspecifics. But it's a little difficult to stay out of the way of anything in a twelve by twenty cage. So, lots of chickens are going to get pecked, and the chances are you are going to be one of them. Indeed, if you are at the bottom of the caged mini-hierarchy, then you may well be pecked to death.

Now, of course, the reason for your debeakings becomes clear. If too many chickens get pecked to death, profits drop. This is a pattern that is repeated time and time again in animal husbandry. An animal is raised in unpleasant and unnatural conditions, and this causes it to behave in unpleasant and unnatural ways. But, do we change the conditions? No, that would be unprofitable. Instead, we butcher the animal so that the damage caused by its unpleasant and unnatural behaviour does not eat into our profits too much.

After a few months of constant rubbing against the cage, and other birds pecking at you, you will have lost many, maybe most, of your feathers. Your skin will be red and raw, especially around your tail. You will be suffering from a severe form of osteoporosis, so much so that even being handled by a human may result in the snapping of your legs or wings, and the caving in of your rib cage. By now, you and your cage-mates are demonstrably hysterical, almost certainly insane, and are very probably developing a penchant for cannibalism.

After a year or two of this (if you are still alive – thirty-five per cent of your cage-mates will not be), your productivity will wane, making it unprofitable for the factory owner to feed or house you any longer. He or she may then try to coax a few more months of egg production out of you by "force moulting." You will be left in the dark for several days without food or water, in the hope that this will shock you into further egg production. But, after a forced moult or two, you are finished, and will be delivered to the processors to be turned into stock cubes, frozen pies, or pet food. Such is the life of a battery hen.

If you are born a broiler rather than a layer, then you are a little more fortunate: you won't live as long. A day-old chick, you will, along with anything from ten thousand to several hundred thousand other chicks, be sent to a broiler house where you receive the mandatory debeaking (and perhaps toe clipping). The broiler house is a large, windowless shed. If you are lucky, you will be allowed to live on the floor of this shed, although some producers use tiers of cages to get more birds into the same size shed. At first, you may have some room in which to move around; you and your shed-mates are still small. As you all grow, however, conditions become progressively more cramped. By the time you reach slaughtering weight, after about seven weeks, you may have as little as half a square foot of space.

As you all grow, of course, what grows with you is the mountain of excrement that covers the floor and the acrid stench of ammonia that fills the air. The ammonia is itself a serious health problem. You will, in all likelihood, be suffering from hock burn and breast blisters. How bad can things get? You are being burned by your own (and others) urine. Also littering the floor in gradually increasing numbers are the bodies of your shed-mates. Naturally enough, you are made unhappy by these unnatural conditions and develop various "vices." Unable to establish a natural social hierarchy in a flock of 50,000 or more, you have a tendency to fight with your shed-mates and, like your laying sister, a rapidly developing proclivity for cannibalism. But cannibalism, if you will forgive the pun, eats directly into the profits of the owner. So what does he or she do? Ameliorate the conditions that cause your behaviour? Allow you to live in more natural conditions? Give you more room? No, that would reduce profits. Instead, you are debeaked, and the light around you artificially controlled. In many systems, this means that the light is reduced to as little as two lux (candlelight is approximately ten lux). Thus, since reduced lighting has been shown to reduce aggression, you are likely to live out your last few weeks in near darkness.

2 PIGS

Pigs are raised in a variety of systems. So, if you are a pig, you may be (relatively) lucky or unlucky. With the increasing application of factory methods to pig husbandry, however, it is becoming increasingly likely that you will be unlucky. It is more and more probable, for example, that you will find yourself raised in a *total confinement* farm system, in which you will never see the light of day, not, that is, until you are sent to your death at the market. You will be born, have a battery of injections, have your needle teeth clipped (i.e. cut down almost to gum level), your ears notched for identification, and your tail cut off without anaesthetic. Then, around weaning time, you may well, if you are a male, be castrated, again without anaesthetic. Then, you will be moved for "finishing" (i.e. fattening) to a large building, designed along the same lines as a broiler house, but divided into pens. You will share this long, windowless, building with several thousand other pigs until you are ready to be slaughtered.

If you were raised in more natural surroundings, you would form a stable social group, and spend your time building communal nests, and rooting around at the edge of the woodland. In fact, of your daylight hours, approximately fifty-two per cent is likely to be spent foraging, and twenty-three per cent exploring your environment.[1] None of this is, of course, possible in your present surroundings. Also, in more natural conditions, you would use dunging areas well away from the communal nest. Again, this is not possible in a total confinement system. The usual method of preventing the inevitable build up of a mountain of excrement is to put in a false, slatted, floor. This is not unlike a cattle grid, except the slats are closer together. Of course, this is not only extremely uncomfortable, but also will result in deformity. Or, rather, it would if you lived long enough (which you won't).

Being the naturally intelligent creature that you are, unremitting boredom is probably your greatest enemy. You can eat, sleep, stand up or lie down. And that's it: the entire gamut of activities available to you. You probably won't have any bedding materials, with which you might make a nest, since this would complicate the task of cleaning. Like factory-raised chickens, because of these conditions, you will, in all likelihood, suffer from stress; and perhaps you might even die from it. The symptoms of *porcine stress syndrome* include rigidity, skin problems, panting, and often, sudden death. Also, and again like factory chickens, you will acquire certain "vices." You and your pen-mates may take to biting each other's tails. This may escalate into outright fighting. This is something that the factory owner must take seriously for two reasons. First, fighting is a strenuous activity and reduces your gains in weight. Second, the tail-biting or fighting may itself escalate into a form of cannibalism. Your pen-mates, for example, might start by biting your tail and then go on eating into your back – literally eating into the profits of the factory owner – until you die.

The cause of this behaviour is multi-factorial, but stress, overcrowding and boredom are centrally implicated. It has been shown conclusively that providing even rudimentary items such as straw bedding substantially reduces the incidence of tail-biting due, at least in part, to the recreational possibilities provided by the straw.[2] However, this would make cleaning the pens more difficult (i.e. the factory owner would have to employ and pay more people), and active pigs put on weight more slowly than bored ones (thus require more feed). So, the preferred method for controlling tail-biting is simple: cut off the tails. Also, total confinement under reduced lighting conditions. We saw exactly the same pattern in the case of factory chickens. Putting animals in unpleasant and unnatural environments produces unpleasant and unnatural behaviour. We combat this not by ameliorating the environments – that would be unprofitable – but by butchering the animals and making their environments even worse.

If you are a male pig, and make it through all this, you can expect to be slaughtered after about twenty weeks, when you reach a market weight of 220 pounds. If you are breeding sow, on the other hand, entirely new vistas of suffering will be opened up to you. Shortly after conception (probably via artificial insemination) you will be moved to a gestation building. On some farms, you may share a small pen with other sows. But, in the more intensive (and increasingly more common) factories you will find yourself restricted to a narrow stall (usually in the region of two feet wide and six feet long), or chained around the neck, or in a narrow stall *and* chained around the neck. Here you will be able to stand up or lie down. But that's about it. You will, of course, not be very happy with this sort of confinement, and are likely to register your disapproval, at least in the beginning, by thrashing your head about in the tether, twisting and turning in an attempt to free yourself. Alternatively, you may smash your body against the sides of your stall. You may persist with this fruitless struggle for up to three hours.[3] Then, perhaps as the hopelessness of your situation begins to sink in, you will lie still for long periods, perhaps with your snout pushed under the bar, emitting the occasional quiet groan or whine.[4] In more normal conditions, you would be a highly active animal, spending several hours a day finding food, eating and exploring. Now, your natural appetite for activity can manifest itself only in a futile gnawing at the bars of your stall.

Here you will remain for about three months, during which time you may be kept in darkness and fed only once every two or three days (a practice itself based on economic considerations: since you are not being sold for meat, not yet anyway, you are fed only enough for you to produce viable offspring). A week or so before your litter is due you will be moved to a "farrowing" building and again restricted to a narrow stall. Here, again, you are able to lie or stand, but you cannot walk or turn around. The function of the stall is to keep you in position only to eat, drink, and keep your teats exposed to your baby pigs. Often, the factory owner will decide that the stall by itself is not enough and will restrict your range of movement further. An iron frame that prevents free movement (a device nicknamed the "iron maiden") is employed for this purpose in many countries. At the very least you will be tightly tethered. The excuse for this practice is to stop you rolling onto and crushing your babies. But, of course, the only reason there is a danger of you doing this in the first place is because you have been provided with so little room. Once again, one of the first rules of factory farming seems to be this: the answer to an inadequate environment is a worse environment.

Only when you are placed with the boar, in a larger pen, do you have a short, and relatively idyllic, break from confinement. With the increasing use of artificial insemination however, even this transient period of porcine pleasure is likely to be denied you. And this is basically it. One period of isolation and severe confinement followed by another period of isolation and even more severe confinement. You can, at present, be expected to produce at least two litters a year. But your reproductive work rate is likely to increase in the near future, since, believe it or not, your suckling duties are likely to be usurped by a mechanical sow tenderly administering to your (now caged) piglets who have been taken from you much earlier than normal. Since your lactation will now cease, you will be fertile again in a few days, and can expect the cyclical confinement regime to begin again. With this mechanical aid, you will be expected to produce, on average, 2.6 litters per year. Such are the days of your life as a breeding sow.

3 CATTLE

In the pantheon of horrors inflicted in the name of animal husbandry, the regime that produces veal calves is surely right there at the top. Veal is the flesh of a young calf. Calves killed before weaning had a flesh that was paler and more tender than those who had begun to eat grass, and the term "veal" originally referred to flesh of unweaned calves. Since such calves are obviously small, veal was expensive. In the 1950s, a method was found of producing the same sort of flesh in older, and, more importantly, larger calves. The method, in essence, was to make the calves severely anaemic, but not so anaemic that they would die, at least not before they reach market weight.

To be a veal calf you must, first, be born healthy and robust. Veal producers seek out the most healthy and robust calves since only they are likely to survive the rigours of the veal production regime. Shortly after you are born you will be taken from your mother, and placed in a wooden stall approximately one foot ten inches wide and four foot six inches long (US standard sizes). This stall will be one of thousands lined up, row on row, in the confinement building. Even when you are very young, these crates will be too small to allow you to turn around, and after you reach a certain size even standing up and lying down will become extremely difficult. For between three and four months you will find yourself confined to this stall or crate, and may well find yourself tethered at the neck to restrict your movement further (we'll see why in a moment). During this time, and this is one of the keys to the process, you will be fed no solid food but only a liquid "milk replacer": a mixture of dried milk products, starch, fats, sugar, additives and plenty of antibiotics. The milk replacer is formulated to be deficient in iron. Not completely devoid of iron, since this would kill you, but deficient enough to produce a severe and pernicious form of anaemia. And it is this anaemia that gives your flesh the pale colour that will fetch a good market price for "prime" veal.

No hay or roughage can be permitted in your diet, for this contains iron and will darken your flesh and reduce your profitability. For similar reasons, you will have no bedding (you might eat it to satisfy your craving for roughage). Instead, you will spend your life on a bare and slatted wooden floor. You may resort to attempting to chew the sides of your stall, in a desperate quest for iron. You will, very probably, develop various digestive disorders, stomach ulcers, and chronic diarrhoea.

But why the small crate? Why the tethering? Because one source of roughage, hence iron, is *yourself*: your fur and your excreta. Any attempts at grooming have to be prevented. And, while, in normal circumstances, you have, like any other calf, a healthy aversion to your own urine and faeces, these circumstances are very far from normal. You might try to satisfy your intense craving for iron by licking your own waste products, and so you have to be prevented from accessing them. Hence the small crate. Hence the tethering.

Like the pig, the physical problems bequeathed to you by this regime are compounded by the psychological ones. Unrelieved boredom is your only companion. Your feeding takes about twenty minutes each day. Besides that there is nothing to do. If anyone looks, they can probably observe you grinding your teeth, wagging your tail, swaying your tongue and engaging in other "stereotypical" behaviour. Like the compulsive pecking of the factory chicken, and the tail-biting of the factory pig, these are recognized symptoms of boredom and boredom-induced stress.

Veal calves are, admittedly, an extreme case. But you should not assume that the lives of other cattle are necessarily tranquil or idyllic. If you are a dairy cow, for example, then there is a significant, and steadily increasing, chance that you will now be kept indoors for much of your time, perhaps even in an individual pen with enough room only to stand up and lie down. To produce milk, of course, you first have to be made pregnant, probably by artificial insemination. Your calf will be taken from you at birth, an experience as painful for you as it is terrifying for your calf. The calf will then will either be reared as a dairy cow, or reared as a beef cow in a feedlot, or sold as a veal calf. After your first calf is taken away, you will be milked twice, or perhaps even thrice, a day for ten months. After the third month or so, you will be made pregnant again and milked until about six weeks before your calf is due, and then again after your calf is removed. You will be capable of keeping up this intense cycle of pregnancy and lactation for, probably, about five years. After this you will be "spent" and, accordingly, slaughtered.

If you are raised for beef, then, in contrast to veal calves (and chickens and pigs), you will get to spend time in the great outdoors. However, with modern beef production methods, the chances are that, at least for most of your life, the great outdoors won't be the prairie but a high-density feedlot (to which you may have been shipped a great distance), where you will probably find yourself sharing a single acre with up to 900 others. Then, after six to eight months of fattening, on corn and other cereals, you too will be sent to the slaughterhouse. And, by the way, during the course of your life you can expect to be dehorned, branded, and castrated without anaesthetic. The typical method of the latter is for you to be trussed, thrown to the ground, your scrotum slit open, and your testicles yanked out. (One's eyes water merely thinking about that one.)

4 FACTORY FARMING AND THE IMPARTIAL POSITION

None of the animal husbandry methods I have described in the preceding sections are in any way unusual. I have not deliberately focused on atypically cruel or unusual methods just to make a point. This is simply what is going on; this is how much of the meat that we find on our plates is produced. This is not to say that all animals raised for food are produced by these sorts of *intensive* or factory methods. But many are. In the United States alone, over 100 million broiler chickens are slaughtered each *week* after being raised in the conditions described in section 1. And in the UK, 719 million chickens a year suffer the same fate. Each year in the United States, at least 160 million male offspring of laying chickens are gassed, suffocated, or ground up alive in the manner described in section 1. Go into any supermarket and look at the relative numbers of free-range versus factory-farmed eggs they stock, and this will give you some idea of the relative numbers of free-range versus factory hens. The vast majority of the pigs we now eat – thirteen million a year are slaughtered in the UK – are produced by the sort of methods described in section 2. And virtually all breeding sows are treated in the ways described in that section. All veal is, of necessity, produced by the methods described in section 3, or slight variations thereon.

In short, factory farming, or intensive production, of the food we eat is the norm; it is the rule rather than the exception. Why? For the simple reason that it is more cost-effective, therefore more *profitable*. Factory farming brings the motivation and the mentality of the automated production line to the production of food. In terms of profitability, the factory farm has the same advantage over small, non-intensive, farms as an automated assembly line has over a workshop that produces hand-crafted items. This is why the trend over the past few decades has been for factory operations to increase in number while small, non-intensive, alternatives (i.e. the traditional farms) go to the wall.

So, if you eat meat then one thing you should know is that, in all likelihood, much of it has been produced by the methods described in the preceding sections. Now, be honest, would you, from the perspective of the impartial position, seriously opt for a world that contained these methods? Would it be rational to choose a world where animals were intensively farmed? In the impartial position, you may be human, but you may also be an animal eaten by humans. (You may also, of course, be an animal *not* eaten by humans, but then you are not relevant to the present issue and so drop out of our calculations.) Whether intensive food production is a rational or irrational choice from the perspective of the impartial position depends on what you stand to gain and to lose from such a choice. So, first of all, suppose you turned out to be an animal eaten by humans. What do you stand to lose from a world that contains intensive food production. Hopefully, the preceding sections have made this clear. If you are animal eaten by humans and are intensively farmed for this purpose then you will live a life of utter misery, wretchedness and desolation, characterized by physical and psychological deprivation and torment. You live a life that is simply not worth living; a life where you would be better off dead. And to live a life where you are better off dead is surely the worst thing that can ever happen to anyone or anything.

Compare this, now, with what you stand to lose if you turn out to be human. Well, *at worst*, you lose out on certain pleasures of the palate. Non-intensive food production results in more expensive food. Not radically more expensive (free-range eggs are approximately thirty per cent more expensive than battery alternatives, for example), but nonetheless significantly more expensive. Perhaps you will turn out to be one of those humans who simply cannot afford this extra expense. Then, you will, in effect, have to give up eating meat and other animal products. But why does this matter? Giving up meat does not require giving up life or health. In most environments at least, humans can live, and live well, without eating meat, a fact attested to by the existence of millions of healthy vegetarians living in almost all parts of the world. There is no doubt, of course, that meat is a valuable source of nutrition, primarily because it provides all of the amino acids essential for human beings. Meat, however, is not essential in this regard since the relevant amino acids can also be obtained from suitable combinations of non-animal protein. And while the knowledge necessary for putting together such combinations is, perhaps, not currently widespread – due largely to the prevalence of meat eating in our society – this knowledge is in no way abstruse or recondite. The necessary knowledge is, in fact, no more complex than that required in order to combine suitable amounts of protein, carbohydrate and fat in one's diet.

If humans beings had to give up eating meat, then the principal thing that would have to be abandoned is neither life nor health, but certain pleasures of the palate. Meat, for most people at least, is delicious. Some vegetarians claim to dislike the taste of meat. Personally, I still dream of rump steaks, and of those heady days when pork ribs would be merrily crackling on the barbecue. However, while meat is undoubtedly tasty, it is easy to make too much of this. Wonderful things can, in fact, be done with the humble vegetable, and it is not as if vegetarianism and palatable food are mutually exclusive.

So, you are in the impartial position and trying to work out if you should choose a world that contains factory farming. To work this out, just focus on your potential gains and losses. If you choose to reject factory farming, then at the very worst you lose out only on certain pleasures of the palate, and at best you gain, potentially, a life worth living. If, on the other hand, you choose to endorse factory farming, then at most you gain certain pleasures of the palate and at worst lose out on a life worth living. Pleasures of the palate cannot be weighed against a life worth living. The two things are just not comparable. After all, how many medium rare rump steaks would you exchange for your life or freedom? Therefore, it would, in the impartial position, be irrational to opt for a world that contained intensive methods of food production.

This claim can be further supported by the fact that since one human being will, in the course of a lifetime, typically eat many animals, there is a much greater chance, from the perspective of the impartial position, that you will turn out to be an animal eaten by humans than you will be a human. So, not only do you stand to lose much more by choosing a world that contains intensive methods of food production, there is also a greater chance that you will in fact lose it.

Therefore, in the impartial position, the rational choice is clear. It would be *irrational* to choose a world that contained factory or intensive methods of food production. Therefore, in the real world, such methods are *immoral*.

5 HOW ANIMALS DIE

A common response to the well-documented horrors of intensive food production is to urge a non-intensive alternative. You often hear people arguing something like this. "OK, factory farming, I agree that's wrong. We should not be cruel to animals, and factory farming methods clearly are cruel. But, as long as animals are treated well when they are alive, as long as they have sufficient space, are able to engage in natural behaviours, and so on, then killing them for food is legitimate." According to this suggestion, we should separate the issue of forcing an animal to live in wretched conditions from the issue of killing that animal. We cannot justify the cruelty involved in forcing a calf to spend the whole of its life in a wooden crate. But we can justify killing calves and other animals as long as this is done in a reasonably humane way.

In order to assess this suggestion, we need to look at two things. First of all, in any system of animal husbandry, there is the fact *that* animals die; and so we need to look at whether, in the impartial position, it would be rational to choose a world where animals die so that humans may eat them. Second, there is the *way in which* animals die; and so we need to look at whether, in the impartial position, it would be rational to choose a world where animals die, *in the way that they currently die*, so that humans may eat them. The first issue is concerned with the fact *that* animals die. The second is concerned with *how* they die. This section looks at how animals die.

The deaths of animals in slaughterhouses are supposed to be quick and painless. They are supposed to be stunned by electric current or captive bolt pistol, and have their throats cut when unconscious. Quick, clean, painless. The reality, however, is quite different. Consider how you are likely to meet your maker if you are a cow. Pretty much the same story, with minor variations, can be told of pigs and chickens.

From a stinking, muddy pen, the air rank with the stench of blood, you are corralled, or more likely, electrically "prodded" up a wooden plank. At the top a worker stuns you with an electric shock to the head. When you fall, someone grabs you, places your rear legs in a metal clamp, and you are hoisted upside-down on a conveyor belt. You are killed by a man who stabs your jugular with a knife. You bleed slowly to death.

Not very pleasant, admittedly. The assumption that an electrical shock sufficient to induce unconsciousness is not painful is, of course, a ridiculous one, as anyone who has had even a mild electric shock will realize. This is why electroconvulsive therapy is usually administered under a general anaesthetic. So, it is very difficult to believe that the cow's death is a painless one. Nor is it neat or quick. The above description is very definitely a best case scenario: if you are a cow about to be slaughtered, that's about the best you can hope for. It may be, for example, that you are incorrectly clamped into the conveyor, in which case you can fall to the ground and regain consciousness (a not uncommon occurrence).

In any event, it is quite likely that you are not fully unconscious. Much of the suffering that occurs in slaughterhouses results from the sheer pace at which the killing line must work. Economic competition means that slaughterhouses must attempt to maximize their number of slaughters per hour. Even the slaughterhouse employees suffer under these circumstances; there is a higher injury and illness rate among slaughterhouse employees in the US than among those of any other industry. In these conditions, then, it is no surprise that sometimes electric shocks are not properly administered, or that rear legs are not properly clamped into the conveyor.

Indeed, you can consider yourself quite fortunate to even get an electric shock. The provision of electric shock is due to the existence of humane slaughter acts in many Western countries. Such countries, however, generally have exceptions to these acts, permitting slaughter in accordance with Jewish and Moslem rituals that require the animals to be fully conscious when slaughtered. Orthodox Jewish and Moslem dietary laws prohibit the eating of dead flesh from any animal that is not "healthy and moving" when killed. The rationale for this was, originally, a good one; it prevents the eating of diseased or putrid meat. As with much religious ritual whose original purpose has been lost, this rule has rapidly descended into meaningless dogma. So, as interpreted today, this rule forbids making an animal unconscious even a few seconds before it is killed. The killing is achieved by way of a slashed jugular and/or carotid artery.

If you are cow killed under this sort of ritual exemption to humane slaughter acts, then you might be in serious trouble, especially in the United States. First of all, the Pure Food and Drug Act of 1906 requires that a slaughtered animal must not, for sanitary reasons, fall in the blood of a previously slaughtered animal. So, what this means is that you must be suspended from a conveyor belt. But, if you are slaughtered under ritual exemption to the humane slaughter act, this means you will be hoisted on the conveyor in a fully conscious state. However, you are a cow weighing between 1000 and 2000 pounds, and your legs simply cannot withstand this sort of strain. Typically, your canon bone will snap, and the skin around it will often tear, and rip away from the bone. Suspended upside-down, with joints rupturing and bones breaking, you will frantically twist and turn in pain and terror. This makes the cutting of your jugular or carotid a little tricky, and so you will then be either gripped by the neck or have a clamp inserted in your nostrils, enabling the slaughterer to kill you with a single stroke as the dietary law requires.

The ASPCA has developed a device that allows a conscious animal to be slaughtered in accordance with US hygiene regulations without being hoisted by the leg, and this is now used for eighty per cent of large cattle undergoing ritual slaughter. However, it is still used for less than ten per cent of calves. Moreover, the large cattle that are killed via ritual slaughter form a larger percentage of the meat in the supermarket than you might think. In order to be classified as "kosher", the meat must not only be from an animal killed in this way, it must also have had forbidden tissues such as veins, lymph nodes, and large nerves removed. Cutting these out of the hindquarters is difficult, and, as a result, only the forequarters of the slaughtered animal are generally sold as kosher meat. The remainder is sold on supermarket shelves without any indication that the animal was slaughtered in ritual manner. The chances are that a significant proportion of the beef you have eaten has been killed in this way.

The lives of food animals are not easy. But suppose we could get around this, suppose we could make their lives idyllic. Pigs would root merrily around on the edge of the woodland, calves would frolic in the fields, chickens would happily peck and bathe in the dust, and so on. Suppose we could do all this. We would still face the problem of death. In order to eat them, we have to kill them. And the way we currently kill them is, at best, merely painful and terrifying. At worst, it surpasses the nastiest excesses of even the most warped horror writer.

Put yourself back in the impartial position. Would it be rational to opt for a world where animals are killed in this way, even if their lives were idyllic? To answer this, you must weigh up what you stand to gain and lose from your choice. Suppose animals were not killed in this way. Then, there are two relevant possibilities. Either you turn out to be human, in which case you lose something. Or, you turn out to be an animal killed and eaten by humans, in which case you gain something. If you turn out to be human, what do you lose? Well, *at worst*, you lose out on certain pleasures of the palate. Suppose the current assembly line methods were the only practical way of killing animals. Or suppose the alternative, less horrific, methods pushed up the price of meat significantly, so that many humans could not afford it. From the perspective of the original position, you could turn out to be one of those humans. In which case, to choose a world where these methods of killing were not employed would be to choose a world where you were unable to eat meat. That's a worst-case scenario. You lose out on certain gustatory pleasures. That's all. You do not lose out on life or health. You simply miss out on certain pleasures of the palate.

If you turn out to be an animal eaten by humans, however, think what you would lose if you opted for the world where animals were killed via current methods and practices. In opting for this world, you would have consigned yourself to one of the most horrible deaths imaginable.

Alternatively, opting for a world where these methods and practices were not employed would save you from such a fate. Surely this more than outweighs the loss of gustatory pleasure you would "suffer" if you turned out to be human. You think not? Well, how many gustatory pleasures would you accept in exchange for a death of this sort? If God or whoever came up to you and said, "I will give you whatever pleasures of the palate you like as long as you agree to be killed in the manner you humans now kill cows, or pigs or sheep or chickens." Would you agree? I wouldn't have thought so. Pleasures of the palate are all very well, but they are not worth dying like that.

If this is right, then it would be irrational, in the impartial position, to opt for a world that contains our current methods and practices of killing animals. Therefore, it is immoral, in the real world, to endorse these methods and practices. Not only is the way the animals we eat live immoral, so too is the way they die. It would be wrong, therefore, to endorse either. And since the principal way of endorsing the way animals live and die is by putting money in the pockets of those who make them live and die this way, we should not do this.

6 THAT ANIMALS DIE

Suppose, however, we could change the way animals live and die. Suppose that we could not only make their lives relatively idyllic, but we could also make their deaths quick and painless. Old MacDonald, let's suppose, has a free-range farm where pigs merrily root, calves happily frolic, hens contentedly cluck etc. And Old MacDonald does not send his animals (perhaps long distances without food and water) to the slaughterers. Instead, he waits until they fall asleep, and then finishes them with a painless lethal injection. Impractical this may be, but surely this would be OK morally speaking?

To see whether it is indeed morally OK, we have to again put ourselves in the impartial position. The choice is between two worlds. World 1, where humans eat meat, but where this is produced by some idyllic free-range system of animal husbandry followed by a quick and painless death for the animals. World 2, where humans are exclusively vegetarian. In the impartial position, which world is rationally preferable? To work this out, we need to assess what you potentially gain and lose from each world. Suppose, first, you turn out to be human. Then, in World 1 you have, and in World 2 you lose, certain pleasures of the palate. If you turn out to be an animal eaten by humans, on the other hand, then in World 2 you have, and in World 1 you lose, your life. Now, even allowing for the fact that the harm of dying consists in losing a future and that animals typically have a future in only a weak sense, there is no way that being deprived of a few gustatory pleasures is comparable with being deprived of your life. Being deprived of certain pleasures of the palate is one thing, but being deprived of your future, even in a weak sense, is being deprived of the possibility of having any pleasures, or having any of your preferences satisfied. Ever.

If this is not clear, think about it like this. Suppose there were – as in H.G. Wells' *The Time Machine* – two distinct groups of humans. One group, the *Morlocks* are cannibals, and they raise and kill another group of humans, the *Eloi*, for food. They raise them, let's suppose, in a free-range manner. That is, the Eloi are allowed to live relatively trouble free and idyllic lives in, roughly, the way they choose to lead them, until, when they reach eating weight, they are slaughtered. Let's also suppose they are slaughtered quickly and painlessly in a trance-like state (as in the 1963 film adaptation starring Rod Taylor) so they have no idea what is happening to them. In the impartial position, you don't know if you will turn out to be Morlock or Eloi. In this position, would it be rational to choose the Morlock/Eloi cannibalistic system, or opt for a non-cannibalistic alternative? Pretty clearly, I think, it would be rational to choose the non-cannibalistic option. Then, if you turn out to be Morlock, you merely lose a certain amount of gustatory pleasure, for (being human) you can live perfectly well on a non-meat diet. On the other hand, if you choose the cannibalistic system, and you turn out to be Eloi, you lose your life and everything that goes with it. Under the cannibalistic system, your potential losses are great, and your potential gains meagre. Therefore, it would be seriously irrational to opt for this system.

Now, from the point of view of the rationality of your choice, what's the difference between opting for the system of cannibalistic *human husbandry* of the Morlocks and the system of carnivorous animal husbandry of humans? The answer is: very little. Even accounting for the fact that animals lose a future in only a weak sense, whereas the Eloi lose it in a strong sense, the two choices are still both very irrational. This is because, in the impartial position, you do not know who or what you are going to be. Therefore, the rational choice is to maximize your potential gains and minimize your potential losses *whoever or whatever you might turn out to be*. The gains from the carnivorous system if you are human, or the cannibalistic system if you are Morlock, are meagre compared to your losses if you turn out to be an animal or Eloi. Therefore, it is irrational to opt for either system.

Moral reflection, aided by the heuristic device of the impartial position, yields unambiguous conclusions. Not only is the intensive or factory farming of animals for food wrong, so too is the free-range alternative. Indeed, the free-range alternative is morally wrong, even if the animals are killed quickly and painlessly. In the impartial position, it would be irrational to opt for any system where animals are raised and killed for food, no matter how they are raised, and no matter how they are killed. Therefore, in the real world, it is immoral to raise and kill animals for food, no matter how they are raised and no matter how they are killed.

Now, let's start looking at the chorus of objections this claim usually provokes.

7 BUT WHAT WOULD HAPPEN TO ALL THE ANIMALS?

"What would happen to all the farm animals if we stopped raising them for food?" This objection is embarrassingly common. It's not a very good one. Some people, perhaps fixating on the slogan "animal liberation" and then taking the word "liberation" far too literally, seem to envisage pigs and cows and chickens roaming the streets or countryside, dying of neglect and starvation. But this is silly. Believing in animal rights or animal liberation does not mean you should open the farmyard gate and shout "shoo!"

That would itself be cruel, and a violation of the duties we have acquired towards these animals. These duties involve being responsible, and caring for, these animals until they are no longer with us.

A more sensible way of developing the "what would happen to all the animals?" question is in terms of the idea that if we were to abandon animal husbandry, then the vast majority of pigs, cows, chickens, and so on, would die out, since the only reason there are so many of them in the first place is because we eat them. This is true. One of the consequences of widespread vegetarianism would be a massive reduction in the numbers of these animals. But what's wrong with this? If, say, there are only 400 cows in the world instead of, say, 400 million, why should this matter? In particular, how does it harm any one of the 400 cows? Answer: it does not. Whether it harms any of these cows depends on the individual interests of each cow, and there is no reason to suppose that the interests of an individual cow in any way involve the numbers of others of its kind, at least not as long as there are enough of these others around to provide it with companionship in a normal social setting. The welfare of each individual cow is completely unaffected by whether there are 400 or 400 million others of its kind. Vain and complex species that we are, we tend to worry about things like "the future of the human race." So, it might be in our interests to have large numbers of humans around, because we worry about such things, and our (overinflated) view of our role in the universal scheme of things demands our continuation. But cows, pigs, chickens, and sheep certainly do not worry about the size of their species. As long as there are enough of them to form a normal social group, they're happy.

It might be true that the elimination of a species or sub-species is a cause for regret, even if that species has been artificially created by a eugenic selective-breeding regime. But vegetarianism does not require the elimination of species. If we are worried about this, then we can always turn over areas of land – maintained by public funds – for grazing by animals that we currently eat. In a vegetarian world, perhaps we might want to do this anyway, as a living memorial to the morally bankrupt ways of our forebears.

8 BUT THE ANIMALS WOULDN'T BE THERE IF IT WASN'T FOR US!

True. But so what? Your children wouldn't be there if it wasn't for you either. But this doesn't mean that you can do whatever you like to your children, simply because you brought them into existence. Generally, bringing something into existence does not mean that you have unrestricted rights over that thing.

9 BUT WOULDN'T THE ECONOMIC CONSEQUENCES BE DISASTROUS?

The livelihoods of many people – farmers, factory owners, meat packers, transporters, retailers, veterinarians, and so on, are bound up with the animal husbandry industry. Should this industry fail, as it would if vegetarianism were to become widespread, these people would lose the proverbial shirts off their backs. So, wouldn't the economic consequences of widespread vegetarianism be disastrous?

There are two answers to this. The first one is: no. The second one is: even if they were (which they won't be), so what? Let's start with the first one.

To begin with, we have to remember that any transition to widespread vegetarianism is likely to be very gradual, indeed it would probably span several generations. Anyone who would lose their job or livelihood through vegetarianism would have a luxury few who lose their job or livelihood have: the time to plan and train for a different vocation. Secondly, everyone still has to eat. Many, perhaps the vast majority of, people employed, directly or indirectly, by the animal husbandry industry will, if they so wish, be able to earn their living, directly or indirectly, from arable farming and the surrounding service industries. Many, although not all, farmers who now raise animals can, instead, grow wheat, corn or barley. Transporters can transport, and packers can pack, grain instead of meat. Retailers can sell vegetables. The only class of people not directly insertable into the arable industry would be veterinarians. But, if you are smart enough to get into veterinary school, then you are presumably smart enough to realize that your vocation is going to be considerably down-sized over the coming years, and so either get into small animal medicine or train for something else. So, why should there be any disastrous economic consequences? Certain corporations heavily invested in the meat trade may go to the wall – but only if they are unable to diversify. Such is life. And these will be replaced with corporations invested in arable farming. Predictions of large-scale economic catastrophe have not, I think, been properly thought out.

Now for the second answer. Practices that are morally wrong cannot be justified by appeal to economic considerations, no matter how pressing and important they are. For example, the abolition of slavery in the southern United States was the morally correct course of action, even though it had a devastating impact on the economy of the South as a whole, and left the region in a devastating economic slump from which, arguably, it is still recovering today. Nevertheless, since slavery is an unjust institution, abolishing it was the correct thing to do, despite the economic consequences. Unjust or immoral practices cannot be justified by appeal to economic benefits. We should always try to do the right thing, even if the economic heavens fall.

The irrelevance of economic considerations to moral justification is, in fact, implicit in the idea of the impartial position. The reason is that economic considerations are not things *presupposed* in the impartial position but one of the things that must be *decided upon* from this position. That is, in the impartial position, the sort of question you should ask yourself is not, "Given that economic resources are directed towards slavery in such a way that a desperate economic slump would result if slavery were to be abandoned, how would I like the world to be?" Rather it is, "How would I like economic resources to be directed in the world I am choosing?" That is, precisely how economic resources are to be directed in your preferred world is one of the things to be chosen in the impartial position. So, the direction and distribution of economic resources is not one of the things that you will *know* in the impartial position; it is one of the things you must *choose* from that position. And this is tantamount to the claim that economic considerations cannot, by themselves, provide a justification for moral rules or institutions. This is not to say that economic considerations are never relevant to our moral decision-making; clearly they are. However, it is to say that economic considerations can apply only *after* considerations of justice have been satisfied. So, economic considerations cannot be used to justify unjust institutions or practices. And this is, ultimately, why economic considerations cannot be used to justify the institution of animal husbandry: in our treatment of the animals we raise and kill for food, even minimal conditions of justice have not been met. Therefore, the argument from economic catastrophe has no moral force.

10 SUMMARY

In working out whether the practice of raising and killing animals for food is morally legitimate, we employ the idea of the impartial position, and follow the *golden rule*: if it is irrational to choose a situation, institution, or course of action in the impartial position, then it is immoral to choose this situation, institution, or course of action in the real world. In the impartial position, it would be irrational to opt for any system where animals are raised and killed for food, no matter how they are raised, and no matter how they are killed. Therefore, in the real world, it is immoral to raise and kill animals for food, no matter how they are raised and no matter how they are killed. Therefore, not only is the intensive or factory farming of animals for food wrong, so too is the free-range alternative. Indeed, the free-range alternative is morally wrong, even if the animals are killed quickly and painlessly. The standard objections to abandonment of the institution of animal husbandry do not work.

6

USING ANIMALS FOR EXPERIMENTS

According to fairly conservative estimates, well over 100 million animals are used in experiments every year. The purposes to which these animals are put are various, but four main categories can be identified:

1. Medical research
2. Product testing
3. Psychological study
4. Military testing

These categories are not entirely distinct. Some medical research is carried out largely with a view to developing new products to be put on the market. Some psychological research is medical in character, some is not. Military research can have medical applications, and can also result in new products being put on the market. And so on. There is a catch-all term commonly applied to all these sorts of practice: *vivisection*. In this chapter, we are going to look at whether experimentation on animals – vivisection in this broad sense – is, or is not, morally legitimate. In doing so, we shall have to be appropriately sensitive to the differing purposes that vivisection serves. So, we have to look at whether all vivisection is morally legitimate, whether some of it is, or whether none of it is. I am going to try to show that none of it is.

USING ANIMALS FOR EXPERIMENTS

1 VITAL AND NON-VITAL INTERESTS

The case against animal husbandry developed in the previous chapter was based on the idea that, by abandoning this practice, humans would lose only certain pleasures of the palate, whereas, by continuing this practice, animals would lose any possibility of a life worth living. We are weighing a vital interest of the animal against a non-vital interest of the human being. In the impartial position, not knowing whether you are human or animal, it would be irrational to choose a world where non-vital interests are allowed to override vital interests, since you may turn out to be one of the things whose vital interests are overridden. Therefore, it is, in the real world, immoral to endorse any institution that involves or requires that non-vital interests outweigh vital ones. This is why the institution of animal husbandry is an immoral one.

The idea that it is immoral to let non-vital interests outweigh vital ones is an idea that applies to other things besides animal husbandry. So, with regard to animal experimentation, we should ask ourselves, "Does the experiment serve any vital human interest?" As we shall see, the animal involved is likely to suffer considerably during the experiment, and will almost certainly be killed after the experiment; and both of these clearly involve the sacrifice of vital interests of the animal. So, if the human interests served by the experiment are not vital ones, then to endorse this experiment would be to endorse a situation where non-vital interests are allowed to outweigh vital ones. And this is irrational in the impartial position, and so is immoral in the real world. So, vivisection that serves no vital human interest can be ruled out as morally wrong, and for precisely the same reasons we have ruled out animal husbandry as morally wrong.

However, it may seem that vivisection is on much stronger moral ground than animal husbandry. For it may seem that at least some vivisection does serve vital human interests. Such interests include staying alive and staying healthy, and if vivisection helps promote or foster these interests, then what can be wrong with it? In fact, it might seem as if we could use the idea of the impartial position to actually support vivisection. In the impartial position, you do not know if you will be human or an animal experimented upon by humans. So, you have to weigh up what you stand to gain from vivisection if you are human and what you stand to lose through vivisection if you are one of the animals experimented upon by humans. If you are an animal experimented upon, then you will suffer and die; your most vital interests will clearly be sacrificed. If you are human, it might be thought, then without vivisection you are far more likely to have your vital interests thwarted, since vivisection results in medical advances that allow us to live longer and healthier lives, and life and health are clearly vital interests. Moreover, we might remember that humans are more closely tied to, and so have more invested in, their futures than non-human animals. So, in dying, the average human tends to lose more than the average non-human. But this means that the vital interest a human has in staying alive outweighs the vital interest an animal has in staying alive. And if this is right, then why wouldn't vivisection be justifiable?

So, at the very least, the moral case for vivisection *seems* much stronger than the case for animal husbandry. With animal husbandry then it is pretty clearly only trivial human interests are at stake. But with vivisection, it could be argued that the human interests involved are genuinely vital ones, ones that outweigh the similarly vital interests of animals. Nevertheless, I am going to try and show that the moral case for vivisection only *seems* a strong one. In reality it is not. First of all, most vivisection is not even remotely connected with vital human interests. Second, even in the comparatively small number of cases where vivisection is even on nodding terms with vital human interests, it is still not morally legitimate.

2 MOST VIVISECTION IS UNCONNECTED WITH VITAL HUMAN INTERESTS

Much vivisection, in fact the vast majority of it, is, from the point of view of human health and happiness, completely useless. Not by any stretch of the imagination does most vivisection have anything to do with vital human interests.

Commercial product-testing. This is most obviously true for vivisection involved in commercial product testing; experiments used to establish the toxicity of newly introduced consumer usables. Before a new product is put onto the market, it must be tested for its degree of toxicity to human beings. This testing is usually done on animals, and many countries have legislation requiring that it be tested extensively on animals. Two of the more commonly used toxicity tests are the Draize and LD-50 tests.

You are most likely to fall victim to the Draize test if you are a rabbit or, increasingly, a dog. If so, you can expect to be placed in a holding device, from which only your head protrudes (to prevent you from scratching at your eyes). Then, one of your lower eyelids is pulled outwards, and a test substance (shampoo, ink, bleach, oven cleaner, etc.) is placed in the resulting gap. Your eye is then held closed. Perhaps the application will be repeated. Then, you will be observed for eye swelling, ulceration, infection, bleeding, and the like. The study can last up to three weeks. The best you can hope for is to spend the next few weeks in various degrees of discomfort, with an irritated eye that you are prevented from scratching, but it is quite probable that you will spend those weeks in agony. In some cases, you might suffer total loss of vision due to serious injury to your cornea. Then, of course, the obvious denouement: you are killed.

The LD-50 test is one of the more common forms of oral toxicity test. The idea is to see what quantity of a substance is required to kill fifty per cent of a given batch of animals, hence "LD" stands for "lethal dose" and "50" stands for fifty per cent. If you are, say, a mouse and fall victim to the LD-50 test, then you can expect the following sort of thing to happen. You will be forced to ingest the product under test, for example, lipstick, tooth-paste, paper, etc. Being a not especially stupid mouse, you will probably not eat these things yourself. So, you will be force fed, either by having your mouth held open and the stuff rammed down it, or by having a tube inserted down your throat into your stomach. This will continue for any-thing between fourteen days and six months (if you survive that long). During this time, you will, in all likelihood, suffer many of the classical symptoms of poisoning, including vomiting, diarrhoea, paralysis, convul-sions and internal bleeding. When half of the members of your batch have died, the experiment has been deemed to reach a successful conclusion, and then you and the remaining half are killed.

This sort of testing pretty clearly involves sacrificing the most vital interests of the animals involved. Weeks of agony followed by death are a thwarting of one's vital interests if anything is. But does this testing serve or in any way promote vital human interests? The answer is no.

Toxicity testing for new commercial products often does not serve or promote vital human interests for the simple reason that the products themselves do not serve or promote vital human interests. No one could seriously claim that it was vital to our interests to have a new brand of shampoo, ink, bleach, lipstick, oven cleaner, or whatever on the supermarket shelves. Nice though it is to have shiny hair, or a sparkling oven, it can hardly be thought of as vital to our life, health or happiness. Especially, when you consider that there are literally hundreds of products already available that will make your hair shiny or your oven sparkly. What drives the testing of most new products are not human interests, vital or otherwise, but the *economic* interests of the corporations, usually large multi-national corporations, that produce such items because they think they can make a fast buck out of it.

In fact, since it is the commercial interests of corporations that drive this sort of testing, and since such corporations are concerned with money rather than human welfare, often many of the products they test not only do *not* promote vital human interests, but actively compromise these interests. Many of the products tested – for example, chemical warfare agents, pesticides, weedkillers – either can or already have seriously compromised vital human interests worldwide (if you doubt this, just think of the continuing effects of DDT and Dioxin). In fact, most of the toxicity studies carried out today are tests on food additives. Perhaps I'm being na ve, but it seems to me that we need new food additives like we need a hole in the head. The more we eat the sort of food that does not have or need additives in it, the better our health is going to be. So, it is difficult to see why testing for food additives has anything at all to do with vital human interests.

Even where products *seem* to serve or promote vital human interests, they usually do not in fact do so. The testing of various medical products provides a good example of this. OK, you might think, new brands of oven cleaner we don't need, but new medicines we definitely do. New medicines, surely, can serve vital human interests? But, the truth is that most new medical products are about as useful as new brands of oven cleaner. The introduction of new medical products, like that of new commercial products in general, is driven not by vital human interests but by the economic interests of the companies that introduce them. And most of the time these are products that we simply don't need. It is hardly in my vital interests that I have yet another way available to me of easing the symptoms of cold and flu, or getting rid of that tense, nervous, headache (which, let's be honest, probably isn't all that bad anyway).

It might be thought that although most products tested for commercial use do not serve or promote vital human interests, the data obtained from such testing can, nonetheless, serve or promote such interests. Many countries, for example, have government-sponsored poison control centres of some description. These centres collate data from toxicity tests on animals, and can advise you if you have happened to ingest something dubious. Surely this is a useful thing to have, and could this not serve vital human interests? If your child, for example, has just drunk a bottle of Domestos, wouldn't you want to know how toxic it is? Maybe. But the chances are that if your child had drunk a bottle of Domestos, you are not going to hang around dialing the number of the local poison control centre. You are going to go straight to the hospital. There, will the doctor call the poison control centre? Or will he use animal data provided by the centre? Almost certainly not. This is because, as Dr Christopher Smith, a physician from Long Beach California puts it:

> The results of these tests cannot be used to predict toxicity or to guide therapy in human exposure. As a board-certified emergency medicine physician with over 17 years of experience in the treatment of accidental poisoning and toxic exposures, I know of no instance in which an emergency physician has used Draize test data to aid in the management of an eye injury. I have never used results from animal tests to manage accidental poisoning. Emergency physicians rely on case reports, clinical experience, and experimental data from clinical trials in humans when determining the optimal course of treatment for their patients.[1]

Most commercial product testing, then, is unconnected with vital human interests. Most of the products tested are ones we clearly don't need anyway, and those that we seem to need, on further analysis, turn out to be ones that we don't really need. The data obtained from these tests are, in addition, of dubious accuracy and play little role in the medical treatment of cases of accidental poisoning.

Military testing. It is difficult to claim that much animal experimentation carried out by the military has anything to do with vital human interests, at least not while keeping a straight face. Here is an example of the sort of thing your tax dollars have been paying for.

You are, let us suppose, a monkey, one unfortunate enough to be inducted into the United States Air Force. You are tied down on what is known as a Primate Equilibrium Platform (PEP). Then you will be given severe electric shocks until you learn to grasp the control stick in front of you. When you have got the hang of this, the platform is tilted forward, and you are given electric shocks until you learn to pull the stick back. Then, when the platform is tilted back, you are shocked until you learn to push the stick forward. This process is repeated about a hundred times a day. Initially, your moving the stick has no effect on the position of the platform, but in the final stage of training the position of the stick controls the position of the platform, and you are given electric shocks until you learn to keep the platform level.

This is all pretty unpleasant, but the real unpleasantness is, in fact, just about to begin. Once you have got the hang of keeping the platform level (basic training takes about ten to twelve days, and then there is an additional period of "advanced" training, lasting about twenty days), you are *irradiated*. That is, you are given a lethal or sub-lethal dose of radiation. Alternatively, you might be given a lethal or sub-lethal dose of chemical warfare agent, like Soman gas. Then, nauseous and probably vomiting, you are strapped back into the platform, and required to keep it horizontal, prompted, of course, by the same system of electric shocks.

This is not a one-off experiment. Experiments of this sort, variations on this general theme (vary the toxic agent, vary the species of monkey, vary the task, and so on) have formed a series that has been running for several decades. What vital human interests does this sort of experiment serve? The rationale for the experiment is to determine the likely effect of nuclear or chemical warfare on the abilities of pilots to fly their aircraft, and thus provide an estimate of second-strike capability. Now, it seems to me that if the Russians, or whoever, had dropped the Big One, then the grim satisfaction that comes from knowing that "we can get the bastards back!" does not really amount to a vital human interest. On the contrary. But, even if we let this go, we have to ask ourselves how valuable this sort of data is going to be. Are the Joint Chiefs of Staff going to start sifting through the data from animal tests to work out whether they should bother putting together a second strike? I seriously doubt it. One person who asked precisely this sort of question was Dr Donald Barnes, who was in charge of these primate equilibrium experiments at Brooks Air Force Base. His supervisor insisted that the data taken from the experiments was invaluable on the grounds that the operational commanders "don't know the data are based on animal studies"! Barnes resigned and became a strong opponent of animal experimentation. The experiments, however, have continued.

This is not an isolated example. The US Army, for example, has regularly experimented on dogs (beagles). One series of experiments, carried out at Fort Detrick in Maryland, involved feeding TNT to a group of sixty beagles. Observed symptoms included dehydration, emaciation, anaemia, jaundice, low body temperature, diarrhoea and death. Nor are experiments that adversely affect the vital interests of animals limited to the United States military. At the Ministry of Defence research facility at Porton Down, England, monkeys and other animals were repeatedly injected with glutaminase, causing vomiting, spasms, lethargy, diarrhoea, dehydration and death.

Indeed, any complete account of military experimentation on animals would itself require something of the size of a book, and, in any event, I don't want to spend a whole chapter listing examples of abuse of animals by the armed forces. My point is that any military experimentation that compromises the vital interests of animals deserves serious scrutiny. We have to ask ourselves whether the goals the military have in conducting such experiments correspond to vital human interests. Is it vital to our life, health or happiness that we know, for example, the effect on a pilot's performance of a lethal dose of radiation? My suspicion is that the answer to this sort of question is usually "no." And, if not, then the knowledge that is the goal of the experiment is questionable. And a questionable goal is, morally, the same as a questionable product. If a product does not serve or promote any vital human interest then we cannot legitimately sacrifice the vital interests of animals to test it. And if a piece of knowledge does not serve or promote any vital human interest then we cannot legitimately sacrifice the vital interests of animals in order to get it.

Psychological research. If we put together a list of the cruelties inflicted on animals in the name of research, then psychologists would occupy many of the higher slots. A whole book – a very large book – could be devoted to what psychologists have done, and still do, to animals.

If you are a dog, for example, you might find yourself in what psychologists call a "shuttlebox." This is a box consisting of two compartments separated by a barrier. You are placed in one of the compartments. Suddenly, you receive an intense electric shock to your feet; the floor on which you stand is an electrified grid. Instinctively, you jump over the barrier into the other compartment. This procedure is repeated over and over again; in fact, hundreds of times in total. Each time, however, the jump is more difficult, since the researchers are gradually increasing the size of the barrier. Then, after one jump you land on the other side to receive another intense electric shock; the researchers have now electrified the floor of the other compartment. No matter where you jump, you are going to be shocked. Nevertheless, the pain of the shock is intense, and so you try to escape, no matter how futile this attempt may be. You jump from one electrified grid to another, and the researchers, when they write up their experiment, will describe you, when jumping, as giving "a sharp antici-patory yip which turned into a yelp when he landed on the electrified grid." Next, the researchers try something new. They block the passage between compartments with glass. You will repeatedly jump forward and smash your head against the glass, before falling back to the electrified floor. Exhausted and defeated, you will lie on the floor urinating, defecating, yelping, shrieking, trembling, occasionally attacking the apparatus, and so on. But after ten to twelve days of trials, you will cease to resist the shock.[2]

This is not a one-off experiment carried out by unusually sadistic researchers at some minor institution. The preceding was a description of a famous series of experiments, initiated in 1953 by R. Solomon, L. Kamin

and L. Wynne at Harvard University, carried on in the 1960s by M. Seligman, J. Geer and S. Maier at the University of Pennsylvania, in the 1980s
by P. Bersh at Temple University, and replicated, for educational or other
purposes, by numerous lesser known researchers at many institutions for
the past four decades.

What is the point of this work? It supposedly establishes the so-called
"learned helplessness" model of depression; the idea that depression is
something that can be learned. This is regarded by many psychologists as a
result of considerable importance and consequently the work of Solomon,
Kamin and Wynne is held in high esteem. Any undergraduate student of
psychology will almost certainly become acquainted with the experiments,
and not in any critical manner. That is, the experiments are not typically
taught as examples of ethical issues raised by dubious experimental procedures, but as examples of the important results that can be obtained by
imaginative experimental psychology. The experiments, in many respects,
made the careers of Solomon, Kamin and Wynne, and also of imitators
like Seligman.

Are these experiments morally justified? To assess this, we have to ask
ourselves whether the learned helplessness model of depression has ever
contributed to the promotion of vital human interests. First consider
the sheer number of these experiments done; this tells us something
important about the mindset of experimental psychologists. Once
Solomon, Kamin and Wynne had put forward the learned helplessness
hypothesis as a model of depression, it had to be "tested." What "testing"
means to experimental psychologists in this context is doing lots of
experiments that differ slightly from the original (to test the "generality"
of the model). So the experiments are repeated with a different method
of restraining the dogs, for example they are strapped in harnesses instead
of being presented with an insurmountable barrier (Seligman). Then,
the experiments are repeated, in differing forms, for different species –
rats (Bersh), goldfish (G. Brown, P. Smith and R. Peters, University of
Tennessee at Martin), and so on. So, after three decades of hundreds
of experiments, subjecting countless numbers of animals to severe and
prolonged physical and mental pain, what do we get? The researchers
are undecided. S. Maier, who with Seligman and Geer was a co-author

of one of the more influential studies on learned helplessness, wrote in 1984:

> It can be argued that there is not enough agreement about the characteristics, neurobiology, induction, and prevention/cure of depression to make such comparison meaningful ... It would thus appear unlikely that learned helplessness is a model of depression in any general sense.[3]

Although Maier does try to salvage something from three decades of work by claiming that learned helplessness may be a model of stress and coping, rather than of depression, he has, in effect, admitted that more than thirty years of inflicting intense physical and mental pain on countless animals has been a waste of time. Not one human being – apart from the researchers who used them to build their careers – has ever benefited from these experiments, for the simple reason that after thirty-one years of work, the researchers involved cannot decide what these experiments *mean* – what the experiments establish one way or the other and what their significance for the treatment of human beings would be.

Nor is this sort of failure unusual. H. Harlow, a very well-known psychologist at the University of Wisconsin, Madison and for many years editor of a leading psychology journal, inflicted many years of torture on various species of monkeys. The alleged purpose of the experiments was to investigate the effects of social isolation in general, and maternal deprivation in particular, on the psychological development of monkeys. If you were a monkey unfortunate enough to participate in one of Harlow's experiments, then a variety of fates awaited you: none of them good. You might for example, be taken from your mother a few hours after birth and raised for the first three, six or twelve months of life in complete isolation, in a bare stainless steel chamber. Alternatively, you might find yourself being raised by a "monster mother." This was a cloth monkey who behaved in disagreeable ways – for example, periodically ejecting high-pressure compressed air, rocking violently, ejecting sharp spikes from the front of its body, and so on. In another experiment, you might find yourself with a *real* monster mother. Harlow and colleagues raised monkeys in complete social isolation, and then made them pregnant (by way of a device they jocularly referred to as the "rape rack"). When the babies were born, some of the mothers simply ignored them. And if you were one of the babies, this was the best you could hope for. If you were less lucky, then you would find yourself with a mother who would crush your skull with her teeth, or smash your face in the ground, and then rub it back and forth.[4]

Did these experiments serve or promote vital human interests? Well, it is difficult to see how they could. The results of social isolation and maternal deprivation on humans were well documented as far back as 1951, *before Harlow and colleagues even began their work*. From the point of view of vital human interests Harlow's experiments were completely unnecessary, therefore worthless. Why were these experiments then performed? Did Harlow not know about the work on humans? Hardly. The work conducted out by John Bowlby, a British psychiatrist, on war orphans, refugees and institutionalized children was not only very well known, but Bowlby had also actually visited Harlow, and viewed his work.

Once again, this was not an isolated experiment. Since Harlow began his maternal deprivation experiments over forty years ago, over 250 of these experiments have been conducted in the United States. These experiments have employed over 7000 animals, inducing physical and mental torture, despair and death.

Why were these experiments done? Who knows? Perhaps simply because they could be. Many psychologists, in the eyes of those who have interacted with them through work, have a peculiar sensitivity to their work being regarded as "unscientific." Some are positively paranoid about it. For many psychologists, being scientific amounts to conducting experiments, lots of them, and so collecting as much data as possible. This not only betrays a very facile conception of the way science works, but also leaves a lot of animals very vulnerable indeed. Thus, M. Reite, of the University of Colorado, a follower of Harlow, justified his experiments on maternal deprivation in chimpanzees simply on the grounds that very little work had been done on them. The experiments should be done on chimpanzees simply because they hadn't been done on chimpanzees. He did not even *attempt* to justify his experiments by showing that they might benefit human beings.

In a book of this sort, it would be impossible to survey all the experiments performed on animals. That would require a bigger book; a much bigger book. The preceding examples were included to provide a flavour of the sorts of things that are done to animals, *even when vital human interests are clearly not at stake*. Much animal experimentation, in fact the vast majority of it, does not, in any way, serve or promote vital human interests. In the case of commercial product testing, the interests being served or promoted are the economic interests of the companies that produce and sell these products. Much military testing involves a seriously warped conception of what is a vital interest for human beings. Much psychological research serves and promotes both the innate intellectual curiosity and the careers of those who carry it out. But, not by any stretch of the imagination does it promote interests that are vital.

In the impartial position it would be seriously irrational to opt for a world where these sorts of experiments are carried out. Not knowing whether you are human or animal, you would be potentially sacrificing your most vital interests to serve and promote interests that are far from vital. Such a choice would be irrational in the impartial position, and, therefore, immoral in the real world. Experiments of this sort are morally illegitimate and should be stopped.

Surely, however, we are on firmer ground with medical research? Medical research is concerned with making humans live longer, and making them healthier – hence happier – while they are living longer, and surely these are vital human interests? I think, on the contrary, that to suppose that all medical research is motivated by these goals is simply naïve. Just like much psychological research, what passes for medical research is often motivated by the intellectual curiosity of researchers, and by the desire to advance their careers. And, just like commercial product testing, much of what passes for medical research is motivated by the straightforward economic interests of companies that sponsor it. But suppose I'm being too cynical. Suppose that all medical research has the goal of serving and promoting vital human interests. It would not matter. Much medical research fails to be legitimate because it is either *unnecessary* for the promotion of vital human interests or it is *ineffective* at promoting such interests. Let's see why.

3 MUCH VIVISECTION IS UNRELIABLE OR POSITIVELY HARMFUL

Even where medical vivisection is connected, even tangentially, with vital human interests, there are serious questions over its usefulness. There are fundamental problems involved in extrapolating results obtained from animal experimentation to human beings, and attempts to do so in the past have often had tragic results.

Consider an example of medical research that is, arguably, connected with vital human interests. A significant proportion of medical research on animals has to do with the study of *shock*. "Shock" here refers not to electric shock, but the physical and mental state of shock that generally accompanies severe injury. So, to study shock, you have to produce it, and to produce it you have to severely injure your test animals. The methods at your disposal are various. A tourniquet will destroy a limb by cutting off blood supply. Alternatively, you could crush the limb in a vice. You could produce muscle trauma by "contusion"; that is, smashing the animal with a hammer. More imaginatively, you could use the *Noble-Collip drum*, a device in which an animal is placed and the drum rotated, causing the animal to tumble repeatedly to the bottom of the drum, thereby injuring itself. Freezing or burning is always reliable. And, for those whose tastes run to the direct, you could always try gunshot wounds. The use of anaesthesia is discouraged, since this might taint results: shock, of course, is not so shocking if you cannot feel the injury that would ordinarily produce it.

After three decades of the study of shock in dogs, produced primarily by "haemorrhage" (i.e. severe injury, usually caused by gunshot, followed by massive blood loss), more recent studies have indicated that haemorrhage-induced shock in dogs is not much like shock in humans. In other words, all the prior studies of haemorrhage in dogs are simply inapplicable to the treatment of human beings; we've been shooting dogs without anaesthetic for nothing! Not to worry. Perhaps shock induced by other means (see the above list) will be similar to that in humans. Or perhaps haemorrhage-induced shock in other animals is like haemorrhage-induced shock in humans. Cue researchers at the University of Rochester who repeat the experiments on pigs, which they *think* might be more like humans in this respect.[5]

Much of the experimental work on animals is, in fact, straightforwardly inapplicable to human beings. Often the attempt to extrapolate results from animal studies to humans has tragic or even fatal consequences. The most famous example of this is the drug *thalidomide*, an anti-nausea drug taken by pregnant women to reduce the symptoms of morning sickness. Thalidomide was extensively tested on animals before it was released, but caused serious deformities in human foetuses. Indeed, even after it was suspected of producing these deformities, further tests on pregnant dogs, cats, monkeys, hamsters and chickens all failed to produce deformities. It was only when a particular strain of rabbit was tried that deformities were produced.

More recently, Opren, thought to be the new wonder drug for arthritis, passed all the usual animal tests before it was released. However, it was suspended from use in Britain after sixty-one deaths and 3600 reports of adverse reactions. A report in the magazine *New Scientist* reveals that many further deaths and adverse reactions may not have been recognized as associated with Opren, and that the real toll could have been much higher. Similarly, Practolol, a drug used to treat heart disease, sailed through the usual animal tests. Nevertheless, it caused blindness in significant numbers of human beings. The Practolol adverse reaction has yet to be seen in any species other than human. The cough suppressant Zipeprol caused seizures and comas in some of those who took it, despite being released only after extensive animal testing.[6]

Two pain killing drugs – Butazolidine and Tanderil – have jointly been cited a bringing about the deaths of as many as 10,000 people, and the unreliability of animal tests seems at least partially responsible. Dogs, one of the test subjects for these drugs, take only a couple of hours to metabolize Butazolidine and only thirty minutes to break down Tanderil. Humans, on the other hand, require seventy-two hours to break down Tanderil, and even longer to break down Butazolidine. Differences in how long a drug remains in the body can be very dangerous, and in certain circumstances fatally so.

The unreliability of extrapolating results from animal tests to human beings also cuts the other way: substances that are known to be harmful to many animals are not harmful to humans. Aspirin, for example, causes birth defects in rats, mice, monkeys, guinea pigs, cats and dogs, but not in humans. The antibiotic Triamcilanone causes birth defects in mice but not humans. And when Alexander Fleming accidentally discovered penicillin in 1928, he tested it on rabbits. It didn't work, and he lost interest in the substance. Still two scientists followed up his work and successfully tested it on mice. This was a lucky choice, because rabbits excrete penicillin too quickly for it to work, and in guinea pigs penicillin is fatal in even very small doses.

In general, extrapolation of results from animal tests to human beings is fraught with difficulty and often danger. Animals are different anatomically, physiologically, genetically, immunologically and histologically from humans. Therefore animals and humans often react very differently to the same substances.

4 MUCH VIVISECTION IS UNNECESSARY

Much vivisection is also unnecessary. This is so for at least two reasons. First, tests are often needlessly replicated. Theodore M. Farber, director of the US Environmental Agency's Toxicology Branch said (in 1987) that, "Many of us in regulatory toxicology see the same studies over and over again." His agency, at that time, had files of 42,000 completed tests. A significant proportion of these were simply repetitions of tests already done because the results were not easily accessible.[7] This needless replication of tests happens in medical testing as much as in any other. Testing of new medical products is largely driven by the economic interests of pharmaceutical companies, and such companies rarely publish details of animal studies they have conducted or commissioned because of commercial confidentiality.

Needless replication of experiments on animals often occurs to such an extent that new studies on animals are commissioned even *after* the product has been tested on humans. To take just one example, in October 1998, the Pfizer laboratories in Sandwich, UK, tested the anti-impotency drug Viagra on beagle dogs. The tests involved the mutilation of the dogs' penises. The penises were skinned and a needle inserted for recording pressure. A nerve to the penis was electrically stimulated, and the effects of various doses of Viagra were studied. Pretty nasty stuff, admittedly. What is even nastier is that these gruesome experiments were permitted – and a licence was granted by the Home Office – even though Viagra had already undergone clinical trials on humans, and was already being administered to patients suffering from impotence!

Second, there are several types of alternatives to animal tests, the power and scope of which have not been fully explored or utilized because of the easy availability of experimental animals. Alternatives to animal testing include:

Tissue cultures. Human cells and tissues can be kept alive in cultures and used for medical research. Since human cells are used, problems of extrapolation do not arise. And production of tissue cultures is cheap and inexpensive. By itself, however, tissue culture analysis is not going to be enough. New drugs need to be tested on all systems of the body working together. A drug that is not poisonous to cells alone may become so after it has been transformed by the liver, for example.

However, tissue cultures can be supplemented by several other techniques, including:

Physico-chemical methods. These include mass spectrometry and gas/liquid chromatography. These allow researchers to identify substances in biological material. For example, a bioassay for vitamin D used to involve inducing rickets in rats and feeding them substances rich in vitamin D. Now such studies can be carried out using liquid chromatography.

Computer simulations. Computer simulations of physiological and pharmacological processes can be used to replace much of the use of animals for educational purposes. Computer-aided drug design can also help design drugs according to required specifications. Computer-aided design is becoming increasingly common in cancer research.

Mechanical models. Mechanical models can again be used in some educational settings. They can also replace animals in certain sorts of tests. For example, an artificial neck has been developed by General Motors for use in car-crash simulations, replacing the apes formerly used. Indeed, the results obtained from these "crash test dummies" are much more accurate and effective than those obtained from study on primates. Similarly, a group of scientists in the Netherlands have developed the "techno-tum" or artificial gut. This mimics the action of the gut, and so facilitates studies of absorption of chemicals. Another example is the "POP trainer", consisting of artificial organs with a simulated blood supply, which can eliminate the need for animal use in many educational contexts.

It would be unrealistic to suppose that these alternatives, even when taken together, can entirely *replace* the use of animals in medical research, at least not at present. But these alternatives, properly employed, can, without any doubt whatsoever, substantially *reduce* the use of animals. Given these alternatives, then, a significant number of animals are used in medical research unnecessarily.

To this general point, it is also perhaps worth adding that many animals, bred for the laboratory, often don't even get as far as that. They are killed as surplus to requirements. On the basis of information contained in answers to Parliamentary Questions asked by Norman Baker MP, the British Union for the Abolition of Vivisection recently estimated that as many as eighty-five per cent of rats and eighty per cent of mice bred for experimentation may be killed without being used. Whether or not you agree with their figures, it is an undeniable fact that many, many experimental animals are slaughtered without even being used for experiments. And to the number of unnecessary experiments we must add these unnecessary deaths.

5 How important is vivisection?

Most advocates of animal rights acknowledge that vivisection has played a *contributing* role in some valuable medical advances. In some cases, it may have even have played an *essential* role in medical advance. However, there is ample historical evidence to show that the importance of vivisection to human health has been exaggerated. First, look at the statistics. Most estimates suggest that at least eighty-five per cent of the animals killed in labs between the 1890s and the 1990s died after 1950. Indeed, in Britain alone, over 144 million animals have died in laboratories since 1950. However, the average life expectancy for people in Britain has not changed since this date. The rise in life expectancy of British people that began in the 1890s was largely complete by 1950, despite the fact that the vast majority of animal experiments occurred *after* that date.[8]

The dramatic increase in life expectancy was brought about by a decline in the prevalence of the old killer diseases: tuberculosis, pneumonia, typhoid, whooping cough, and cholera. But, without exception, the declines in these diseases came about through improvements in housing, working conditions, water supply, and hygiene. Specifically medical procedures like immunization cannot, logically, be given much credit here since they only became available *after* most of the declines were complete.

The big killers today are cancer and heart disease. And despite the huge numbers of animals sacrificed at the altar of these diseases, gains have been meagre at best. Although quite dramatic results have been obtained for some cancers (child leukaemia being an obvious example), when the whole array of cancers are taken into consideration, any gains are far less convincing. Indeed, death rates from many sorts of cancers have stabilized or even increased. And where there is an overall decrease in death rate from a specific form of cancer, this is usually the result less of medical intervention and more of effective education about the causes of the cancer (consider, for example, lung cancer, colorectal cancer, etc.).

6 CLEARLY ILLEGITIMATE VIVISECTIONS

Any experiment that involves an animal and violates or sacrifices that animal's vital interests is morally illegitimate if any of the four conditions hold.

1. The experiment does not even attempt to serve or promote vital human interests but, instead, is concerned only with non-vital ones.
2. The knowledge that the experiment seeks to acquire is already available.
3. The knowledge that the experiment seeks to acquire can be obtained by other means, ones that do not involve the use of animals.
4. The difficulties involved in extrapolating the results of the experiment to human beings are so great that they render these results of questionable importance, or the extrapolation can only be carried out on the basis of extensive human testing that makes the results of the animal tests superfluous.

All these conditions can be justified on the basis of the impartial position. In this position, you would not choose a world where the vital interests of animals are violated by experiments that do not even attempt to serve or promote the vital interests of humans (condition 1). You may turn out to be one of those animals, and so it would be irrational to choose a world where your vital interests are thwarted for the sake of the comparatively trivial interests of another species. It would be equally irrational to choose a world where your vital interests are (potentially) violated by way of an experiment that was unnecessary for the promotion of vital human interests, either because the knowledge was already available or because it could become available by other means, ones that did not violate your interests (conditions 2 and 3). Finally, it would be irrational, in the impartial position, to choose a world where your interests are (potentially) violated by experiments that are simply ineffective in promoting vital human interests because the results obtained from them cannot be extrapolated to human beings (condition 4).

In short, experiments on animals that do not attempt to promote vital human interests, are unnecessary for the promotion of vital human interests, or that are ineffective at promoting vital human interests are morally wrong. They are what I shall call *clearly illegitimate vivisections*. Clearly illegitimate vivisections are morally wrong because it would, in the impartial position, be irrational to choose a world that contained them. From the perspective of the impartial position, you might turn out to be an animal experimented upon. And it would be irrational to choose a world where your most vital interests are violated by way of an experiment that does not serve or promote a vital human interest, either because it does not attempt to do so, or because it is unnecessary for doing so, or because it is ineffective at doing so.

Many, in fact the vast majority of, experiments carried out on animals are ones that do not attempt the promotion of, are unnecessary for the promotion of, or are ineffective at the promotion of, vital human interests. These experiments are all *clearly illegitimate vivisections*. They should be stopped.

7 Vivisection that promotes vital human interests

You might accept that clearly illegitimate vivisections are morally wrong but also think that nevertheless there is a small core of animal experiments that do attempt to promote vital human interests, that are necessary for the promotion of such interests and that are effective at this promotion. I agree. These experiments, I think, make up a tiny portion of the total number of experiments conducted on animals. Indeed, if only the experiments that are neither necessary for, nor effective at, the promotion of vital human interests were eradicated in my lifetime, I would die a happy man. Nevertheless, I am willing to concede that there exist experiments on animals that do effectively promote vital human interests. I am also willing to concede, at least for the sake of argument, that these experiments might promote vital human interests better than any non-animal-based alternatives. The question we now have to ask ourselves is this: are these experiments morally legitimate? I'll try to show that they are not. These experiments may not be *clearly* illegitimate, but they are *illegitimate* nonetheless.

The idea that vivisection that serves or promotes vital human interests is morally legitimate stems from the intuitive feeling that human lives are, in some sense, more valuable than non-human ones. As we saw in chapter 4, this intuition can, to a considerable extent, be rationally defended. Most humans, being strongly tied to their future, tend to lose more than most non-humans when they die. Being more strongly tied to their future, humans typically have more invested in their future than animals have in theirs. Accordingly, humans typically, but not always and not necessarily, lose more when they die than animals lose when they die. So, if humans typically lose more when they die than animals lose when they die, wouldn't it be right to sacrifice the lives and other vital interests of animals, in order to promote the lives and other vital interests of humans? The answer, I am going to argue, is an unequivocal "no." In morality, lives and vital interests are not transferable in this way.

Let's begin to erode the confidence we have in the idea that the lives and interests of one thing can be sacrificed for the lives and vital interests of another. If you think vivisection of non-human animals is legitimate when it serves vital human interests, do you think it would be legitimate to practice vivisection on, say, human orphans under six months old? Why would anyone want to do this? Well, the most important consideration might be avoiding the problems of extrapolation that persistently dog experiments on animals. The results we glean from human experimentation would almost certainly be more reliable than those obtained from animal experimentation. So why not? Most higher mammals, certainly apes, monkeys, pigs, dogs, cats, rats and the like, are more aware of their surroundings and what is happening to them, at least as intelligent, and at least as sensitive to pain and other noxious stimuli, as a human infant. We can remove any misgivings the children's parents would have about this by only selecting orphans. If you are worried about potential, then we can further stipulate that the infants should be brain-damaged, where this damage is of a sort to ensure that they will never develop the intellectual and emotional capacities beyond the level of a six month old infant. There are, unfortunately, many such human beings. So, why not experiment on them?

Now, please don't think for a minute that I am advocating this. On the contrary, in line with most other people, I think such a plan is morally obscene. My point is that if experimenting on orphaned human infants, brain-damaged or not, is morally obscene, then how can experimenting on apes, monkeys, pigs, dogs, cats and rats be any different? As I argued in chapter 2, there are no morally relevant differences between these sorts of animals and the orphaned human infants that could justify the claim that experimenting on the former is morally legitimate while experimenting on the latter is obscene. No difference without some relevant other difference; and here there simply is no relevant other difference. So, if experimenting on orphaned human infants is morally wrong, so too is experimenting on animals.

This, hopefully, should be enough to erode at least some of the confidence we have in the idea that vivisection of animals is morally legitimate. Nonetheless, it does create something of a puzzle. If humans lose more in dying than do animals, or brain-damaged human infants for that matter, then why shouldn't it be right to sacrifice the lives and vital interests of animals and brain-damaged human infants in order to promote the lives and vital interests of "normal" humans? Let's try and work out why.

You are sitting at home one day, minding your own business, when a group of men burst in, kidnap you, and drag you off to a laboratory. Why? Your neighbour has had a hang-gliding accident, has punctured his liver, and needs a new one. And he has decided that you are going to provide him with it. A little unfair? Not in this world. You screwed up in the impartial position, you were a little less than fully rational, and you chose *risk transferability world*. The basic rule of risk transferability world is this: whenever someone suffers as the result of a risk they voluntarily undertook, someone *else* must pay the piper.[9]

So, you fall off your horse and break your neck. No problem; other people can be forced to undergo the medical testing that might restore your movement. You have unprotected sex with lots of people and catch a rather nasty disease. You're in luck; other people can be forced to take part in the clinical testing of drugs that might alleviate your condition. You sit on the couch all day smoking, drinking and eating pork rinds. Consequently you have a serious heart problem. Don't worry; other people can be forced to undergo the vivisection that might save your life. Such are the vicissitudes of risk transferability world.

If you were in the impartial position, would you choose risk transferability world? Not unless you were terminally stupid. Risk transferability world is just too *risky*. In particular, risk transferability world seems to ride roughshod over something we value very highly: our autonomy. In chapter

1, we distinguished various forms of autonomy. Here, I am using the idea in only the minimal sense. Autonomy, that is simply the ability to do what you want to do. Most humans, but also most animals, have autonomy in this sense.

Doing what you want is, ultimately, what makes life worth living. Different people, of course, want very different things. Some want to surf all day, others want to help starving people. Some want to create the greatest work of art the world has ever seen, some just want to have fun. A life where you could never do what you wanted would be a life with no point; it would be a tragedy. This is not to say that such a life is not worth living (and, anyway, wanting to die would be cruelly self-defeating in such a life). But the only thing that might make this life worth living is the hope, even the faint hope, that some day, some time, you might be able to do what you want.

We all want many different things. And to get these things, we typically have to sacrifice and to gamble. We have to sacrifice, at the very least, our time. Satisfying desires usually takes time, and our time is a finite and non-renewable commodity. We gamble because we sacrifice. It may be that the thing we wanted wasn't really worth wanting, and that the sacrifice of our time was misguided. Or it may be that the thing we wanted was something that we could not get, and that our sacrifice of time was futile. Satisfying desires, then, is a *risk*: satisfying desires requires a sacrifice which entails a gamble, the taking of which is always a risk. The trading off of desire and risk is what autonomy, in the minimal sense used here, comes down to. What is really objectionable about risk transferability world is that it undermines this sort of autonomy. In risk transferability world, the risks we take – whether we know it or not – are to satisfy not our desires but those of other people. Accordingly, we have no control over the risks we take, and the way we take them. Indeed, most of the time we will be completely unaware that we are even taking a risk. We will simultaneously be taking a potentially infinite number of risks, ones of which we are totally ignorant, and which play no role in shaping our own lives.

So, risk transferability world is both risky and abhorrent. It is risky because we are simultaneously taking a potentially infinite number of risks that we know nothing about, therefore that we cannot in any way mitigate. It is abhorrent, because it takes away from us any genuine possibility of autonomy, understood as the trading off of desire and risk. In the impartial position, therefore, one principle that you should endorse is this: *risks are not morally transferable to those who do not voluntarily choose to take them.* To choose otherwise would not only be irrationally risky; it would also undermine your autonomy that, at the end of the day, is what makes life worth living.

Notice that nothing in the argument against risk transferability world depends on the *size* of the risks taken by others. If you are required for experiments on, say, paralysis, it does not matter whether this was because your neighbour injured himself sky diving or because he was hit by a bus while crossing the street. The objectionable nature of being forced to pay for the risks voluntarily undertaken by others does not seem to depend on the size of the risks they take.

If it would be irrational to choose a world that followed the risk transferability principle, then it would be immoral to endorse this principle in the actual world. And this means that at least some medical research is morally wrong, even if this research is genuinely aimed at, and genuinely effective at, promoting vital human interests. Any medical research on animals that has the aim of mitigating problems that humans have brought on themselves through risks they have voluntarily taken is morally illegitimate, even if those problems impinge on the most vital interests of those humans. Consider, for example, medical research into drug addiction. At the University of Kentucky, beagles were used to study withdrawal symptoms from Valium and Lorazepam.[10] The dogs were forced to become addicted to the drugs and then, every two weeks, the tranquilizers were withdrawn. Withdrawal symptoms included twitches, jerks, gross body tremors, running fits, rapid weight loss, fear and cowering. After forty hours of Valium withdrawal, numerous seizures were seen in seven of nine dogs. Four of the dogs died, two while convulsing, and two after rapid weight loss. In a laboratory at Downstate Medical Centre, rhesus monkeys were locked in restraining chairs.[11] The animals were then taught to self-administer cocaine by pushing a button. According to one report, the test monkeys pushed the button over and over, even after convulsions. They went without sleep, and ate five to six times their normal amount while still becoming emaciated. In the end they began to mutilate them-selves and died, often in convulsions. Sometimes, after withdrawal of the cocaine, they would pluck out their own hair and bite off their own fingers and toes.

Drug addiction is nothing short of a human tragedy. Addicts should be helped by whatever means possible, *as long as these means are morally legitimate.* However, research that endorses, whether explicitly or implic-itly, the risk transferability principle is not morally legitimate. Being treated for his or her addiction is, I think, pretty clearly one of the addicts most vital interests. Nevertheless, it is not morally legitimate to promote such an interest by way of the risk transferability principle. To choose this principle in the impartial position would be irrational. Therefore, to endorse this principle in the real world would be immoral.

We all take numerous risks every day, some large, most small, and most of the time we have no idea that we are doing so. Life is a gamble. When-ever I plug in my kettle, drive (or walk) to work, drink water from my tap, breathe in the air of a smoke-filled bar, I take a risk. The big killers today are heart disease and cancer, which have a significant lifestyle component. We know that the chances of someone suffering from heart disease and many forms of cancer are significantly affected by the choices he or she makes. If he does not exercise and eats a high-fat diet, the chances of heart disease are significantly increased. If she smokes, the chances of lung cancer and heart disease rise accordingly. No one is contesting this. The chances are, then, that many of the ailments from which we suffer result, to a considerable extent, from our own choices. Consequently, many of the animals experimented upon suffer because we think it is legitimate that those animals should bear the brunt of harms we inflict on ourselves, as the result of our own choices. It's high time we started taking responsibility for the choices we make, and not expecting someone or something else to suffer for those choices. To do otherwise is to endorse the risk transferability principle, and this principle is morally iniquitous.

However, it would be ludicrous to claim that all the harms from which we suffer are the result of our choices. There is a world of difference between the case of the person addicted to heroin and the child suffering from leukaemia. What about research into diseases – like child leukaemia –

that cannot be regarded as stemming from our own choices? Is the use of animals here not morally legitimate?

Ultimately, I think it is not, although this is more contentious. Again, we have to ask ourselves, "Would we be willing to conduct this research using orphaned six-month-old children?" If we would not, what is the difference between using these and using, say, six-month-old beagles. It is difficult to identify any morally relevant difference, and if there is no such difference, then the two proposals are equally immoral. Or, suppose, your neighbour requires a new liver not because he punctured it hang gliding but for reasons beyond his control; he was shot by an intruder, for example, or suffers from a congenital liver disorder. This makes not one bit of difference to your loss of autonomy. Your autonomy is undermined by this just as much as if he had lost his liver through a risk he voluntarily undertook. So, if the risk transferability principle is irrational because it is too risky in general, and undermines your autonomy in particular, then so too must be the generalized *harm transferability principle*: the idea that harms can be transferred to those who do not willingly accept them. It would be irrational, in the impartial position, to choose a world where individuals are made to suffer in order to ameliorate the harms suffered by someone else – however these harms came about. And, if this is correct, then it is wrong, in the real world, to endorse such a practice.

8 SUMMARY

Most vivisection does not serve or promote vital human interests. This is for one of three reasons. First, much vivisection does not even *attempt* or *aim at* promoting vital human interests, but concerns itself with interests that are peripheral to human life, health and happiness. Second, much vivisection, although it does attempt to promote vital human interests does not *effectively* do so. Animals differ anatomically, physiologically, genetically, immunologically, and histologically, from humans. So, extrapolation of results from animal tests to human beings is fraught with difficulty and, often, danger. Third, vivisection is often *unnecessary* to the promotion of vital human interests, either because the knowledge it attempts to produce is already available, or because it can be obtained by other means. This is born out by epidemiological studies which show that most of the great killer diseases of the nineteenth and early twentieth centuries were successfully overcome not by medical research but by improvements in housing, working conditions, water supply, and hygiene. Moreover, despite huge expansion in the number of animals used for medical research in the second half of the twentieth century, gains against the great killers of that epoch have been comparatively meagre.

Vivisection that does not attempt to promote vital human interests, that does not effectively promote such interests, or that is unnecessary to the promotion of these interests is *clearly illegitimate vivisection*. It would be irrational, in the impartial position, to choose a world where vivisection of this sort occurs. Therefore, it is immoral in the real world, to endorse such vivisection.

At least some vivisection, however, may effectively promote vital human interests, and may even be necessary for the promotion of such interests. Such vivisection is not *clearly* illegitimate, but it is, nonetheless, still *illegitimate*. The rationale for this sort of vivisection lies in principles – like the *risk transferability principle* and the *harm transferability principle* – that it would be irrational to choose in the impartial position since they are far too risky and impinge unacceptably on one's autonomy. These principles are, therefore, immoral, and so cannot be used to justify the practice of vivisection, even if this does effectively promote vital human interests.

7

ZOOS

We have spent a lot of pages looking at two things we do to animals: eating them and experimenting on them. These are hard issues. We have, historically speaking, spent so much time eating animals that it can seem a perfectly natural and appropriate thing to do. And we have been told for so long that animal experimentation is essential to human health and happiness that we can't help believe it must be justifiable. Consequently, undermining these practices takes a lot of time, and a correspondingly high word count. There are other things we do to animals, however, and on these we can afford to spend less time. This chapter is concerned with *zoos*.[1]

1 ZOOS AND THE IMPARTIAL POSITION

A zoo (or zoological garden to use the full name) is, roughly, a public park that displays animals to humans. Are zoos morally justified? To see this, we again put ourselves in the impartial position. Here, would it be rational to choose a world that contains zoos? If so, zoos are morally legitimate; if not, they are morally wrong. In the impartial position, applied to the case of zoos, you do not know whether you are a human who may visit the zoo, or an animal who may be confined in it. So, we have to work out what you stand to gain and lose in each case. When we have done this, we can assess the rationality or otherwise of choosing a world that contains zoos.

2 WHAT ZOOS TAKE FROM ANIMALS

If you are an animal confined in a zoo, the most obvious thing that you lose is your liberty. In chapter 1, the idea of *weak autonomy* was explained as the ability to do what you want, or what you choose, to do this intentionally, with understanding, and without controlling influences that influence the action. Clearly, being confined in a zoo will cut deeply into any animal's autonomy. Many of its most natural behaviours will be thwarted by its unnatural environment. It will not be able to hunt or gather its own food, nor engage in the activities – moving around, sometimes over great distances, stalking, and so on – that allow it to do this. Many social animals will not be able to develop appropriate social orders; indeed, many of them may be forced to live solitary existences. Many of the things that animals want to do are the result of millions of years of evolution. These sorts of behaviour we call *natural*. It's a truism that you cannot have natural behaviour in an unnatural environment, and zoos are, typically, very unnatural environments. Therefore, in zoos, many of the things animals want to do they cannot do. And this is a harm of deprivation; a deprivation of autonomy.

All of this is obvious. Almost as obvious is the idea that a deprivation of an animal's autonomy is a thwarting of one of its most vital interests. Being able to do what you want, at least some of the time, is ultimately what makes life worth living. Therefore, a serious deprivation of autonomy strikes at the core of what makes a life worthwhile. So, one of the things you will know in the impartial position is that confinement in a zoo is, almost certainly, a thwarting of one of the most vital interests of an animal.

Many zoo environments are not simply unnatural; they are positively abysmal. To take just one example, a wolf is a sensitive social creature who will roam up to fifty miles in a night when hunting. When you have a wolf in a Spanish zoo confined, in isolation, in a small, sterile, concrete run, then it does not take much intelligence or imagination to realize that the life of that unfortunate creature is going to be one of overwhelming misery.

In addition to the loss of autonomy, we also have to consider how animals get to be in zoos in the first place. When chimpanzees, for example, are taken from the wild, the usual procedure is to shoot the mother and capture the child. All animals face a traumatic capture and equally traumatic transport, usually over long distances, to their place of confinement. In short, zoos typically thwart some of the most vital interests of animals, and the route by which many animals get to be in zoos in the first place is one that often involves considerable suffering. This is one of the things you will know in the impartial position.

3 WHAT ZOOS GIVE TO HUMANS

Do zoos supply any benefits, of remotely comparable importance, to human beings? Indeed, what are the benefits for humans that zoos supposedly bring with them? Attempts to justify zoos typically appeal to four benefits: amusement, education, scientific research, preservation of species.

Most people visit zoos for a "day out." They go to be entertained, and zoos that wish to remain financially secure need to cater for this. So, most zoos have some sort of "children's corner," etc. And even highly rated zoos like San Diego have or have had dancing bears and the like. But while being entertained is surely an interest of human beings, it is not on a par with our interest in autonomy. Being autonomous is a vital interest, being entertained is not. It's as simple as that. It would, in the impartial position, be irrational to choose a world where the vital interest of autonomy was routinely overridden by a relatively superficial interest in entertainment: you might turn out to be one of the things whose autonomy is overridden. Therefore, it is, in the real world, immoral to endorse an institution that is based on the idea that vital interests can be overridden by superficial ones. And the "entertainment" defence of zoos is based precisely on this idea.

In any event, most zoo curators dismiss the idea that the primary function of zoos is to provide entertainment. They are far more likely to stress the educational aspect of zoos. Zoos, it is often claimed, are valuable because they educate the public about animals, their nature and behaviour, and so are likely to stimulate people to care more about the natural world, about the importance of species conservation, habitat preservation and so on.

It is difficult, truly difficult, to take this idea seriously. This is, in part, because the claim that zoos succeed in any serious educational mission is simply factually untrue. Thus, one study indicates that zoo-goers express the usual prejudices about animals; seventy-three per cent dislike rattlesnakes, fifty-two per cent dislike vultures, and only four per cent dislike elephants. The same study shows that zoo-goers are only slightly more knowledgeable than those who claim to know nothing at all about animals.[2] Another study indicates that the most common expressions used to describe animals (this was a US study) are "cute," "funny-looking," "lazy," "dirty," "weird" and "strange."[3] Hardly edifying stuff. The complete failure of zoos to succeed in their supposedly educational mission seems to stem in part from the fact that many of them make no real effort at education, but also, in part, from the apathetic and unappreciative character of the majority of the zoo-going public.

Even more serious than the fact that zoos fail miserably in their educational goals is the fact that we have no real idea of what would count as success. What is it that zoos are supposed to teach people? Facts about the physiology and behaviour of animals? But why does this require keeping animals in captivity? Couldn't we achieve this through films or lectures? Do we want them to acquire certain attitudes towards endangered species? Again, why does this require keeping animals locked up? Compassion for animals? How does locking them up help achieve this? Zoos not only fail in their stated educational goals, it is utterly mysterious why those stated goals require keeping animals in captivity in the first place.

Even if we could make sense of the idea that the function of zoos is educational – which we can't – this still leaves the problem that being educated about a certain aspect of the world cannot plausibly be construed as a vital interest on a par with the interest in autonomy. And, if this is right, we would again be trying to justify violating a vital interest of an animal for the sake of a less than vital interest of a human. In the impartial position, it would be irrational to choose a world where this sort of violation routinely occurs. Therefore, it is, in the real world, immoral to endorse such violations.

Another oft asserted benefit of zoos is the possibilities they bring for scientific research. We have, in effect, already dealt with this in the previous chapter. The use of animals in zoo settings for scientific research will be clearly illegitimate if it does not attempt to promote vital human interests, is ineffective at promoting such interests, or is unnecessary for the promotion of these interests. Even if it satisfies these conditions, experimentation on animals is still morally illegitimate, although probably less clearly so.

So, what sorts of scientific research are funded by zoos? There are two broadly different types. On the one hand, there is field research: some zoos fund the study of animals in their natural environment. On the other, there is study of animals already confined in zoos.

There is, of course, absolutely nothing wrong with field research, properly conducted. However, there is also absolutely no reason why it should be funded by zoos, and, mostly, it isn't. Very few zoos, in fact, support any real scientific field research, and the funding for these sorts of studies provided by zoos is extremely small compared to funding provided by governmental and non-governmental organizations. Of more significance is research that is actually conducted on animals in zoos. This can, again broadly, be divided into two sorts: behavioural studies and anatomical/physiological studies.

The value of behavioural studies conducted on zoo animals is extremely dubious. The problem is that zoos provide very unnatural environments for their animals, and these unnatural environments inevitably produce unnatural behaviour. So, if our goal is to learn about the behaviour of animals, then it is unclear, to say the least, why the study of captive animals is the way to go. More accurate, hence more important, results can always be obtained through studies of animals in the wild.

Anatomical and physiological studies are the most common forms of zoo research. What is the purpose of this research? One goal is to improve the health of animals in zoos. This would be a laudable goal – but only if you accept that animals should be in zoos in the first place. You can't, without being seriously confused, justify keeping animals in zoos on the grounds that they provide useful research subjects for improving the lot of animals in zoos. That would be what, in the philosophy industry, is known as a *circular* argument; you are assuming the conclusion – that it is legitimate to keep animals in zoos – that you are supposedly arguing for.

Another aim of zoo-based anatomical and physiological studies is, allegedly, to contribute to human health. How? By providing animal models of human ailments. How is this supposed to happen? It doesn't. The reason is that you are very likely to get any results from zoo animals that have not already been obtained from clinical studies, either of animals or human beings. The laws being what they are, you are allowed to get away with far more in your treatment of laboratory animals than in your treatment of zoo animals; your research on laboratory animals can, accordingly, be far more manipulative, invasive and downright brutal. This means that almost all the anatomical or physiological research done on zoo animals is superfluous or trivial. To take just one example, some studies have been based on the idea that both humans and zoo animals, living in essentially urban environments, will suffer from the same ailments – for example, lead toxicity – through inhaling polluted city air (and also, actually, chewing the paint on their bars or enclosures). Suppose this is true. Then there will also be available for study plenty of humans who suffer from lead poisoning. That zoos make available some additional non-human subjects for this research is, at best, completely unimportant.

However, even if zoo-based studies were useful in providing models of human ailments – which they are not – this would no more justify zoo-based studies of animals any more than it legitimates laboratory studies. And, if the arguments of the previous chapter are anywhere near correct, such studies are morally wrong, even when they effectively promote vital human interests.

A final aim of zoo-based anatomical and physiological research is, allegedly, to gain knowledge about animals for its own sake. I have nothing against knowledge; all things being equal knowledge is a good thing to have. But the end does not justify the means. We would not justify painful experiments on young children on the grounds that the experiments yielded interesting knowledge. Humans, perhaps, are essentially inquisitive creatures. And for some humans, perhaps, a life not dominated by the quest for knowledge is a life not worth living. Perhaps. But there are other channels for our intellectual curiosity, ones that do not require such a high price in terms of animal suffering.

The final reason often used to justify zoos is their role in helping preserve endangered species. Zoo breeding programmes have had important successes; without them the Pere David Deer, the European Bison and the Mongolian Wild Horse would all now be extinct. However, we should not make too much of this role of zoos. First, most zoos do very little breeding, or breed only species that are not endangered. So, at most, this argument could justify the existence of only a tiny number of presently existing zoos. Second, many of the major breeding programs are located in facilities specifically created for this purpose, and far from the attention of zoo-goers. The Bronx Zoo, for example, operates its Rare Animal Survival Center on St Catherine's Island off the coast of Georgia; and the National Zoo runs its Conservation and Research Center in Virginia's Shenandoah Valley. Most zoos have neither the staff nor the facilities to pursue any meaningful breeding programmes. So, if the purpose of zoos is to help preserve endangered species, then we should replace them with these sorts of large-scale breeding centres.

4 BACK TO THE IMPARTIAL POSITION

In the impartial position, not knowing if you were a human or an animal typically put in zoos by humans, would you choose a world containing zoos? If you did, you would be irrational. To choose a world with zoos would be to allow the vital interest an animal has in its autonomy to be overridden by the relatively trivial interests humans have in zoos. And you may turn out to be that animal. This is a depressingly familiar pattern, one that emerged in the discussions of both animal husbandry and animal experimentation, and is repeated in the case of zoos. Entertainment is not a vital interest of human beings; so to justify zoos on this basis is, from the perspective of the impartial position, irrational. And even if education and scientific research were vital interests of humans – which, typically, they are not – zoos do not effectively promote them. So, again, to justify zoos by appeal to these considerations would, from the perspective of the impartial position, be irrational. Preservation of endangered species is, arguably, a vital interest of humans (at least many environmentalists have argued this). However, once again, zoos are neither necessary for, nor effective at, the promotion of this interest. So, to justify zoos by appeal to these considerations would, in the impartial position, again be irrational.

The four attempted justifications of zoos all have the same failing. They try to justify the sacrifice of interests that are vital to an animal by appealing to interests that are either not vital to humans or that are not effectively promoted by zoos. In the impartial position, to choose a world where this sort of trade-off is made would be irrational. Therefore, in the real world, to endorse such a trade-off is immoral.

5 Summary

The existence of zoos sacrifices some of the most vital interests of animals to try to promote interests of humans that are either not vital or are not effectively promoted by zoos. It would be irrational, in the impartial position, to choose a world where this sort of trade-off happens. Therefore, it is immoral, in the real world, to endorse this sort of trade-off. Zoos are morally illegitimate, and should be abolished.

8

HUNTING

In the impartial position, it would be irrational to choose any situation where a non-vital human interest is served or promoted through the violation of a vital interest of an animal. This is because, in the impartial position, you do not know whether you will be the human or the animal. Therefore, it is immoral, in the real world, to endorse such a situation. This is what makes animal husbandry, zoos, and vivisection, wrong. The same is true of hunting, at least in almost all circumstances. Hunting, of course, involves killing animals, and getting killed necessarily entails a thwarting of every vital (and, for that matter, non-vital) interest the animal has. So, unless the hunting serves or promotes human interests that are similarly vital, a world that contained hunting would be an irrational choice in the impartial position. Most hunting does not serve or promote vital human interests, therefore most hunting is immoral.

1 WHEN IS HUNTING LEGITIMATE?

Hunting is legitimate only when it serves or promotes vital human interests. And this means, roughly, that hunting is permissible only when it is necessary for the preservation of the life or health of the human hunters. For the vast majority of humans, this is not the case. However, there are certain human societies, operating on the *margins of existence*, where eating meat is essential to their survival. This is for the simple reason that supplies of vegetable protein are scarce or non-existent. The *Innuit* provide an obvious example. In such cases, the humans involved must be classified as, for all practical purposes, carnivores, creatures unable to survive without eating meat. The impartial position allows that it is morally acceptable for such people to eat meat. In the impartial position, to adopt a rule that proscribed eating meat for people such as the *Innuit* would be irrational; it would be to adopt a rule that potentially sealed one's own fate. More generally, the class of human beings who, for whatever reason, are unable to survive without eating meat should be treated along the same lines as any other carnivore. As we shall see in a moment, it is perfectly acceptable for such individuals to eat meat, nor do we have any obligation to assist the animals upon which they prey.

The scope of this rule, however, is strictly limited. It allows that humans who absolutely have to kill in order to live and be healthy may do so. But they may kill only what they need to satisfy their vital interests. If you are entitled to kill, say, fifty seals a year because you need these to survive, that's one thing. But it does not then follow that you have the right to kill a thousand seals so you can sell their pelts, or because someone else is paying you to do this because they want to take more fish. This falls outside the bounds of what is necessary for survival and health, and thereby falls outside the bounds of acceptable use.

In an ideal world, where everyone had the luxury of choosing where they lived, we might question someone who chooses to live in a place where killing animals was essential to survival. But it is, of course, not an ideal world. And, most people do not have this luxury. Certainly those living on the margins of existence don't. We have, it seems, far more pressing things to worry about – the animal husbandry techniques of big agribusiness, for example – than small numbers of humans, living on the margins of existence, who have to kill a small number of animals in order to survive.

In specifying when hunting is permissible, I mentioned life and health. But what about something else that is, arguably, a vital human interest? What about *happiness*? Some people claim that hunting is absolutely essential to their happiness, that a life without hunting is no life at all. Therefore, for those people at least, isn't hunting a vital interest? There are two points that count against this suggestion. First of all, it is not clear that happiness, in any full-blooded sense, is a vital interest on a par with life and health. Most people profess to be not particularly happy at all; there are very few people, however, who think that their lives are not worth living. Second, human interests are, if not infinitely, then at least indefinitely plastic. Whenever someone claims that one interest they have is of overriding importance and that, without it, life wouldn't be worth living then, basically, *they need to get out more!* Human happiness can be accommodated in various ways, and thinking that one particular way is of overriding importance almost always stems from the fact that one's experience is too narrow to provide an adequate basis for comparison.

2 Animals kill and eat each other, so why shouldn't we kill and eat them?

One of the most common defences of hunting is based around the idea that, in hunting animals, we are simply doing the same sort of thing that they do to each other. If the wolf's preying on the caribou is not morally wrong, then why should our preying on caribou be wrong? On the other hand, if our preying on caribou is morally wrong, then why would the caribou not have a case against the wolf?

One difference between us and wolves, of course, is that we are, while they are not, moral agents. They are unable to morally assess their actions by dispassionately evaluating them by way of the moral principles they adopt. Hence the wolf cannot be morally blamed for killing caribou for the simple reason that it is not the sort of thing that can be blamed. However this point, by itself, is not enough. For while the wolf may not be doing anything for which it can be blamed, we might still be obligated to render assistance to the caribou, in the same way that we might be obliged to prevent a person being harmed by any innocent threat. If a baby, for example, has come into possession of a loaded gun, and is firing it in the direction of passers-by, then the baby, since it is not a moral agent, is not doing anything for which it can be blamed. It is what we can call an innocent threat. Nevertheless, if I am, at fairly minimal risk to myself, able to dispossess the baby, then it seems I am morally required to do so; I have a duty to render assistance to the endangered passers-by. Similarly, even if the wolf can't be blamed for what it does to the caribou, we might still have a duty to assist the caribou.

The idea that we have a general duty to assist prey animals is, I think, just silly. Fortunately, it is not an idea we need accept. There is a big difference between humans and most carnivorous non-humans: we can survive without eating meat, they can't. Carnivorous animals simply do not have the right sort of digestive system – to begin with, their digestive tracts are far too short – to survive on vegetable matter. They must eat meat or die. With this in mind, put yourself in the impartial position. There, one of the things you do not know is whether you are going to be incarnated as a carnivore or herbivore. Given that this is so, how would you like the world to be? In particular, would you like it to be a world where humans routinely interfered with the attempts of animals to catch their prey?

To choose such a world would be irrational. If you turn out to be a carnivore, then your choice in the impartial position has condemned you to a slow death through starvation. But even if you turned out to be a herbivore, it would be irrational to make this choice. One of the things you would know in the impartial position – since you are in possession of all general laws relating to the natural world – is the role predators play in culling the weaker members of any group of prey animals. When a pack of wolves is hunting caribou, for example, they first spend a considerable amount of time making false attacks on the herd. This is for one purpose only: to find out which members of the group are weakest. Then, they go to work on one of those members. This is a general feature of the behaviour of most predators, and its evolutionary justification is obvious: killing a weak animal takes less effort than killing a strong one. One consequence of this is that predators generally kill the weaker members of any group of animals. This means that the limited food supplies available to any group of herbivores do not become exhausted through overgrazing. It also inhibits the spread of disease, since older, weaker, animals are more likely to carry disease than younger, healthier, ones. In any situation where a prey animal's natural predator has been eradicated – almost always by the hand of man – then the number of such animals explodes drastically, and disease and starvation are the result. All these things you will know in the impartial position. So, even if you turned out to be a prey animal, in choosing a world where humans routinely interfere with the attempts of predators to catch you, you choose a world where you are far more likely to succumb to disease and starvation. So, to choose such a world would be irrational. If you turn out to be predator, you suffer a slow death through starvation. If you turn out to be prey, you suffer a slow death through starvation or disease, instead of the relatively quick end at the hands of a predator. Therefore, we need not suppose that we have a general duty to assist prey animals. With regard to the relations between predator and prey, the best advice is simply: *leave them alone*.

With regard to hunting, then, the crucial difference between humans and animals is that, in the vast majority of cases, we don't have to hunt in order to survive, they do. Except in the case of certain human beings, like the *Innuit*, occupying the margins of existence, vital human interests are not at stake. But when animals hunt, their vital interests are very much at stake. Therefore, human hunting practices cannot be justified by appeal to animal hunting practices.

3 HUNTING IS NECESSARY TO ERADICATE "PESTS"

One of the most common defences of hunting is based on the idea that it is necessary in order to keep down the numbers of "pests." What makes something a pest? Its characteristic behaviour impacts adversely on human interests, typically economic ones. This is probably the most common argument in favour of fox hunting in Britain. Foxes are pests, since their activities adversely affect the interests of farmers. Therefore, their numbers must be kept down. And, so the argument goes, hunting with dogs is the most effective way of doing this. Is this a good argument?

There are several things wrong with it. First, even if we accept that the numbers of foxes should be kept down (which, for reasons that will become clear in a moment, we should not), the question is not what is the most *effective* way of doing this, but what is the most *humane*. It is difficult to take seriously the claim that chasing an exhausted and terrified animal for miles across the countryside, before digging it out of its hole and either shooting it and/or allowing the hounds to tear it apart constitutes the most humane method at our disposal.

Second, just what is the farmer doing that his interests are adversely impacted by the activities of the fox? It's not as if the fox is nibbling away at his corn or wheat or barley. Rather, he is raising animals for food. Specifically, he is raising sheep. The vast majority of sheep are not raised for their wool; that would be a financially unviable. They are raised for food. When they have reached market weight, they will be killed (if you want details of their death, they're pretty much the same as those described in chapter 5). Before this, many of them will be transported, indeed exported, often great distances in hot, cramped conditions, sometimes without food or water. If the arguments developed in this book in general, and in chapter 5 in particular, are correct, then raising and killing animals for food is not a morally legitimate enterprise. And you cannot defend a practice like fox hunting on the grounds that it is necessary to preserve the profits you get from a morally illegitimate enterprise. That would be like a mafia boss defending his killing of rivals on the grounds that it was necessary to protect his profits. If gains are ill-gotten, or earnings immoral, they cannot be used to justify a practice that is necessary in order to get or keep them.

Some animals, of course, do eat arable crops. Rabbits and rats, for example, will eat barley. Is it legitimate to hunt these in order to protect one's barley crop? Well, the first thing to do is compare the interests at stake. In most healthy arable systems – to the extent that one can use the term "healthy" in connection with the systems produced by modern arable production methods – the damage inflicted by rats, rabbits and other pests is fairly minimal. So, here we are looking at the vital interests of the rats and rabbits versus the economic interests of the farmer. So, this is a case of vital versus non-vital interests and, therefore, no contest. In certain circumstances, however, the number of rats, rabbits or other pests can get out of hand, and the economic damage they inflict can reach vital proportions. But then we have to ask why this happened. And the answer is, almost inevitably, because their natural predators – like, for example, foxes – have been hunted out of the locale.

The expression "shotgun diplomacy" was often used in the days of the British Empire, and referred to the almost reflex tendency of sending in a gunboat or equivalent whenever there were even the faintest mutterings of dissent from the natives. Well, in most of the developed world, we also suffer from what we might call "shotgun ecology." Look at what we have done in Britain. We first eradicated the large predators – wolves and bears – and have been gradually working our way down the ecosystem ever since. Foxes, they kill sheep, so lessen profit, so we'll keep their number down. Badgers, well they *might* – the evidence is unclear – carry TB, and while they are not really a threat to human health, might conceivably be a threat to cattle, hence to profit, so we'll start culling them. We don't learn our lessons. Whenever you remove a predator, the things it eats, and the things with which it competes, increase in number. And our answer, every time, is to bring out the shotgun (or equivalent). This never solves anything, it merely pushes the problem one level down the ecosystem. You kill foxes, then rabbits increase. You shoot rabbits, there's more for rats to eat. You poison the rats, there's more for mice to eat. You get rid of them, there are more insects which eat the very crops you were trying to protect by shooting the rabbits. The most egregious example of this was probably in China, during the comically misnamed "green revolution" of the 1950s. A government sponsored bird eradication involving millions of people took place. The birds were eating crops, so millions of people were organized to beat drums and generally make a lot of noise on a 24/7 basis. The birds were all scared off, were unable to feed properly, and died in huge numbers. Result: insects, which were normally eaten by the birds, exploded in numbers and *they* ate all the crops! It was one of the worst crop failures in modern Chinese history! It is difficult to know what to say to this sort of comic ecological myopia, but the word "Duh!" springs to mind.

We have to stop trying to squeeze every ounce of yield we can out of our land. Then, reintroduce predators, wherever possible: foxes, polecats, wildcats, even the wolf and the bear. Not only will they make the British countryside a much more interesting place to be, they will also remove the need for any human culling of "pests."

4 HUNTING IS NECESSARY FOR CONSERVATION

Of all the arguments used to justify hunting, perhaps the most risibly perverse is the claim that it is necessary for conservation. Here's how the argument goes. If a certain number of animals are not hunted, there will be too many animals belonging to a given species for a given environment to support. The environment will then suffer through overgrazing, and the animals will die of starvation and disease.

What makes this argument so laughable, I think, is its wilful ignorance of certain basic facts, ones familiar to even young schoolchildren. Take, for example, the idea of the *balance of nature*. Very roughly, a given environment will settle down into a reasonably steady state, where the numbers of any given species are determined, therefore, kept in check by the numbers of members other species that are related to it in sometimes complex relations of predation, competition, cooperation, and symbiosis. An environment that contains a certain amount of plant mass, for example, will support a certain number of, say, deer. But how many there of these depends on how many members of directly competing species there are in the same environment and, of course, vice versa. It depends also on the numbers of predators there are and, again, vice versa. The relations of dependence are sometimes quite staggeringly complex, even awe-inspiring. But the basic idea is simple and well understood.

The idea that human intervention is generally necessary to prevent one species in an environment getting out of control is just ecologically ignorant. Sometimes this happens but when it does it is always because humans have first done something else: removed a major predator from the ecosystem. If you remove wolves from a given environment – as, for example, when humans systematically slaughtered virtually all the wolves in the contiguous forty-eight US states – then of course deer numbers will explode exponentially. *That was the whole point of the exercise!* Or, at least one of them. That is, almost the only situations in which human culling of a given species is necessary in order to safeguard the environment, are situations that have been explicitly engineered by humans so that they can go and shoot lots of animals! The eradication of wolves from the contiguous forty-eight states in the early part of the twentieth century was partly to protect livestock but largely to increase the numbers of deer so that "sportsmen" would have more to shoot.

This is the whole philosophy – and I use the term loosely – behind game management. Take an environment. Remove the major predator or predators. Then you will have more "sport" animals to shoot. Shooting is then necessary, for, with their natural predators gone, their numbers would explode with devastating environmental consequences. However, you don't want to shoot all the sport animals. This would leave you with nothing to shoot next year. So, how many do you shoot? Kill only as many animals as will allow you to kill the same number next year. Then, in the long run, you will be able to kill *more* animals.

The idea that hunting animals can be justified on environmental grounds is a joke. Only if we remove large predators would this form of culling ever become necessary. And why would we remove large predators? Two reasons. Either we are protecting the profits from another morally illegitimate practice like animal husbandry. Or, we are deliberately creating the conditions under which we will have large numbers of animals to shoot. Not content with shooting deer, we want to stop everything else killing deer. Why? So we can shoot *more* deer. So, we shoot the wolves to stop them competing with us, and thereby create the conditions where we can claim that killing deer is necessary on environmental grounds. This claim should be treated with the contempt it deserves.

5 SUMMARY

Hunting thwarts the most vital interests of the animals hunted. However, in the vast majority of cases, it does not serve or promote any similarly vital human interest. In the impartial position, choosing a situation where vital interests are outweighed or overridden by non-vital interests would be irrational. Therefore, hunting, in the vast majority of cases, is morally wrong. The traditional arguments used to support hunting do not work, and some of them are positively risible.

9

PETS

One issue that is seldom discussed by moral philosophers is our use of animals for pets. There are obvious reasons why this receives little attention. First, when you compare the horrors of factory farming or vivisection, the situation of pets seems positively enviable, and our treatment of them comparatively benign. Second, our attitudes towards pets are backed up, and enforced, by various laws, ones that prohibit cruelty in at least some of its forms, and our treatment of farm and laboratory animals is (shamefully) exempt from many of these laws. With pets faring so much better than farm or laboratory animals, then, it makes sense to concentrate on the latter rather than the former. Nevertheless, the issue of pets does add some interesting wrinkles to our overall account of the moral status of animals, and we can consider some of them, at least briefly, here.

1 NATURAL AND ACQUIRED OBLIGATIONS

In moral philosophy, it is common to distinguish between what are known as natural (or unacquired) obligations and acquired ones. A natural, or unacquired, obligation is, very roughly, one that you have independently of anything that you have done. An acquired obligation is the opposite; it is one you pick up or acquire because of what you do. A promise is a classic example of an acquired obligation. Making a promise is an action, and in virtue of this action you thereby acquire an obligation to keep the promise. To treat others with equal consideration, on the other hand, is an example of a natural obligation; you have this obligation to everyone independently, and irrespective, of what you do or how you act.

A common, though far from universal, position is that natural obligations trump acquired ones, at least typically. My promise to you to give you a Maserati for your birthday does not justify my stealing the car from someone else. If this is right, then, when you act, you have to first make sure that you are not violating any of your natural obligations before you start worrying about fulfilling your acquired ones.

Many of our natural obligations are *negative* ones; that is, they are not obligations to do something but to *not* do, or refrain from doing, something. This is clearly true in the case of animals. Most of our obligations to them are negative ones: to not kill them unnecessarily, to not inflict unnecessary suffering on them, to not imprison them, and so on. These are all natural obligations – ones that we have independently and irrespective of our voluntary actions – they are also all negative ones. Indeed, I think that in the case of wild animals, all our obligations to them are negative ones. In any event, the specific natural obligations we have to animals can, I have tried to show, be worked out using the imaginary idea of the impartial position. We pretend, with regard to a specific situation like factory farming, vivisection, hunting that we do not know whether we are a human or an animal likely to be centrally involved in that situation. Then we ask ourselves, "How would I like the world to be?" And this, in effect, is a way of working out the obligations we have to those animals.

With pets, however, a new type of obligation comes to the fore: acquired obligation. To take on a pet, to bring it into one's home, is something we do; and in virtue of this we acquire extra obligations to the animal, ones that we do not have with respect to wild animals. This is not to say that we have no acquired obligations to farm, laboratory, or zoo animals; in my view we clearly do. It's just that with pets, it is far more likely to be recognized or accepted that we have acquired obligations. So, pets provide a useful forum to work out what obligations we might acquire with respect to animals. The idea of the impartial position again proves useful.

2 WHAT ACQUIRED OBLIGATIONS DO WE HAVE WITH RESPECT TO PETS?

At a minimum, to take on a pet is to acquire the obligation to take care of its basic needs. These may be both physical and psychological. A dog, for example, has physical needs such as those for food and shelter. However, it has also evolved as a social creature and, accordingly, requires companionship of some sort, provided either by other dogs or by humans. This is a baseline requirement, implicated in the assumption of responsibility inherent in the act of taking on a pet.

What further duties do you have? Your dog, let's suppose, would like to go for a walk. It's been in the house all day, while you have been at work, and it would like to run around for a while, perhaps meet some other dogs, smell some interesting smells, and so on. You have every reason to suppose your dog would like this since (i) it is exhibiting the usual behavioural signs – jumping up at the door, walking over and staring at you intently, or whatever – and (ii) this is all perfectly natural dog behaviour, at least in the ancestral home of the dog. You, on the other hand, don't really feel like it. It's cold outside, a little wet, and you're tired from work. Do you have an obligation to take your dog for a walk?

To see this, put yourself in the impartial position. Pretend you do not know if you are you or the dog, and the ask yourself, "How would I like the world to be?" This is not an exact science, not even close. You simply have to do the best you can under what are, in effect, conditions of profound uncertainty. But, what you are trying to do is work out how important the walk is to the dog compared to how important not going for the walk is to you. How much does the dog lose by not getting exercised? And how much do you lose by forcing yourself out on this unpleasant evening. And there are many, many factors you have to consider. How long has it been since the dog's last walk? How unpleasant is it outside? How tired are you? Is there anything worthwhile you have to do this evening, or are you simply killing time? Is the dog on its own during the day, or does it have company? The list is a long one, and there is no guarantee you will succeed in correctly weighing each factor. You can, ultimately, only guess at how important the walk is to the dog. But there are honest guesses and there are self-serving ones. And, at the end of the day, you can just try your best to arrive at an honest answer. The same sort of method can then be applied to other decisions you must make about how to treat your pet.

There is also a second baseline condition implicated in the act of taking on a pet. The animal must not be made worse off by becoming a pet. That is, the animal must, as a pet, have a life that is at least as good as it would have had if it were not a pet. Again, this idea does not lend itself to precise evaluation. And, in most cases, the principle does not have much effect. The hopelessly domesticated Shih-Tzu would not have much of a life not being a pet; its life in the wild would be, as the philosopher Thomas Hobbes once put it, nasty, brutish and short. However, there are some pets for which this second baseline condition is crucially important: animals that are either captured in the wild or ones that, though bred in captivity, are closely related to wild animals. Monkeys and snakes provide obvious examples of animals of the first sort; wolf-hybrids provide a good example of the second.

Consider the case of wolf-hybrids. These are the result of the cross-breeding of wolves and dogs, the latter usually being ones – like Siberian Huskies, Alaskan Malamutes, and German Shepherds – that are closely related to wolves. The amount of wolf in the hybrid is measured in terms of percentages reflecting its lineage, and many of the high-percentage hybrids (eighty-five per cent plus) are physically and behaviourally almost indistinguishable from their pure-blooded relations, and they are clearly capable of surviving in the wild.

Many would argue that keeping captive wolf-hybrids is morally unacceptable. They argue that since a high-percentage hybrid is so close to a wolf, it would always be happier in the wild. I don't agree, but I do accept that keeping a wolf-hybrid is morally justifiable only if the life it would have in a human home is at least as good as the life it would have in the wild. And often this condition is not met. The major problem is allowing the hybrid to express its natural behaviour, since it will almost certainly be unhappy if it does not. It needs to hunt, and it needs to roam. A wolf in its natural habitat may travel up to fifty miles in a night when hunting. So, taking on a wolf-hybrid requires making arrangements for it to roam and for it to hunt. (Any hint of incompatibility between this and the idea of animal rights has, hopefully, been dealt with in the previous chapter. Just because humans are obligated to be vegetarians does not mean that wolves – hybrid or otherwise – are similarly obligated.) Obviously, hunting and roaming are not things the animal can be allowed to do on its own. So, you have to get yourself a mountain bike, or get seriously good at running, and get fit enough to stay with it. Subsidiary problems include training it sufficiently well to not be a danger to other dogs, and inappropriate forms of prey. Wolf-hybrids are notoriously difficult to train, and proper training takes months at best.

So, arguably, much time and effort are required if the life of the high-percentage wolf-hybrid is to be as rewarding as life in the wild. Many people simply don't have the time, and simply won't make the effort. The result is that hybrids are often shut outside in a smallish enclosure living a life of unrelieved monotony. And that, for these magnificent creatures, is no life at all. Certainly it is nowhere near as rewarding as a life in the wild, and so fails the second baseline condition for taking on a pet.

3 Pets and vegetarianism

As many people have pointed out, there is an undeniable tension between being a vegetarian on the one hand and keeping carnivorous pets on the other. Is the tension a contradiction? That is, if you are a vegetarian, should you frown on the practice of keeping pets that eat meat?

We should, first, get clear about why there is a potential problem here. When your dog or cat eats meat, it is not doing anything for which it can be blamed. Dogs and cats are not moral agents – are not capable of evaluating their actions in the light of impartial moral principles – and so can be neither praised or blamed for what they do; at least not in any moral sense of praise or blame. If moral questions are to be raised here, they concern not your carnivorous pet, but you, its owner. The problem is that in taking on a carnivorous pet, and feeding it meat from a can, packet, or bag, you are helping sustain a system of food production that inflicts untold misery on millions and millions of animals every year. And, your complicity in the system is something that should be subject to moral scrutiny. Your pet cannot be praised or blamed for what it does, but you can be blamed for taking on the pet that does what it does. Or so the argument goes.

Of course, it is true that there are many unwanted pets in the world. And if you had not taken on your dog or cat, it may well have turned out to have a much worse life than it has with you. Nevertheless, to some extent, people breed dogs and cats because there is money in it. If people did not take on pets, then the demand would drop, and potential revenue decline. So, people would stop breeding so many of them. And then the number of animals that die in order to feed these pets would diminish. So, in the long run, it would be better if people did not take on carnivorous pets. At least, so the argument might go.

I don't think the argument is particularly effective. To begin with, we must ask. "To what extent do *additional* farm animals suffer and die because of the existence of pets who eat them?" And the answer, I think, is very few. It is not as if prime cuts of beef, lamb, or chicken go into making dog or cat food. The meat that goes into pet food is, almost invari-ably, what is known as "mechanically reclaimed" meat; animal matter that has been stripped off the bone and contains a high proportion of gristle, sinew, and nerve fibre. This is meat that humans would not eat anyway (especially now when doing so might lead to a very nasty death by vCJD). In addition, various parts of the animal carcass that have been declared unfit for human consumption, cancerous tumours for example, regularly find their way into pet foods. The animals are killed because humans want to eat the "choice" parts of animal bodies. Pets eat the left-overs that would otherwise be thrown away (or fed back to pigs and cattle, actually).

So, it is very unclear that *more* farm animals suffer and die because of the existence of pets that eat them. At worst, taking on a carnivorous pet contributes to the *profitability* of the meat industry. Still, this is some-thing worth thinking about. Are there any ways of avoiding this, or at least moderating its effects? To an extent, yes; at least in the case of dogs. Most evidence suggests that dogs can be raised on a non-meat diet. Turning your dog vegetarian, however, is not something to be undertaken lightly, and should only be undertaken after getting detailed veterinary advice. If you decide to go down this road, then a gradual, rather than abrupt tran-sition is probably to be recommended. Another option, one that can be combined with the gradual phasing out of meat, is to let your dog eat fish. At this point, many committed vegetarians will be choking on their lentils, or whatever it is that us stereotypical vegetarians are supposed to eat. And this suggestion is, of course, far from ideal. Fish can suffer, and therefore they count morally. But the fact is that fish, at least if they are not factory farmed – which, unfortunately, a steadily increasing number are – have a life that is substantially better than the squalor and misery to which many pigs, chickens and cattle are routinely subjected. I don't eat fish, because I don't have to. But, because of the difference in digestive tracts, the transition to a vegetarian diet for a dog is a lot more difficult than for a human. If you go this route, make sure that the tuna is dolphin friendly. And try to avoid the most over-fished species. Fish, obviously, also provide a more acceptable alternative for cats.

In any event, moving your dog away from the standard can of meat plus bag of mixer diet is to be recommended independently of moral considerations. In addition to the questionable parts of animals that go into these things – and would you really want your dog eating diseased parts of animals – there is also the fact that most brands of dry dog food contains additives – anti-oxidants like ethoxyquin – that are known carcinogens, and that have been banned from human food for precisely this reason. If you are living in Europe, you see this on the packet or bag. It'll say something like, "Contains EEC permitted levels of anti-oxidants." Permitted for pets, that is; not for humans.

4 Summary

Our obligations to wild animals are natural and negative ones. However, in the case of pets, we have additional – acquired – obligations, and many of these are positive. With regard to our pets, we have the baseline obligations to take care of their basic physical and psychological needs and to ensure that the life they live as a pet is at least as good as the one they would have led in the wild. Questions concerning specific obligations that arise in day-to-day living can be examined by using the impartial position. Finally, contrary to popular belief, being a vegetarian is not incompatible with having carnivorous pets, although if you would like to counter any profits your pet is creating for the meat industry, certain steps can be taken.

10

ANIMAL RIGHTS ACTIVISM

Suppose you are convinced by the arguments of this book, or by other arguments not dealt with here. You come to believe, as I did several years ago, that our current treatment of animals is very wrong indeed. What should you do about it? To what extent should you become an animal rights *activist*? And if you become an activist, how far should you go?

1 THE VARIETIES OF ANIMAL RIGHTS ACTIVISM

The expression "animal rights activism" conjures up images of nose-ringed, roll-your-own radicals manufacturing letter bombs in some seedy inner-city squat. The reality is very different. There are, in fact, many different types of activism, and these can be divided up into three broad categories.

One important type of activism consists simply in various *lifestyle changes*, changes in the things you do in, and with, your life. These include:

Become a vegetarian (or vegan)

Refuse to buy products tested on animals

Refuse to buy and wear leather and fur

Avoid investing in companies that exploit animals

Educate yourself about animal rights issues

Another type of activism consists in what we might call *spreading the word*. This can include:

Tell your family and friends (indeed, anyone who will listen) about your beliefs

Write letters to government officials, newspapers, etc.

Write books and articles

Give talks at schools, public meetings, etc.

Join an animal rights organization

Demonstrate, picket and protest at appropriate sites (e.g. live animal export firms, animal testing laboratories)

The final category of activism is the most contentious: *civil disobedience*. Acts of civil disobedience can include:

Sit-ins and occupations

Obstruction of people engaged in animal cruelty (e.g. sabotaging foxhunts)

Trespass on property associated with animal abuse (e.g. animal research laboratories) for the purposes of gathering evidence, release of animals, etc.

Destruction of property related to abuse of animals (e.g. destruction of equipment at an animal research laboratory)

Intimidation of people involved in animal abuse (e.g. research scientists, foxhunters, etc.)

Terrorism

If you believe that our current treatment of animals is very wrong, there are two questions you should probably confront. First, am I committed to doing any of these things in the above list? Second, how far can I acceptably go? That is, which, if any, of the things on the above list are morally unacceptable?

2 POSITIVE AND NEGATIVE OBLIGATIONS

In trying to answer these questions, one distinction that we ought to keep in mind is between *positive* and *negative* obligations. A positive obligation is an obligation to do something, to act in a certain way. A negative obligation is an obligation to *not* do something, to refrain from acting in a certain way. Most of the forms of activism labelled *lifestyle changes* are negative obligations: obligations to *not* eat meat, to *not* wear fur or leather, to *not* use products tested on animals, etc. There is a crucial difference between positive and negative obligations: fulfilling positive obligations takes time, fulfilling negative obligations generally does not. This is for the obvious reason that doing something takes time, while not doing something does not.

If someone or something is morally entitled to certain treatment, and if all you have to do to respect this moral entitlement is *not* do something, then just about any moral theory that has ever been devised will tell you that that is what you should do (or, rather, not do). This stems from the whole idea of moral entitlement. If someone is entitled to something, then it follows, by definition, that you should respect this entitlement if you can. This is precisely what it means to be entitled to something; others should let you have that thing if they can. Sometimes, they won't be able to, sometimes matters might be beyond their control. But it is a simple point of definition that if you are entitled to something – whether this is a certain type of liberty, a type of treatment, a commodity, or whatever – then others should let you have that thing if they can.

If this book is right, animals are entitled to certain things – to a life free from unnecessary physical and psychological suffering, for example. If they are entitled to this, then we are under an obligation to let them have this if it is within our power to do so. But if all we have to do in order to fulfil this obligation is *not* do certain things, then that is certainly within our power. It is always within our power to *not* do something. If our eating animals contributes to a husbandry system that inflicts unnecessary physical and psychological suffering on millions of animals, and it is always within our power to *not* eat animals, then that is what we should do: *not* eat them. If our buying products tested on animals helps prop up a medical-industrial complex that inflicts unnecessary physical and psychological suffering on animals, and it is within our power to not buy such products, then that is what we should do: *not* buy them.

Generally, it is always in our power to *not* do something, however much we may want to do it. Therefore, given the connection between what animals are entitled to and what we are obligated to give them if we can, we are morally required to at least fulfil our negative obligations to animals. The sort of lifestyle changes that involve not doing something then, these are all morally required of us.

The positive obligations we have towards animals are more difficult to work out. Indeed, there is a well-known argument that can be used to cast doubt on whether we have many, if any, positive obligations at all, not just to animals but to anyone. Here, let me be clear that I am talking about what, in the previous chapter, I called *natural* or *unacquired* obligations, not acquired ones. Most philosophers have no problem with the existence of acquired positive obligations. Nonetheless, many of these take a dim view of the idea that we have many, or even any, definite natural positive obligations. If this is right, the positive courses of action we might take on behalf of animals are not, in themselves, things that we are morally obligated to do. They are not, that is, moral obligations at all.

The argument against unacquired positive obligations begins with the idea that *ought implies can*. That is, it makes little sense to say that someone morally ought to do something if they are physically incapable of doing it. There's no way, for example, that you can be morally obligated to give say $100 to each and every charity in the world if you don't have enough money to go around, nor the means of getting the money. Nor, can you give your time to each and every charity because your time, like your money, is strictly limited.

Positive obligations, if we had them, would take time. But the time anyone has is strictly finite. No one has the time to fulfil all of his or her potential positive obligations. Remember that if we have positive obligations to animals, then we will also have them towards humans – obligations to help feed starving people, shelter the homeless, and so on. No one is capable of fulfilling all these obligations, or supposed obligations, they simply would not have enough time. Ought implies can; so if you cannot, you oughtn't. So, we cannot be obligated to fulfil all our potential positive obligations.

However, and here's the rub, in the case of many positive obligations at least, there seems nothing to choose between them, morally speaking. Why should feeding the starving be any more worthy than sheltering the homeless? So, at least in the case of many supposed positive obligations, there is nothing to choose between fulfilling the one and fulfilling the other. You cannot do both, but there is no reason why you should have to do one rather than the other. But if this is right, it would seem to indicate you are not obligated to do either. You cannot, let's suppose, do both, because of, say, time constraints. But there seem no grounds for saying that you should do one rather than the other. And if this is right, it would seem that you are not obligated to do either. At least, this is the lesson many moral philosophers have drawn.

I am not convinced that this argument works, but I am not convinced that it does not either. The argument does not prove that you have no positive obligations at all. But what it does show is that you are not committed to any *particular* positive obligation, an obligation to do one thing rather than another. At the very least, I think we should conclude that proving that we are committed to any of the positive obligations listed at the beginning of this chapter is going to be difficult at best, and perhaps it is impossible. And this means that many of the positive courses of action we might take on behalf of animals are not really obligations at all; they are not things we are morally obligated to do.

There is no reason for the defender of animal rights to be particularly worried about this. First, the argument applies quite generally, to our treatment of humans as much as our treatment of animals. So, there is no way that animals are especially disadvantaged by this conclusion. Second, the changes in quality of the lives of animals would be drastic and immense if people were only to follow up on their *negative* obligations towards animals. Think of how their lives would change – for the better – if we were to *not* raise them for food, or *not* experiment on them. Whether or not we also have any positive obligations towards them is a question of comparatively minor importance. Third, most moral philosophers recognize the existence of a type of action they refer to as *supererogatory*. A supererogatory action is defined as one that it is good to do, but not bad not to do. Such an action is, as we might say, one that goes *over and above the call of duty*. It is an action that is good to do, but that cannot really be expected of anyone in the normal run of things. Positive actions we take on behalf of animals may be of this type. They may be good things to do even if they are not bad things not to do. Also, we tend to take a dim view of someone who merely fulfils their moral obligations, doing only the bare minimum that is necessary to satisfy the demands of morality. Such a person is, in effect, a *moral miser*. There is, as Aristotle put it, no *greatness of soul* about such a person. Going above and beyond the call of duty is not only a good thing to do, it also says a lot about the person who is willing to go this extra mile.

The question then is, "How many of these positive actions we may take on behalf of animals are good ones?" The actions listed under *spreading the word* may not be obligatory, but, if the arguments of this book are correct, they are certainly *supererogatory*; they are not only good things to do, they also say a lot about the sort of person who is willing to do them. But are all actions we may take on behalf of animals good ones, or do some of them "cross the line"? How far is it morally acceptable to go in defence of the interests of animals?

3 BREAKING THE LAW

The actions listed under *civil disobedience* are all illegal. This is a point of definition; an action can count as civil disobedience only if it is illegal. Lawful picketing, for example, may be a form of civil *disturbance*, but it is not a form of civil *disobedience*. So, in order to work out if these actions are good ones, we need to look at the question of whether it is ever morally right to break the law.

Most political philosophers think we have what they call a *prima facie* obligation to obey the law. That is, the fact that some rule is enshrined as law gives us at least some reason to obey it. However, to say that our obligation to obey the law is *prima facie* is to say that it can be overridden in certain circumstances (that is what *prima facie* means; it is Latin for "on first appearance"). What are the circumstances in which a law can be overridden? There are several, but one circumstance, most political philosophers agree, is if the law is fundamentally *unjust*. This is why the campaigns of civil disobedience orchestrated by, for example, Gandhi in India, and by Martin Luther King in the US, are widely accepted as morally legitimate. So, the question we must ask ourselves is: "Do we have any reason for thinking that the laws pertaining to human treatment of animals are fundamentally unjust?" If we answer this question in the affirmative, then breaking these laws can be morally legitimate.

If the arguments of this book are correct, then our current treatment of many non-human animals is, morally speaking, very wrong indeed. It is wrong because it is incompatible with very fundamental moral principles that we hold, the principles of equality and desert. These principles run deep; they are essential to our moral thinking and to our sense of what counts as right and wrong. Our treatment of animals, then, ignores two of our most central and deeply held moral principles. This treatment is, also, made possible by certain laws, ones that specify what we can and what we can't do to animals. Does the fact that our treatment of animals is immoral – in the sense of incompatible with some of our most fundamental moral beliefs – entail that these laws are unjust?

Ultimately, it does. To see this, ask yourself, "What are laws?" And the answer is, ignoring some conceptual frills and extras, that laws are those moral rules that we consider important enough to be enforced. There are many moral obligations that we do not consider sufficiently important to elevate to the status of law. You have a moral obligation to be loyal to your friends, for example, or faithful to your partner. But neither of these widely accepted moral obligations are given legal sanction. Laws, legal statutes, are those moral rules that we consider important enough to require enforcing. That is the basis of, and ultimately the justification for, law.

The principles of equality and desert are not marginal or insignificant moral principles. They are absolutely central to morality, absolutely foundational to our moral thinking and the moral tradition built on this. In terms of moral principles, they are about as important as you can get. So, if these principles are not worthy of enforcement as law, then it is difficult to imagine any moral principle that would be.

So, this is the situation. Take the laws that facilitate our present treatment of animals: laws that permit animals to be bred for the laboratory, to be kept in miserable conditions, and then be subjected to appalling experiments, laws which permit animals to be raised in atrocious conditions on the factory farms and then killed in a grisly and horrifying manner. These are laws that are incompatible, logically inconsistent, with our most fundamental moral principles. We fail to see this only because we fail to properly understand, and so grasp the consequences of, these moral principles. But this is simply a failure on our part. The laws that permit our current treatment of animals are incompatible with absolutely central components of our moral tradition. These laws are, therefore, as unjust as any laws can be. And we are, therefore, under no overriding obligation to obey them. Just because an act of civil disobedience is illegal does not mean that we should not do it.

4 ACTS OF RESCUE AND ATTEMPTS TO CHANGE SOCIETY

Any adequate account of what you should and should not do as an animal rights activist has to be properly sensitive to a crucial distinction between *acts of rescue* and *attempts to change society*. Acts of civil disobedience perpetrated by animal rights activists can have two quite different functions, and, accordingly, they have to be morally assessed in two quite different ways. Take, for example, breaking into a laboratory, destroying equipment, and releasing the captive animals. This can, broadly, be construed as what we can call an *act of rescue*. The laboratory animals are rescued, and the destruction of property makes it more difficult (although perhaps only marginally) for animals to be similarly confined and tortured in future. It is sometimes claimed that acts of sabotage of this sort are only *symbolic* ones, empty gestures that make very little difference in the long run. Nothing could be further from the truth. To the animals rescued this act makes all the difference in the world, although it is perhaps incumbent on those who release them to make sure that the situation of the animals does not become worse because of their release. Finding them a home of some sort would, of course, be ideal. And, in many cases, though unfortunately not all, this is precisely what happens. Acts of rescue, when you consider the impact on animals saved from wretched conditions and transported to something better, are about as far from empty gestures as it is possible to get.

Suppose now that the perpetrators of this act of rescue notify the press of their actions, turn themselves in to the authorities, and try to ensure maximum exposure for their case in the media. Now, something quite different is going on. Now, the attempt is to change the way society thinks about animals. The goal is now to work on society's sense of justice, to educate people about what's going on, and to massage the public's sense of what's right and wrong. In short, the act of rescue has now been followed by an *attempt to change society*. Such attempts can take a variety of forms, ranging from illegal demonstrations, sit-ins, and occupations on the one hand to intimidation and terrorism on the other. Understood as attempts to change society, these actions have several functions, but most obviously they are attempts to garner publicity; since making the public aware of a situation is a necessary first step in making the public disapprove of that situation.

In order to be legitimate, attempts to change society seem to need to satisfy more requirements than acts of rescue. This is for several reasons, and, to see what they are, consider the following situation. Suppose you live in a society that condones slavery. You, however, having understood the role of the principles of equality and desert in the moral thinking of your society, oppose this. One day you witness a slave owner beating one of his slaves, and you decide to rescue the slave. This sort of situation has a certain, what we can call, *immediacy*: action is called for as a matter of urgency. You could try an alternative approach – for example, seeking to convince your fellow citizens of the injustice of slavery – but this would take time, and will in no way improve the predicament of the slave who is now being beaten. Therefore, you decide to step in and rescue the slave.

This is, then, an act of rescue.

Two features of the situation are, I think, important. First, given the immediacy of the situation, you have no effective legal recourse. Appealing to law – for example, laws prohibiting cruelty to slaves – takes time, and in the present situation you have no time. You could try and prosecute the slave owner, but a successful prosecution might take years, and this will in no way help the slave who is now being beaten. Second, suppose the slave owner resists your intervention, perhaps attacking you. Then, I think it is plausible to suppose that you would have every right to meet his violence against you with violence. That is, you would have every right to use whatever violence is necessary to, first, defend yourself against his attack, and, second, to get the job you are trying to do done. This is justified by your right to self-defence; and this right can be properly exercised in your attempt to put right a serious injustice. At least, you are entitled to use violence if this is *necessary* to protect yourself and *proportionate* to the violence used against you.

Suppose, following the incident with the slave owner, and consequent liberation of the slave, you decide to follow up with an attempt to change society. You and your co-activists, let's suppose, decide to stage a demonstration in the city centre, one intended to draw publicity to your anti-slavery charter, and which causes a certain amount of inconvenience to a large number of people, many of whom might agree with your position anyway. Now, you have to understand, you are doing something completely different. In taking on this sort of action, you are implicitly consigning yourself the "long haul." This sort of situation does not have the same immediacy or urgency as an act of rescue situation. The goals you are pursuing are, indeed, urgent and pressing, but the tactic you have now adopted is not one that is going to bring quick results, and this is one of the things that you have to accept in buying into this strategy in the first place.

In buying in to the long haul of attempting to change society, you have, I think, abrogated any recourse to violence. It is not as if the goals are any different, they are still as urgent and pressing as they ever were, it's just that the methods you are now adopting do not lend themselves to rapid or immediate solutions. And if you are to adopt these methods, you should acknowledge this: it would be an act of the most acute bad faith to adopt a strategy that cannot yield quick solutions while, at the same time, demanding that it does yield quick solutions.

Both acts of rescue and attempts to change society can be morally legitimate if the laws they seek to subvert are unjust. And the laws that permit our current treatment of animals are precisely that. But these strategies work in different ways, and the violence that is justified by an act of rescue is not similarly justified by an attempt to change society.

The distinction between an act of rescue and an attempt to change society is, I think, particularly important in assessing the legitimacy of animal rights terrorism (if there is such a thing). It is to this that we now turn.

5 How far is too far?

I am going to argue that animal rights terrorism is too far. The idea that such terrorism is legitimate is based on a confusion of acts of rescue and attempts to change society. More precisely, it assumes that the sorts of means and methods that are appropriate to acts of rescue are appropriate to attempts to change society. And, as we've seen in the previous section, they're not. First, however, we have to work out what terrorism is.

Discussions of the moral status of terrorism are clouded by the fact that the word "terrorism" is typically used in such a loose and sloppy way. Certainly, in the way the word is commonly used it covers too many things. Destruction of property, for example, is often prosecuted under prevention of terrorism laws – just ask the *Meibion Glyndwr*. And it is difficult to believe such wilful misuse of the word "terrorism" is not politically motivated.

So, in order to work out the moral status of animal rights terrorism, we first have to be clear on what terrorism is. Unfortunately, there is no generally accepted definition of the word "terrorism." Nevertheless, there is a general degree of consensus as to the core features of terrorist acts. These include:

The acts involve the use of violence or the threat of such use

The acts have a political motive

The objective of these acts is to produce a state of terror in a victim or group of victims

This terror has the goal of modifying behaviour

The selected target is often symbolic

One point worth noting, since this is particularly relevant to so-called animal rights terrorism, is that destruction of property does not qualify as terrorism. Why? Because on just about any accepted account of terrorism, terrorism involves violence or the threat of violence. And destruction of property is not violence. You cannot be violent *to* a table. You can be violent *with* a table – as when you hit somebody over the head with it – but your violence is then directed against the person and not the table. In any reasonable sense of the term, you can be violent only against things that can suffer.

Even with this common misconception removed, however, problems of interpretation remain. Suppose you throw a can of red paint over a woman (or man, for that matter) wearing a fur coat, and then proceed to verbally abuse her. This might be interpreted as an attack on her person (rather than her coat), hence an act of violence. It might be construed as having a political motive. It might, in appropriate circumstances, induce feelings of terror in her. It certainly has the goal of modifying her behaviour. And the selected target is certainly symbolic (it's not going to do the mink much good now, for example). But it would certainly be a little harsh, I think, to regard this as a terrorist act. Certainly, if you were sent down for life on the basis of this act, you could justifiably feel a little aggrieved. At most, this is intimidation, not terrorism.

What's the difference between intimidation (employed for political purposes) and terrorism? There probably is no hard and fast distinction; the difference is one of degree rather than kind. The reason your throwing paint on the fur coat is an act of intimidation, rather than terrorism, is simply that it does not produce *enough* terror, or does not involve enough violence. Contrast your action with those of a *bona fide* terrorist group.

One of the IRA's reputed methods of administering a, euphemistically named, "punishment beating" has been by way of what is known as a "six pack." You take your victim, jam the barrel of a pistol in the crook of his elbow, bend his forearm upward so that the barrel rests snugly in the crook. Then you pull the trigger. Due to the position of the arm, the shot blows most of the elbow away. Then you repeat with the other elbow. Then you do the same for the knees. Finally the ankles. The episode with the coat, clearly, pales in comparison.

There is no clear line between terrorism and intimidation, and, to the extent that there is a distinction, it can, I think, turn only on the severity of the terror or the degree of violence involved. In order to be classified as terrorist, the act or threat has to produce a sufficient amount of fear and/or involve a sufficient amount of violence. And this means that most of the acts carried out by militant animal rights groups cannot plausibly be regarded as terrorist acts. The public stance of Animal Liberation Front (ALF), for example, is anti-violence. To the extent that their activities are destructive, it is property, equipment and, sometimes, the results of research that are destroyed; not people. The Animal Rights Militia (ARM) has been associated with the use of bombs. But even then, for the most part, these have been small devices, usually contained in cigarette packs, that were left in department stores and timed to go off only when the stores were closed. Such acts are designed to inflict economic loss, rather than terror. This did not prevent Barry Horne, convicted of one such attack, being sent to prison for eighteen years, much longer than he would have received for rape, child abuse or, in many cases, murder.[1]

The ARM has also been associated with various high-profile hoaxes involving the alleged adulteration of Mars bars with rat poison, mercury in turkeys and bleach added to shampoo. I remember most of these. And let's be honest, they can hardly be considered to have evoked any genuine feelings of terror in anyone. It is not as if we all wandered around in terror at the prospect of not being able to eat Mars bars for a while. The principle effect, and the intended effect, was economic not psychological. Mars lost an estimated ten million dollars through this hoax.

Possibly the most militant animal rights group is the Justice Department. This has been associated with a variety of bombs, including letter bombs, car bombs, and incendiary devices. While both their car bombs were (intentionally) exploded while their owners – individuals connected to animal experimentation – were not in their cars, and while no serious injuries have, as yet, resulted from their activities, the Justice Department might legitimately be regarded as at least a nascent terrorist organization.

So, only a tiny, tiny fraction of the activities of even the most militant animal rights groups qualifies as terrorism in any genuine sense. Nevertheless, we can still ask the question, "Is terrorism – and, by this, I mean genuine terrorism, not property damage or intimidation – on behalf of animals ever justified?" I think it probably isn't, although the reasons for this are not as straightforward as one might suppose.

Some people say that killing humans is always wrong, no matter what. Some people even claim that violence against humans is always wrong no matter what. I don't think any of these positions can be taken seriously. At least, they fly in the face of what passes for common sense in these matters, and so cannot be used to condemn animal rights terrorism. Most people are willing to allow that violence, and even killing, is, under certain circumstances, legitimate. The circumstances might include self-defence, defence of an innocent third party (e.g. your sister who is being raped), and war. What unites these, very roughly, is the idea that violence, even killing, is morally legitimate when it serves "the greater good." Of course, different people have different ideas about what constitutes the greater good, and when this happens we run into problems. But the idea that violence and killing are justified if they are necessary for the greater good is still pretty much accepted wisdom.

Any animal rights terrorist is likely to be convinced that what he or she is doing is justified on the grounds that it is necessary for the greater good. Millions and millions of animals, he or she is likely to argue, are living lives of abject misery, followed by a hideous end. This is a morally deplorable situation, and if a few humans have to die to help bring an end to it, then so be it. These deaths are justified because they contribute to the greater good. What we have to work out, is whether he or she is right.

I think they are wrong. To assess this, we should put ourselves in the impartial position. Here, there are three relevant possibilities. The first is that you turn out to be an animal eaten, vivisected, hunted or whatever, by humans. The second is that you turn out to be a human targeted by animal rights terrorists. The third possibility is that you turn out to be one of the terrorists. The terrorist actions are likely to harm both humans targeted by the terrorists and, unless they are very good at evading capture, the terrorists themselves. So, in the impartial position, choosing a world where there is genuine animal rights terrorism would be irrational unless there is a significant chance that your lot as an animal is going to be significantly improved by the terrorist acts. That is, suppose we have two worlds. One that contains animal activists who commit genuine terrorist acts; the other where the activists restrict themselves to acts that are illegal (e.g. destruction of property, release of animals) but not terrorist. Then, we have to ask ourselves, "Would animals be any better off in the first world than in the second?"

To answer this, we have to look at the function of animal rights terrorism. In particular, we have to look at the question of whether acts of terrorism committed on behalf of animals are best understood as acts of rescue or as attempts to change society, or both. If they are acts of rescue, then the use of *necessary* and *proportionate* violence may be justified. If, however, they are attempts to change society, then the use of violence is not justifiable. I am going to argue that if understood as an act of rescue, animal rights terrorism would be ineffective. Therefore, the best way of understanding terrorism committed on behalf of animals is as an attempt to change society.

It is sometimes claimed that extreme animal rights action of the terrorist sort is counterproductive since it gives the "legitimate" (i.e. non-violent) animal movement a bad name. And this is likely to create a backlash against animal rights in all its forms. I think this objection, as it stands is far too simplistic, and is contradicted by most historical evidence. But it does contain an important grain of truth. Terrorist movements have achieved significant and long-term success only when they have substantial support in the wider community, in particular in the community not directly affiliated to the terrorist organizations themselves. As things stand, the animal rights movement, even in its non-violent forms, simply does not have this level of support. If animal rights terrorists understood themselves to be fighting a war, this would be a war they could not win.

Fighting a war is not the real purpose of animal rights terrorism. If it was, then it could be construed as sort of act of rescue, in a way similar to the way in which wars can be fought to liberate nations. The real purpose of animal rights terrorism is far more subtle. In fact, three distinct functions can be discerned. First, animal rights terrorism dramatizes issues and places them in the public eye when they would otherwise be ignored in the media. Second, such terrorism applies pressure to companies and government departments that would be able to resist pressure from mainstream, law-abiding, organizations. Third, animal rights terrorism broadens the public's conception of activism and prevents mainstream animal rights groups being painted as "militant extremists" by organizations committed to the exploitation of animals.

The third function is, I think, the most important. A common strategy, adopted by the husbandry and pharmaceutical industries in particular, is to paint themselves as the true believers in animal welfare. "We have trained veterinarians on our staff, and every care is taken to make sure the animals have as comfortable a life as possible." Sentences of this sort constituted a virtual litany of the large pharmaceutical companies in the 1980s and early 1990s. The strategy was straightforward: marginalize the mainstream animal welfare movement by portraying them as unreasonable extremists. Philosophers like Peter Singer and Tom Regan, two of the most logical and reasonable people you could meet, received similar treatment. This strategy is still employed, but doesn't work anywhere near as well, thanks, largely, to the efforts of people who engage in extreme action on behalf of animals. People, such as myself, who, from the comfort of their own homes, develop a case for animal rights based (hopefully) on clear and meticulous reasoning, owe a great debt of gratitude to those who put their freedom on the line for what they believe.

But to see the function of animal rights terrorism in this way is to see it as a complex, sophisticated, and multi-faceted *attempt to change society*. And, as such, the use of violence is not legitimate. The crucial point is that if the three purposes described above – to publicise, apply pressure that could otherwise not be applied, and broaden the public's conception of what counts as legitimate campaigning – provide the rationale or justification of terrorism, then terrorism, understood in the genuine sense as acts that provoke extreme terror or use extreme violence, is unnecessary. Any form of extreme action will be equally effective; the specifically terrorist version of such action is not necessary. Publicising of issues can be achieved by a variety of means. Pressure can be applied by a variety of devices. The public's conception of what counts as legitimate campaigning can be expanded by a range of methods.

In the impartial position, then, it would be irrational to choose a world that contains, in addition to non-violent, illegal, attempts to change society, animal rights terrorism. Such terrorism is not necessary for achieving the goals that provide its *raison d'etre*. If you turn out to be an animal, you will, in all probability, not be helped by terrorist action. And if you turn out to be human, you may be harmed by it. And, any suffering that you thereby endure, is gratuitous and unnecessary. Therefore, in the impartial position, it would be irrational to choose a world that contains animal rights terrorism. Therefore, in the real world, it is immoral to endorse such terrorism. And that, I think, is why animal rights terrorism is not morally acceptable.

It is perhaps worth re-emphasizing that this is an argument only against genuine terrorist acts, characterized as ones that must involve the production of extreme terror and/or involve sufficient amounts of violence. At most, only a tiny fraction of extreme animal rights action qualifies as terrorism. Most of it involves only damage to property and release of animals, many of which are found homes. For these animals, such illegal acts of rescue are vitally important, and nothing I have said here in any way counts against them. And this is true, I think, even if such acts involve violence, as long as this is necessary and proportionate.

5 SUMMARY

Animal rights *activism* covers a variety of activities, ranging from lifestyle changes at one end of the spectrum to terrorism at the other, and these activities are underpinned by a variety of obligations or potential obligations. You are morally required to fulfil your *negative* obligations to animals, but there are few, if any, definite (unacquired) *positive* obligations. Accordingly, the forms of activism that involve doing things for animals, as opposed to *not* doing things to animals, are *supererogatory* rather than *obligatory*. That is, they are the sorts of things that it is good to do, but not bad not to do. Many of the positive actions we can take on behalf of animals are morally legitimate even if they are illegal, because the laws that they flout are fundamentally unjust. *Acts of rescue* should be distinguished from *attempts to change society*. Acts of rescue can justifiably involve violence, but only if this is *necessary* for self-defence and *proportionate* to the violence used against you. Animal rights terrorism, however, the most extreme form of animal rights activism, is not morally acceptable. Extreme acts such as these are best understood as attempts to change society, since they would be ineffective as acts of rescue. But, as attempts to change society, their use of violence is morally wrong. However, only a tiny fraction of what animal rights activists do could even remotely be regarded as terrorism. Most other forms of animal rights activism are morally legitimate.

11

WHAT GOES AROUND COMES AROUND

In *The Lives of Animals* J.M. Coetzee skilfully expresses the sense of
disorientation that accompanies the realization that our treatment of animals is very, very wrong:

> I seem to move around perfectly easily among people, to have per-
> fectly normal relations with them. Is it possible, I ask myself, that
> all of them are participants in a crime of stupefying proportions?
> Am I fantasizing it all? I must be mad! Yet every day I see the evi-
> dences. The very people I suspect produce the evidence, exhibit it,
> offer it to me. Fragments of corpses they have bought for money.

Can it really be true? Are we all co-conspirators in a crime of monstrous
proportions? Such a suspicion is likely to engender a sense of bewilder-
ment. Our family, our friends; they have their faults, we all do; but, by and
large, they are kind people, good people. Are they not? Yes, they are.
As far as they can be. But you can be kind and good only within the
framework of possibilities laid down to you by your intellectual and cultural inheritance. We have, all of us, inherited a world-view that makes us
twisted, selfish, spiteful parodies of what we might have been, and what
we might become. And, ultimately, we are the victims of this, as much as
anything else.

1 THE "DARKENED" OF THE WORLD

The philosopher Martin Heidegger, with his characteristic penchant for colourfulness and ungrammaticality, described the late twentieth century as a *darkened of the world*. What he meant by this was that we have all come to see, and understand, the world around us in one predominant way: as a *resource*. We understand nature as a collection of, as we put it, *natural resources*. The mountain is a source of ore, the river a source of hydroelectric power, the forest a source of paper. To be sure, we worry about our resources, we want them to be *renewable*, for if they are not this is bad for us. But we see them as resources nonetheless. Not all resources need be nakedly fiscal. The pleasure we get from the beauty and majesty of an old broadleaf forest is explained in terms of its being a *recreational* resource, perhaps even a *spiritual* resource. Recreational or spiritual they may be; they are still resources. The roots of the resource-based conception of the world run deep; if Heidegger is right, they run over two thousand years back into our intellectual history.

There are many problems with viewing the world and the things in it simply as resources. The arrogance involved is, of course, breathtaking. But, from the point of view of human beings, there is a more pressing drawback. It is impossible to view the world and everything in it primarily as resource without this infecting the way we view each other. This is the logical culmination of the resource-based view of nature: humans are part of nature, and therefore humans are resources too. And whenever something – human or otherwise – is viewed primarily as a resource, things generally don't go well for it.

The logic of the situation, and its implications for human beings, is exemplified in our treatment of animals. Almost every facet of this treatment screams out the idea that they are nothing more than renewable resources. They are things to be eaten, things to be experimented on, things to be stared at, hunted or killed for our entertainment. In most countries, farm and laboratory animals are classified, in law, as *property*. A recent attempt by Compassion in World Farming and other animal welfare groups to have animals reclassified as "sentient beings" – a change that would have enormous ramifications for the way animals are raised and transported – was recently thrown out of the European High Court because of the anticipated economic consequences. What makes this particularly staggering is that the claim that animals are sentient creatures is undeniably true. In the European Union, apparently, truth comes a poor second to profit.

However, when you are talking about fundamental ways of conceptualizing and understanding the world, *what goes around comes around*. The instrumental view of animals necessarily infects our view of humans. In philosophy, the industry term for the logic that characterizes the development of a situation is *dialectic*. This final chapter, then, examines the dialectic by which the instrumental view of animals becomes transformed into an instrumental view of human beings, and the unfortunate consequences this transformation yields. The focus will be on our most widespread instrumental use of animals: for food.

2 BIG AGRIBUSINESS

The dialectic starts with the introduction of what we can call *big agribusiness*. The factory producer, of eggs, broiler chickens, pigs or whatever, introduces himself into an area. Of course, intensive farming facilities – huge buildings full of specialized floors and feeding equipment – do not come cheap. Not counting the cost of land and animals, a modern, smallish, pig factory is going to cost several million pounds, and a modest laying facility about the same. The start-up costs are often so great that factory farmers must often keep the facilities running at peak capacity on a year round basis.

Intensive farming practices are designed to bring animals to market weight as quickly and cheaply as possible. The animals produced have at least four major drawbacks. First, animals are kept closely confined. Exercise means burning of calories which means that more food, hence more money, will be needed for the animal to reach market weight. So animals are not allowed to exercise, and this means the meat that comes from them will contain, compared to a free-range animal, a high percentage of fat.

Second, as we have seen, the animals raised in intensive facilities are typically very unhealthy (both physically and mentally). The factory farmer cannot, of course, allow them to die before they reach market weight, and so tends to rely heavily on antibiotics. The US Office of Technology Assessment reported (in *Drugs and Livestock Feed*) that nearly all poultry, most pigs and veal calves, and sixty per cent of cattle get regular antibiotic additives in their feed.

Third, the use of growth hormones is a relatively common practice in many factory farms.

Fourth, animals in intensive facilities are often given the cheapest feed available, and so are forced to eat things they would never naturally eat. Not many cows have a natural proclivity for cannibalism, but this is precisely what they have been forced to become by modern intensive farming methods.

Factory farming is a prime example of an institution that treats animals as renewable resources. What are the consequences of this for human beings?

3 THE TRADITIONAL FARMING COMMUNITY

The first people to suffer from the introduction of big agribusiness are traditional farmers, and, of course, their wider community. As I have said, the start-up costs of an intensive facility are considerable, and this often necessitates running buildings at peak capacity even when there is a surplus of the product they produce. This tends to create chronic overproduction in the pork, poultry and dairy industries. Overproduction keeps the market depressed, and traditional, non-intensive, farmers have a hard time making ends meet with their small flocks and herds. The depressed markets are often exacerbated by tax breaks given to agribusiness companies and urban investors. The tax laws in many countries allow investors to write off a certain percentage of money invested in factory buildings. Some of these investors are often interested more in tax write-offs than profits and tend to keep producing even when prices are low. This, of course, further depresses the markets. Therefore, the tendency is for small, traditional, farmers to go to the wall, while more and more of the market falls into the hands of intensive producers. If you want to understand the so-called "crisis in the countryside", you need look no further than the role played by big agribusiness. (It, emphatically, has nothing to do with fox-hunting. Bear that in mind next time you see the self-styled Countryside Alliance making a nuisance of themselves.)

4 CONSUMERS

The ripples spread. The next to suffer are consumers. They are increasingly forced to buy meat that is unnaturally high in fat, and laden with antibiotics, growth hormones, and other chemicals. This has serious consequences for consumer health, the most obvious being heart disease and cancer.

There are, of course, various forms of heart disease, some congenital, some not. But, in Western countries, the major form of heart disease is *atherosclerosis*. Fatty deposits, called plaque, composed of cholesterol and fats build up on the inner wall of the coronary arteries. Gradually this restricts blood flow and eventually triggers a heart attack. The build-up of plaque is at least partly associated with excessive intake of animal fats in the diet. And, the more fatty the animal, the more fat you will intake.

High intakes of animal fat are also associated with various forms of cancer, for which the fat appears to act as a promoter or trigger. These include cancer of the breast, colon, uterus, and prostate. Again, animals with the unnaturally high-fat content associated with intensive production methods cannot do someone who is genetically prone to these cancers any good at all. But there are other cancer worries prompted by intensive farming practices. Although farmers are required to withdraw additives, such as nitrites and growth hormones, from the animal feed before shipping, it is far from clear how effective this is. According to one US report, fourteen per cent of the meat it inspected contained illegally high levels of drugs and pesticides. And of the 143 identified drugs and chemicals, forty-two were known to, or were suspected of, causing cancer, twenty of causing birth defects, and six of causing genetic mutations.[1] The US Food and

Drug Administration has expressed fears that as many as 500 or 600 toxic chemicals may be present in the country's meat supply.[2]

There are, however, less obvious, but perhaps even more disturbing, health issues raised by intensive production methods. Since the Second World War, due to the widespread use of antibiotics in the animal husbandry industry, many of these substances have been unloaded into the soil. Consequently, a large number of micro-organisms that are harmful to humans have been exposed to these antibiotics, and the micro-organisms have consequently mutated and developed a resistance to these antibiotics. The bacteria that cause diarrhoea, septicaemia, psittacosis, salmonella, gonorrhoea, pneumonia, typhoid, tuberculosis and childhood meningitis have all evolved antibiotic resistant strains. The chances are that, if you are infected with one of these strains, you will have a lot more difficulty becoming well again than you would have had even ten years ago.

Even more disturbing than this is the fact that one type of bacteria has developed a strain that is resistant to every antibiotic except one. That bacterium is *Staphylococcus aureus*, a bacterium that is usually harmless but that can cause pneumonia and septicaemia in susceptible individuals. This is now resistant to all antibiotics except vancomycin, and it is only a matter of time before it evolves a resistance to this drug too. It is difficult for people of my generation to imagine what the world was like before the development of antibiotics. According to some epidemiologists, we may be about to find out.

The most famous example of a public health problem caused by intensive farming practices, however, is undoubtedly the BSE crisis. Bovine spongiform encephalopathy, a disease that was endemic in British cow herds from the late 1970s until at least the mid 1990s, is spread by giving cattle feed made from the mashed up remains of other cattle, ones infected with the rogue prion that causes BSE. Humans who eat infected cattle get a version of the disease known as New Variant Creutzfeld-Jakob Disease (vCJD). This, as everyone now knows, is a very nasty disease whose symptoms include progressive dementia and which inevitably ends in death. Original estimates of the toll of vCJD were at least eighty but not more than 1000 human deaths. These estimates have recently been upgraded: at least a thousand but not more than 140,000 human deaths! Quite a jump, and who knows if these estimates will not be further upgraded. Humans are dying from vCJD because cattle were fed an unnatural cannibalistic diet. Why? Money. Intensive production demands that animals be brought to market weight as quickly and cheaply as possible. Cannibal feed is cheaper than traditional feed, and cheap, in factory farming, carries the day. Other, non-intensive, producers are then forced to follow suit or go to the wall. At the time of writing, nearly 100 people have died or are dying from vCJD in Britain, and the toll continues to rise.

5 The environment

Intensive farming practices also have some fairly dire environmental consequences. Some of these are direct, the more serious ones are indirect. One of the direct environmental consequences is water pollution. The major difference between intensive and traditional methods is that the excrement that builds up at intensive facilities is much more localized, since there is a much greater concentration of animals per acre. Consequently, it is much more difficult for this to be absorbed by the land. Often the unabsorbed waste runs off and pollutes rivers and ground water. In the United States, for example, farm animals produce two billion tons of manure a year, and more than half of this comes from intensively produced animals. Pollution of rivers around such facilities is common. In Holland, where intensive facilities are widespread, the land is capable of absorbing less than half the excrement produced by animals. The excess is still being dumped on the land where, of course, it pollutes water supplies, kills off vegetation and so on.

The indirect environmental consequences of meat production are, however, even more alarming. Alarming, but not unexpected; they can be predicted on the basis of some simple calculations. A bull is, in effect, a *protein converter*. He is fed vegetable protein and converts it to animal protein. We then eat the animal protein. The bull is a sort of nutritional middleman; a greedy one. It takes twenty-one pounds of vegetable protein fed to a calf to produce a single pound of animal protein that is then avail-able for us to eat. More than ninety per cent of what we put into the bull is lost. That is, for every pound of cattle protein that is available for us to eat, we could have twenty-one pounds of vegetable protein instead.

Or look at it this way. Suppose you have an acre of land at your dis-posal. You could use it to grow a high-protein plant food like lentils or beans. If you do this, you will get anywhere from 300 to 500 pounds of protein from your acre. Alternatively, you could use your acre to grow a crop that you could feed to your bull, and then kill and eat him. If you did this, you would end up with between forty and fifty-five pounds of protein from your acre.

Other animals are not quite as inefficient at converting protein as cattle. The conversion ratio for pigs, for example, is around eight to one. But this is offset by the fact that cattle can make use of sources of protein that are indigestible for pigs. Averaging out over the common species we use for food – cattle, pigs, chickens, sheep – we get a commonly accepted conversion of ratio of somewhere in the region of ten to one, that is ten pounds of vegetable protein for every pound of animal protein.

The same pattern emerges when we look at other necessary compo-nents of food. An acre that is used to grow oats, for example, will yield six times the number of calories as an acre dedicated to producing food for pigs, and more than twenty-five times as many calories as an acre dedicated to producing beef. And even an acre used to grow broccoli will yield three times the number of calories of an acre dedicated to pigs. That same area of broccoli will produce twenty-four times as much iron as an acre dedicated to producing beef. Indeed, the acre of broccoli will even produce five times more calcium than an acre dedicated to feeding dairy cows.

Animals that we eat are the nutritional equivalent of middlemen. We put things in – protein, carbohydrates, iron, calcium and so on – and we get a lot less out than we put in. This means that raising animals for food is an extremely inefficient use of land. And to satisfy our prodigious appetite for meat, much land has to be turned over to the production of food that otherwise wouldn't be needed. Land, however, is not the only thing ineffi-ciently used in the production of meat; so too is water, energy and topsoil. It has been calculated that to produce one pound of beef from cattle raised in a feedlot requires 2500 gallons of water (including not only the water consumed directly by the animal but also the water that went into growing the plants that it eats). Or, as *Newsweek* put it, "The water that goes into a 1000 pound steer would float a destroyer."[3] More than half of all water consumed in the United States goes to livestock. This demand is drying up the huge underground aquifers upon which many of the drier regions of that country depend.

Consider, now, energy. In most industrialized countries, growing anything typically involves quite a high investment of fossil fuels (chiefly in the form of fertilizers and the fuel used to power agricultural machinery). So, corn grown in Mexico, for example, produces eighty-three calories of food for each calorie of fossil fuel invested, whereas in the United States, where the reliance on fossil fuels is much greater, corn will produce something less than 2.5 calories of food for each calorie of fossil fuel invested. But, this pales into insignificance compared to the situation in meat production, for here the conversion ratio is actually *inverted*. The most inefficient method of production is feedlot cattle production, and here each calorie of food produced takes thirty-three – I repeat thirty-three! – calories of fossil fuel investment. By far the most efficient is range cattle production, but even here each calorie of food produced takes three calories of fossil fuel investment. So, even in the United States, where, in terms of the investment of fossil fuels, the cost of growing crops is much higher than in other countries, growing vegetable food is at least five times more energy efficient than grazing cattle and fifty times more efficient than feedlot cattle production.

Meat production, then, is an extremely inefficient use of land, water and energy. Because of the inefficiency built into the nature of the process – deriving from the use of animals as nutritional middlemen – huge amounts of land, water and energy have to be dedicated to growing food for animals. Throughout human history, the practice of grazing animals has always led to the clearing of forests; and it still does today. Over the past twenty-five years, almost half of Central America's rainforests have been cleared, largely to provide beef to North America. Deforestation leads to extinction of species, erosion of topsoil, and flooding. Most importantly, destroying a forest releases huge amounts of carbon into the atmosphere, in the form of carbon dioxide. This is a greenhouse gas, and so intensifies the greenhouse effect, which increases global warming, which causes melting of the ice caps, which raises sea-levels, which causes flooding of low-lying regions, droughts, disastrous climatic changes, and so on.

6 BACK TO ANIMALS

The ripples produced by the introduction of big agribusiness have been slowly spreading outwards; first to traditional farmers, their dependants, their communities, then on to the wider community, then to the environment. At each stage in the dialectic, things go badly for someone. Whether it's the loss of a livelihood or way of life of traditional farmers, adverse impacts on the health of consumers, or environmental consequences that will, eventually, affect us all. Everyone is suffering, or will suffer, in some way. Our standard way of coping with this, and this really does not reflect well on us at all, is to try and deflect some of that suffering back onto animals; to get them to do some of our suffering for us.

Heart disease and cancer are the biggest killers in western countries today. Both these diseases have genetic components, but both of them, almost always, require an environmental promoter or trigger. Sometimes, the environmental promoters or triggers are things beyond our control – exposure to a chemical in our environment of which we were unaware, for example – but often the triggers are very definitely within our control. In the case of heart disease, the two most important environmental promoters are smoking and, even more importantly, the amount of fat in one's diet. The seriousness of a genetic predisposition to build up fatty plaque on the walls of your coronary artery, for example, can be significantly mitigated by the removal from your diet of fatty substances, red meat being the most obvious candidate. But do we do this? Some of us do. Most of us do not. Instead, we consign literally millions of animals to vivisection and then death every year in the attempt to design drugs that will do our job for us: take the fatty deposits of our artery walls without us having to lift a finger.

Obesity is strongly implicated in several common forms of cancer, including cancer of the breast, colon, uterus and prostate. This is not to say that everyone who gets one of these forms of cancer is obese, or even if they are that this is the reason they got it. But it is to say that if you take steps to ensure that you are not obese – regular exercise and cutting down the amount of animal fat in your diet are obvious, and simple, steps – then, statistically speaking, the chances of you getting one of these forms of cancer are significantly reduced. But do we do this? Again, some of us do; most of us don't. Instead, we send a few more million animals off to vivisection and death, in the hope that preventative or curative drugs can be developed that mean we don't have to lift a finger.

The effectiveness of antibiotics has been reduced by their widespread and sloppy use in the meat industry? Indeed, some bacteria are close to developing immunity to all known antibiotics? No problem. Send a few million more animals off for vivisection and death; we'll develop new antibiotics. Of course, we'll soon need more new ones, because we will continue to use antibiotics in a sloppy and irresponsible way in the meat industry. But this is no problem: there's an unlimited supply of experimental subjects.

The earth is warming and seas are rising. This is because we like driving our cars, but also because we enjoy our hamburgers, and rainforests in South and Central America are being cleared at a rate of between nine million and twenty million hectares a year, depending on who you believe, so we can go on enjoying our hamburgers at a "competitive" price. So what if fifteen million people in Bangladesh are displaced by flooding accompanying a half metre rise in sea level? What's that got to do with me? I'm just minding my own business, and eating my burger. Besides, it's a free market isn't it?

Do you see a pattern emerging?

7 DECISION-MAKING IN THE GESTELL: THE CASE OF BSE

Heidegger, with whom we began this chapter, talked of the view of nature as a resource as stemming from a conceptualization of the world he called a *gestell*, which can be translated "framework" or "matrix." The danger of the gestell, or one of its dangers, is its tendency to universality. If we view nature, and all things in it, as simply resources, then it is inevitable we eventually acquire the same view of human beings. But viewing human beings as resources has two facets. Obviously, one thing it means is that you will view other human beings as resources. Less obviously, you are yourself a human being, and you will come to think of yourself as a resource also.

That humans are typically viewed as resources by governments and governmental bodies is, by now, so obvious, as not to need much defence. Social policy, at the end of the day, is dictated by cost-benefit analysis. How many pensioner deaths are "acceptable" before it is worth the eco-nomic risks of a hike in winter fuel allowance? You won't ever hear a government reasoning publicly in these terms, but this cost-benefit analy-sis always, but always, provides the framework for their decision-making. Nowhere is this more obvious than in a recent, animal-related, matter: the tragic and shameful story of the British government's response to BSE. The recent publication of the Phillips Report tells us something deeply disturbing, but not particularly unexpected, about the perceived value of human life.

At some time in the 1970s, the Phillips Report speculates, a genetic mutation occurred in a cow somewhere in Britain. The cow developed *Bovine Spongiform Encephalopathy* – BSE – a degenerative brain condi-tion caused by an abnormal prion protein. In Britain, cows have been fed the mashed up remains of their relatives since 1926, and this practice increased during the course of the century. The diseased cow was fed to other cows, and the disease spread like wildfire throughout the 1970s and 1980s. Due to BSE's long incubation period, thousands of cows were infected long before the first was diagnosed.

In September 1985, the brain of a diseased cow number 133 was delivered to the Central Veterinary Laboratory (CVL) of the Ministry of Agriculture, Fisheries and Food (Maff). Tests on its brain revealed the char-acteristic sponge-like pattern that we now know is the hallmark of BSE. It was not until the end of 1986 that Raymond Bradley, head of the CVL's pathology, speculated that the disease might be a form of bovine scrapie, which, as he pointed out, would have severe repercussions for the export trade and possibly human health. According to the Phillips Report, Bradley's work should have been sent immediately to the Neuropathogenesis Unit (NPU) in Edinburgh. It was delayed by William Watson, the director of CVL, for six crucial months. The CVL was not only slow; it also covered up what had been found. According to Phillips, a "policy of suppression of all information on the subject" was put in force. Why? Watson did not want to tell Maff until he was sure. In fact, during the period from 1984 to 1988 – almost certainly the period of peak infection – uncertain findings were suppressed by scientists and ministers. This was combined with a propaganda campaign to sedate the increasingly jittery public.

Finally, in 1988, John Wilesmith, the CVL's only qualified epidemiologist deduced correctly that cannibal feed was the source of the infection. Did this result in an immediate ban on the use of such feed. Not at all. Farmers were given a five-week period to clear their feed stocks. According to Phillips, this concession was seriously abused by both farmers and suppliers, and old feed stocks continued to be used long after this period. The result was that thousands of cattle were infected after the ban had, theoretically, taken effect.

The delay in banning cannibal feed was mirrored by a delay in removing infected animals from the food chain. By February 1988, 264 cases of BSE from 223 farms had been confirmed. At this time, Derek Andrews, permanent secretary at Maff, proposed a policy of compulsory slaughter, and removal from the food chain, of infected animals. John MacGregor, then Agriculture Secretary, demurred, and referred the matter to Sir Donald Acheson, the Chief Medical Officer. Acheson disagreed. Why? According to Phillips, because he feared a food scare. Instead, he suggested referring the matter to a working party of experts. The working party, chaired by Sir Richard Southwood, a zoologist, first met on 20 June 1988. The result of all this procrastination, was that the ban on infected animals suggested by Maff was not given the final go ahead until 8 August, 1988, six months after Maff suggested it. Then, a decision to give farmers only fifty per cent compensation almost certainly resulted in diseased cows slipping in under the wire (the compensation was later increased to 100 per cent).

The Southwood working party, although supposedly composed of experts, did not, in fact, contain a single expert on prions. The recommendations of the working party were, largely, predicated on an unproven assumption – that BSE was a form of bovine scrapie, which could not be transmitted to humans. Despite their lack of expertise, they still felt competent to conclude that the risk to humans was "remote" provided that action was taken to remove affected cattle from the human food chain. There are two things notable about this. First, the qualification that infected animals be removed from the food chain was largely forgotten in subsequent public pronouncements by the government. Second, the lack of confidence the working party had in their own findings was manifest in the fact that they also, inconsistently, advised that offal be removed from baby food. If action had to be taken on baby food, why not other food?

Throughout 1988 and most of 1989, Acheson, according to Phillips, resisted imposing a ban on offal in human food because of the possibility of a food scare. In fact, Pedigree Masters Foods – manufacturers of dog and cat food – had decided to remove offal from their product before Acheson came to accept the necessity of a ban on offal in human food. It wasn't until November 1989 that this ban went into effect.

Throughout this, the principal efforts of the government went into reassuring consumers about the safety of beef. In 1990, the credibility of the government was severely cast into doubt by the fact that BSE had, in the laboratory, been transmitted to a number of different species, including mice, a puma, and an oryx. This showed that BSE could cross the species barrier, and thus undermined one of the central premises of the Southwood Report. The government then sought to downplay the significance of these experimental findings. The experimental conditions, they argued, were not reproduced in nature, so no implications of a risk to humans could be drawn. Their credibility was finally destroyed in May 1990 when a cat was diagnosed as having BSE from eating contaminated beef. Between then and 1994, fifty-seven other cats were infected in this way.

Did the government then start to do anything about the growing risk to human health. Of course not, that might cause a food scare. Instead, they redoubled their efforts at reassuring the public. Around this time, we have the rather ugly public spectacle of John Gummer, Agriculture Minister, feeding a hamburger to his four-year-old daughter, Cordelia. But increasingly the government reassurances were without foundation. Shortly after the discovery of cats infected with BSE, Keith Meldrum, Chief Veterinary Officer, attempted to reassure the public by claiming that there was no likely connection between this and BSE. Phillips notes: "There was no basis for this degree of reassurance." In March 1993, after the news that a dairy farmer with a BSE herd had died the previous October, Dr Kenneth Calman, new Chief Medical Officer, repeated the claim that beef is safe, almost certainly after pressure from Maff. In 1994, after the press had seized on the case of Vicki Rimmer (who died of vCJD in 1998), Calman reiterates, "There is not the slightest evidence that eating beef or hamburgers causes CJD." According to Phillips, this was "somewhat more emphatic than desirable." Others might say that it was simply wrong; that the evidence was mounting all around him.

Throughout this sorry incident the same shabby story repeats itself. It is a story that the Phillips report tells as gently and non-emotively as possible, but one that can be seen crawling out diffidently from either side of each line of that report. We cannot, of course, look into the souls of the people involved in making these decisions, but we can draw reasonable inferences from their actions. And, on the face of it, the government – in the form of Maff and connected ministries – certainly *seemed* to be more concerned with allaying fears of a food scare than with finding out the truth and protecting human health. This *seems* to be why Watson delayed the sending of the brain of cow 133 to the NPU for a crucial six months. This *seems* to be why Acheson delayed the ban on infected animals entering the food chain and, instead, referred the matter to the Southwood working party. This *seems* to be why Acheson also delayed the ban on offal in human food even until after it had been removed from certain pet foods. This *may* have been why the qualification "provided that infected cattle are removed from the food chain" tagged onto the Southwood party's insistence that BSE posed only a "remote" threat to human health tended to be lost in subsequent government pronouncements. This *seems* to be why government officials were quick to debunk the significance of the production of BSE in different species in the laboratory. This *seems* to be why, despite mounting evidence to the contrary, the government, throughout the early 1990s, continued with its mantra that there is no evidence linking BSE to vCJD.

These are not evil men. They live their lives and love their families just like everyone else. They are simply men doing what they have been trained to do, and think in the way they have been trained to think. They are children of the *gestell*. What is the value of human life in the gestell? All along, there was a possibility that human health would be affected by BSE. As time went on, the possibility increased, and eventually became a probability. But human life is only one factor in the equation, one more thing to be included, alongside economic gain and loss, in the overall analysis. This is life in the *gestell*. Humans are renewable resources, one resource amongst others, to be balanced, weighed, evaluated, and traded off, against other resources. This is the instrumental view of human beings that Heidegger saw as a culmination of two and a half thousand years of intellectual and cultural development.

8 WE NEVER LEARN

The problems of vCJD, real and horrific though they are, will be a stroll in the park compared to those that will arise from the next major exploitation of animals by humans. Xenotransplantation is the transfer of live organs, tissues, or cells between different species. The idea is to compensate for the widespread reluctance of humans to donate their vital organs after they die by breeding animals – pigs – to do the donating for us. The major technical – as opposed to moral – problem is that the human immune system rejects these alien organs. Cue large numbers of experiments designed to find a way around the problem of rejection. Consider, for example, what the nice people at the Huntingdon Life Sciences (HLS) research laboratory in Cambridgeshire have recently been doing along these lines: contract work for the company Imutran, a subsidiary of the giant pharmaceutical company Novartis.[4]

The experiments were conducted on at least forty-nine baboons, and 424 cynomologus monkeys. Six baboons had piglet hearts grafted onto their necks. Twenty-seven baboons had piglet hearts inserted into their abdominal cavities. Sixteen baboons' hearts were replaced with piglet hearts. The public position of Imutran has always been that the animals do not suffer; the reality is very different. More than thirty per cent of the baboons died within the first twenty-four hours after surgery, due to technical failures, some of which were due to sheer incompetence. For example, a mismatch in size between pig heart and baboon body, or the source piglet being too young. One baboon was sacrificed when research-ers forgot to unfreeze the piglet heart. The remaining baboons all died as a result of infections, toxic effects of immuno-suppressant drugs, heart failure as result of rejection, or heart failure for unknown reasons. The cynomologus monkeys suffered a similar fate. Around eighty of them were killed so that their hearts could be transplanted to baboons. Sixty-one had piglet hearts grafted into their abdomens; and thirty-three of these died due to technical failures, the rest on average twenty-five days later. The claim that these animals did not suffer is as bare-faced a lie as you are ever likely to hear, and this is borne out by the researchers' own reports, ones laced with phrases such as "huddled, eyes swollen, body tremors, reluctant to use legs", "very laboured breathing", "severe tremors upper torso and head", "sudden collapse", "bloody discharge from penis", "vomit during dozing", "found dead."

The suffering of these animals was monstrous. Who stands to benefit? Not us. Xenotransplantation poses one of the greatest risks to human health imaginable. Pigs, for example, the most likely donors, carry a variety of viruses. Many of these are poorly understood by us, some have probably not even been identified. Viruses, when they pass from one species to another, typically do something rather inconvenient: they mutate. The result is that a virus that has little effect on an animal can, following its transmission to humans, mutate into something very deadly indeed. Thus, to take just one example, HIV derives from SIV – Simian Immunodeficiency Virus – and a recent account of how we came to con-tract HIV even claims the source was a polio vaccine made from the crushed kidneys of infected chimpanzees. (As a matter of interest, seven of the baboons used at HLS were infected with Simian Herpes B, a virus that is lethal to humans.)

Xenotransplantation, far from promoting vital human interests is one of the most serious threats imaginable to such interests. In fact, the only interests being promoted by xenotransplantation are the economic interests of giant pharmaceutical companies like Novartis, subsidiaries like Imutran, and contract research institutions like Huntingdon Life Sciences.

9 ACCEPTABLE LOSSES

We are literally killing ourselves, and killing each other. We foul our water, our air and our food. The great killers of today – cancer and heart disease – are increasingly inflicted on us by the corporations that churn chemicals out into our air, our rivers and our groundwater, and by the food producers that pile our plates full with food high in fat and laced with poisonous chemical cocktails. Do we fight this? Do we rage against what is being done to us and to our world? On the contrary, our complicity in the dialectic is unquestionable. What are we in this great scheme of things? *Acceptable losses.* As long as not too many of us die, then our deaths are an acceptable trade-off for economic gain and material luxury. Environmental degradation on an unprecedented scale? Ditto. In the *gestell* everything is a resource – ourselves and our world included. Everything is up for grabs, anything can be traded off against anything else. And, in this process, a loss – whether human or environmental – that is not too great, and which procures something else that is valued more, is an acceptable one.

We are *acceptable losses.* Why don't we do anything about it? Because, implicitly, we have come to understand and accept this fact. Not only do we understand other people as resources, this is also how we understand ourselves. This is the culmination of the resource-based view of the world; the logic of the *gestell.* We are simply one resource amongst others. Our position is hopeless, and we are, consequently, helpless. We are not responsible for what we do, and what we let others do to us, because we are just *acceptable losses.* Why should we pretend otherwise?

We are killing ourselves, and killing each other. If I were religiously inclined – which I am not – I would be tempted to describe these as our *sins.* And what do we do with sins? We get someone else to take our sins upon them. Whether they want to or not! Animals can suffer for us, not only for those things that have been thrust upon us, but also for those things that we have brought upon ourselves. They suffer for our smoke-induced lung cancer, for our obesity-induced heart disease, for the sloppy and irresponsible way we have used antibiotics. We, their self-styled masters, are lazy and stupid and, above all, ungrateful. But that's OK. If anything, these are just other sins, and someone, or something, else can be made to take our sins upon them, and suffer so that we might not have to. Jesus is, apparently, live and well, but somewhat unwilling this time around. He's living as a Draize rabbit, and LD-50 mouse, a heroin monkey, and a smoking dog.

NOTES

Chapter 1: Do Animals Have Minds?

1. Descartes' most famous (and relevant) works are *Discourse on Method*, first published in 1637, and *Meditations*, first published in 1641. Both can be found in Haldane, E. and Ross, G. eds, *The Philosophical Works of Descartes*, vols 1 & 2, Cambridge: Cambridge University Press.

2. *See* Kitchell, R.L. and Erickson, H. eds, *Animal Pain: Perception and Alleviation*, Maryland: American Psychological Association, 1983.

3. Bitterman, M. "The Evolution of Intelligence", *Scientific American*, vol. 212, 1965.

4. The philosophers, in this case, are very good ones, and include Donald Davidson and Stephen Stich. Davidson's most explicit treatment of this issue can be found in his paper, "Rational Animals", in LePore, E. and McLaughlin, B. eds, *Actions and Events: Perspectives on the Philosophy of Donald Davidson*, Oxford: Blackwell, 1985, pp. 473–80. Stich discusses this issue in "Do Animals have Beliefs?", *Australasian Journal of Philosophy*, vol. 57, 1979.

Chapter 2: The Moral Club

1. In fact, in another work, I try to develop a case for the claim that non-conscious things have a form of intrinsic value. *See* Rowlands, M. *The Environmental Crisis: Understanding the Value of Nature*, London, Macmillan, 2000.

2. The idea of equality figures quite centrally in most arguments for animal rights. For an especially clear discussion, *see* Singer, P. *Animal Liberation*, London: Thorsons, 1990, Chapter 1.

Chapter 3: Justice for All

1. Rawls, J. *A Theory of Justice*, New York: Oxford University Press, 1971. The

theoretical basis of my neo-Rawlsian account is developed more fully in Rowlands, *Animal Rights: A Philosophical Defence*, London: Macmillan, 1998.

Chapter 4: Killing Animals

1. Nagel, T. "Death", *Nous*, vol. 4, no. 1, 1970. Reprinted in Nagel, T. *Mortal Questions*, Cambridge University Press, 1979, 1–10. All page references are to the latter.
2. *Ibid.* p. 6.
3. *Ibid.* pp. 6–7.
4. *Ibid.* p. 9.
5. Regan, T. *The Case for Animal Rights*, London: Routledge, 1984, p. 308.
6. Regan also thinks that humans lose more in dying than do dogs, but for different reasons than me. For his discussion of this, *see The Case for Animal Rights*, p. 324.

Chapter 5: Using Animals for Food

1. Stolba, A. and Wood-Gush, D. "The Behaviour of Pigs in a Semi-natural Environment", *Animal Production*, vol. 48, 1989.
2. Van Putten, G. "An Investigation into Tail-biting among Fattening Pigs", *British Veterinary Journal*, vol. 125, 1969.
3. Cronin, G. "The Development and Significance of Abnormal Stereotyped Behaviour in Tethered Sows", PhD. thesis, University of Wageningen, Netherlands, p. 25.
4. Ewbank, R. "The Trouble with Being a Farm Animal", *New Scientist*, October 18, 1973.

Chapter 6: Using Animals for Experiments

1. PCRM Update (Newsletter of the Physicians Committee for Responsible Medicine, Washington, D.C.) July–August 1988, p. 4. Quoted from Singer, *Animal Liberation*, p. 56.
2. *Journal of Abnormal and Social Psychology*, vol. 48, 1953.
3. *Progress in Neuro-Psychopharmacology and Biological Psychiatry*, vol. 8, 1984.
4. *Engineering and Science*, vol. 33, 1970.
5. Hobler, K. and Napodano, R. *Journal of Trauma*, vol. 14, 1974.
6. On Zipeprol, *see* Moroni, C. *et al.*, *The Lancet*, January 1984. On Practolol, *see* Inman, W. and Goss, F. eds, *Drug Monitoring*, New York: Academic Press, 1977.
7. "Industry Toxicologists Keen on Reducing Animal Use", *Science*, 17 April, 1987.
8. Report of the Littlewood Committee. Report cited in Ryder, R. "Experiments on Animals", in Godlovitch, S., Godlovitch, R. and Harris, J. eds., *Animals, Men, and*

Morals, New York: Taplinger, 1972.

9. The importance of risk transferability in this context is emphasized by Regan, *The Case for Animal Rights*, pp. 377–81.

10. *Journal of Pharmacology and Experimental Therapeutics* vol. 226, 1983.

11. *Health Care*, vol. 2, 1980.

Chapter 7: Zoos

1. Some of the arguments developed in this chapter owe much to Dale Jamieson's "Against Zoos", in Singer, P. ed. *In Defence of Animals*, Oxford: Blackwell, 1985, pp. 108–17.

2. Stephen Kellert, "Zoological Parks in American Society", *Proceedings of the American Association of Zoological Parks and Aquariums*, 1979.

3. Edward Ludwig, "A Study of Buffalo Zoo", *International Journal for the Study of Animal Problems*, 1981.

Chapter 8: Hunting

1. If you doubt that this was one of the principal motivations for the eradication of wolves, read Aldo Leopold's *A Sand County Almanac*, in particular, the essay "Thinking like a mountain."

Chapter 10: Animal Rights Activism

1. Barry Horne recently died in prison, the result of repeated hunger strikes.

Chapter 11: What Goes Around Comes Around

1. *Problems in Preventing the Marketing of Raw Meat and Poultry Containing Potentially Harmful Residues*, US General Accounting Office, 1979.

2. *New York Times*, 15 March 1983.

3. "The Browning of America", *Newsweek*, 22 February 1981.

4. Details of procedures and results are taken from the excellent expos by the *Daily Express*, 21 September 2000. For more information, *see Stop Huntingdon Animal Cruelty*, Newsletter 7. (www.shac.net).

INDEX

INDEX

INDEX

marginal cases, argument from, 57
    intelligence, 43, 44–7
    potential, 47–8
medical sciences *see* vivisection
Meldrum, Keith, 209
mental states
    autonomy, 22–3, 153, 154
    beliefs, 19–22
    conditioning, 17–19
    consciousness, 27
    desires and preferences, 16–19, 22–3
    fear and anxiety, 9–11
    happiness and pleasure, 12–14
    individual dispositions, 13
    intensity of suffering, 14–15
    practical reasoning, 16–19
    subjectivity and morality, 23–5
Mexico
    land use, 203
military, 130–2, 136
mind
    Cartesian mechanism, 3–5
    see also mental states
Ministry of Agriculture, Fisheries and Food
    and BSE, 206–10
monkeys
    desires and preferences, 19
    drug addiction, 148–9
    as pets, 172
    psychological research, 134–5
    xenotransplantation, 211
morality
    agents and patients, 63–6
    appearance, 41–2
    consequential theories, 35
    considerability, 41
    deontological theories, 35
    differential entitlements, 52, 56
    entitlement/desert, 48–51
    excellence, 36
    illegitimate vivisection, 142–4
    intelligence, 42–4
    interweaving equality and desert, 58
    laws and moral principles, 183–4
    in and out of the club, 26–8, 51–4
    philosophical argument, 28–31
    quantifying, 98–9
    relevance of being human, 39–41
    subjectivity of animals, 23–5
    validity of equality, 34–7
    see also equality

Nagel, Thomas
    death as deprivation of possibilities,
      72–6
New Variant Creutzfeld-Jakob Disease
    (vCJD), 200–1, 209, 210
Newsweek, 203
Nietzsche, Friedrich
    eternity of joy, 84
    excellence and morality, 35, 48
Novartis, 210

obligations
    natural and acquired, 169–73, 180
    positive and negative, 179–82, 193–4
Opren, 138

pain
    awareness of, 5–6
    behavioural evidence, 6–7
    evolutionary argument, 8–9
    intensity, 14–15
    and mind, 3–4
    pain-controlling substances, 7–8
Pedigree Masters Food, 208
perfection
    and desert, 48–9
Peters, R., 133
pets, 174–5
    acquired obligations to, 169–73
    laws against cruelty, 169
    meat for, 173–5, 208
    natural obligations to, 169–70
    in the wild, 172
Pfizer laboratories, 139–40
pharmaceutical industry, 139–40
    and animals rights activism, 192
    see also drugs; vivisection
Phillips Report (on BSE), 206–10
pigs, 104–7, 116
    after "liberation", 120
    intensive farming, 197
    land use, 202
    porcine stress syndrome, 105
    slaughter, 112
    vivisection, 137
    xenotransplantation, 210–12
pleasure, 12–14
Practolol, 138
Primate Equilibrium Platform (PEP), 130
psychological research, 132–6
Pure Food and Drug Act (1906), 115

INDEX